Spirit AND Power

Foundations of Pentecostal Experience

A Call to Evangelical Dialogue

Spirit AND Power

Foundations of Pentecostal Experience

William W.
Robert P. MENZIES

ZondervanPublishingHouse
Grand Rapids, Michigan

A Division of HarperCollins*Publishers*

Spirit and Power
Copyright © 2000 by William W. Menzies and Robert P. Menzies

Requests for information should be addressed to:

📖 ZondervanPublishingHouse
Grand Rapids, Michigan 49530

Library of Congress Cataloging-in-Publication Data

Menzies, William W.
    Spirit and power : foundations of pentecostal experience / William W. Menzies and Robert
P. Menzies.
       p. cm.
    Includes bibliographical references.
    ISBN 0-310-23507-3 (alk. paper)
    1. Pentecostalism. 2. Theology, Doctrinal. I. Menzies, Robert P. II. Title.
BR1644 .M46 2000
270,8'2—dc21
                                                00-028975
                                              CIP

This edition printed on acid-free paper.

Interior design by Todd Sprague

Printed in the United States of America

00 01 02 03 04 05 06 / ❖ DC/ 10 9 8 7 6 5 4 3 2 1

To Jessica, Sarah, Samuel, and Lucas—
the next generation—
the generation we pray will be powerful
in its witness for Christ

Table of Contents

Abbreviations

Introduction

The advent of the modern Pentecostal movement is, without doubt, one of the most dramatic developments of the twentieth century. From a small, ostracized band in the early 1900s, the movement has grown to be a significant force within Christendom. Along the way, Pentecostals have impacted many other Christian traditions and, similarly, they also have been influenced. Yet, today, in spite of its vitality and growth, the future of the movement is uncertain. This is largely due to the fact that theology gives direction to our experience and praxis, and the theological legacy of Pentecostalism is ambiguous. Pentecostals have been known for their spiritual vitality, not their theological prowess or intellectual rigor. But history tells us that without a strong theological base, enthusiastic movements dissipate or evolve in other directions. Thus, the future of the Pentecostal movement remains uncertain. As this movement heads into the twenty-first century, it faces a genuine challenge: Will Pentecostals be able to hand on to the next generation a solid rationale for their belief and practice?

Paradoxically, just as the Pentecostal movement faces this significant theological challenge, so also it finds itself with unparalleled opportunities for fresh theological reflection. The present context is proving to be fertile soil for the growth of a truly Pentecostal theology. This book is an attempt to chronicle this remarkable story, to lay out the challenges and the opportunities that stand before the Pentecostal movement. The authors also hope that this book will in some small way contribute to the dynamic explosion in Pentecostal theology that is beginning to take place around the world.

Although this book has been written with the needs of Pentecostal Bible schools, seminaries, and pastors in mind, the authors believe that it will also serve well those who wish to understand Pentecostals and their beliefs better. While the book represents a contemporary approach, one that speaks the language of the Pentecostal movement's present-day theological environment, the authors believe that it remains true to the traditional values that have given dynamism to the movement. As such it offers insight into Pentecostal perspectives, but seeks to do so in a coherent and compelling way.

This book is essentially a theology of Pentecost. The Pentecostal bestowal of the Spirit recorded in Acts 2 has given definition to the movement. The dynamic experience that has given cohesion to the movement—an experience Pentecostals describe as "baptism in the Spirit"—is rooted in the promise of power associated with the Pentecostal gift (Acts 1:8). In spite of its significance, the nature of the Pentecostal gift and its relationship to a wide range of experiences and theological concepts have not been clearly explicated. In the following pages, the authors hope to begin working toward this end. We are certainly indebted to others, frequently non-Pentecostals, who have gone before us. Nevertheless, a number of the questions discussed have received scant attention in scholarly literature to date. We hope that this volume, in addition to serving the needs of students and pastors, might stimulate fresh work in these areas.

Most of the chapters are interrelated and build on the material presented in previous portions of the book. Nevertheless, each chapter is also designed as a self-contained unit. Thus, the reader interested in a specific topic can turn immediately to the chapter of interest and read with profit. We have attempted to keep the duplication of material to a minimum, and yet at the same time we have written each chapter so that it may be read and understood independently.

Spirit and Power is divided into two parts. Part One lays out the theological foundations for our enterprise. We begin with a summary of the origins of the modern Pentecostal movement (chapter 1), which provides an appropriate context from which to view the following chapters.[1] Chapters 2–4 deal with various hermeneutical issues; they help the reader understand the contemporary context and the major issues that now need to be faced. Chapters 5–6 respond to exegetical questions raised by two prominent Evangelical biblical scholars. James Dunn, as we will see, began the Evangelical-Pentecostal[2] dialogue back in 1970 with the publication of his *Baptism in the Holy Spirit*.[3] And, in terms of New Testament pneumatology, Max Turner has emerged as the most prolific scholar of the past decade. In many respects he can be viewed as the heir to James Dunn, the champion of an updated Evangelical appraisal of the Pentecostal movement and its theology. Chapters 5–6, then, dialogue with these two key figures respectively. History, hermeneutics, and exegesis— the foundation is thus laid.

Part Two builds on this foundation and seeks to deal with a wide range of questions related to the Pentecostal experience. Chapter 7 deals with the heart of the matter, where the authors seek to define more specifically the character of the Pentecostal gift. What does it mean to be baptized in the Spirit in the Lukan sense (Acts 2)? Can this experience be equated with conversion? Chapter 8 follows by dealing with a related question. Pentecostals have generally maintained that glossolalia is evidence that one has been baptized in the

Spirit; how shall we evaluate this doctrine and its claims? Chapter 9 also addresses an issue related to the controversial tongues issue. Is the gift of tongues available to every believer? What does the evidence from Paul's hand suggest?

Chapter 10 seeks to dialogue with "Third Wave" theology and presents a Pentecostal perspective on power evangelism. Chapter 11 follows by treating the controversial question concerning whether or not healing should be located in the atonement. Chapter 12 seeks to treat a theme much neglected in Pentecostal circles by way of theological reflections on suffering. Chapters 13–14 treat various aspects of gifts of the Spirit. Chapter 13 focuses on foundational principles, while chapter 14 discusses the nature of the relationship between baptism in the Spirit and spiritual gifts. Finally, chapter 15 discusses an issue that has been widely misunderstood and has caused undue division in the church: What is the nature of the relationship between baptism in the Spirit and the fruit of the Spirit?

A final chapter that looks out into the future seeks to stimulate further thought and serves to tie the book together by way of conclusion.

Notes

[1] Chapter 1, the postscript in chapter 13, and the conclusion were written by William Menzies; the remaining chapters were written by his son, Robert Menzies. For this reason we have often retained the use of the first person pronoun in these chapters. Nevertheless, the entire work has been edited and revised by both authors. Thus the book is in its entirety a cooperative work. A number of chapters are modified versions of Robert Menzies' earlier publications: Chapter 3 was adapted from "Pentecostals, Evangelicals, and the Distinctive Character of Luke's Pneumatology," *Paraclete* 25 (1991): 17–30; chapter 4 is essentially "Jumping Off the Postmodern Bandwagon," *Pneuma* 16 (1994): 115–20; chapter 5 contains much of the material from "Luke and the Spirit: A Reply to James Dunn," *JPT* 4 (1994): 115–38; chapter 6 contains material from "The Spirit of Prophecy, Luke–Acts and Pentecostal Theology: A Response to Max Turner," *JPT* 15 (1999): 49–74; chapters 7 and 8 draw on material published in *Empowered for Witness: The Spirit in Luke-Acts* (JPTSup 6; Sheffield: JSOT Press, 1994); much of chapter 10 appeared in "A Pentecostal Perspective on 'Signs and Wonders,'" *Pneuma* 17 (1995): 265–78; and chapter 14 appeared in *Pentecostalism in Context: Essays in Honor of William W. Menzies*, ed. Wonsuk Ma and R. Menzies (JPTSup 11; Sheffield: Sheffield Academic, 1997).

[2] Although Pentecostals represent a diverse subgroup within Evangelicalism, for the purpose of this book we will distinguish between Pentecostals (assuming their identification with traditional evangelical values) as those who affirm a baptism in the Spirit subsequent to conversion and Evangelicals as those who do not subscribe to this view.

[3] James Dunn, *Baptism in the Holy Spirit* (London: SCM, 1970).

Part One

Theological Foundations

Chapter One

History: Understanding the New Context

When sufficient time has elapsed for the twentieth century to be reviewed in perspective, the astounding growth of the modern Pentecostal movement worldwide will certainly be listed among the significant religious phenomena of the century. In 1900, the Pentecostal movement did not exist. At the end of the century, if one includes Charismatics along with Pentecostals, the collective movement embraces a larger number of people than all the Reformation bodies together and is surpassed only by the Roman Catholic Church in sheer magnitude among the church families of Christendom.[1] In some parts of the world, Pentecostal missions and ministry account for a significant proportion of all the new converts to Christianity. While many of the classical Christian denominations have diminished in strength, Pentecostal bodies have grown rapidly. Although the influence of Pentecostalism has not matched its numerical growth, nonetheless, the contours of Christianity have been shaped increasingly by Pentecostal values. It should be noted at the outset, however, that the dramatic rise of Pentecostalism is not without dangers and challenges; but it also carries great opportunities. At this moment of reflection, it is appropriate to consider the stewardship of opportunity required. Pentecostals should avoid falling prey to the risk of triumphalism.

In this chapter we will endeavor to outline briefly the origins and development of the modern Pentecostal movement. In addition, we will examine the emergence of the sister revival movement, the Charismatic Renewal. We will identify some of the challenges and opportunities currently facing Pentecostals today, occasioned in part by the rapid growth of interest around the world in the work of the Holy Spirit. This background chapter is provided as a historical context for the chapters that follow. The intention is to provide a perspective for viewing the development of Pentecostal theology and for charting the challenges Pentecostals face.

1. The Emergence of the Modern Pentecostal Revival

On January 1, 1901, in Topeka, Kansas, Agnes Ozman experienced the baptism in the Holy Spirit, accompanied by speaking in tongues. She was not the first to speak in tongues. Episodes of isolated outpourings of the Spirit have been chronicled as early as the 1850s, not only in the United States but also in various parts of the world. What was unique about the experience of Miss Ozman, a student at Charles F. Parham's Bethel Bible College, is that her experience occurred within a conscious theological understanding that baptism in the Spirit, an empowering of the Spirit for ministry, an experience subsequent to new birth, is marked by the accompanying sign of speaking in other tongues. Parham's Bible school furnished the environment in which a theological self-understanding was developed for appreciating the significance of this spiritual experience. This is the beginning of a connected history of the modern Pentecostal movement.

Students at Parham's short-term Bible school had been studying the Bible with a view to learning what it teaches about the evidence that one has indeed been baptized in the Holy Spirit. These students concluded that the book of Acts teaches that the baptism in the Spirit is accompanied by speaking in tongues. They understood that this experience was intended to empower recipients to be effective witnesses for Christ. It is significant that this revival began in the context of Bible study and that its theological identity was given form here. People had been known to speak in tongues in a variety of places in the late nineteenth century, and many Evangelicals employed the terminology of baptism in the Spirit prior to 1901, to be sure. But it was in Topeka, under the direction of Charles F. Parham, that the connection between baptism in the Spirit as an enduement of power and the accompanying sign of tongues was established.

Following a succession of local revival campaigns in the Midwest, Charles Parham in 1905 opened a short-term Pentecostal Bible school in Houston, Texas. This became for a time the new headquarters for Parham's ministry. A black Holiness preacher, William J. Seymour, became convinced of the truth of the Pentecostal experience during the school year of 1905–6 in Houston. In the spring of 1906, in response to the invitation of a black Holiness woman in Los Angeles, Seymour went to Los Angeles to hold meetings. At the Holiness mission, his proclamation of the Pentecostal experience was rejected by the local leaders, requiring Seymour to seek a fresh venue for his ministry.

Seymour and his followers then moved to a humble dwelling on Bonnie Brae Street, where he continued his proclamation of the Pentecostal message. The power of God fell among these earnest believers. That home on Bonnie Brae Street soon could not accommodate the crowds who came. Seymour and his cluster of followers moved to a two-story frame structure in an industrial area of Los Angeles. Once a Methodist church, the dilapidated building was later converted into a livery stable. This primitive structure on Azusa Street became the launchpad for projecting the modern Pentecostal revival around the world.

Between 1906 and 1909, meetings were conducted at the Azusa Street hall continuously. Striking during the Jim Crow era in American social history is the mixed-race character of the Azusa Street meetings. Blacks and whites worshiped together, united by the power of the Holy Spirit. Because of the strategic location of Los Angeles for international travel and because of publication in the local papers about the sensational happenings at Azusa Street, travelers from various nations gravitated there. Some of the visitors were missionaries attached to various sending agencies. Many of these curious seekers received the Pentecostal experience. On fire for God, these new Pentecostals, often ostracized from parent bodies, scattered to spread the gospel, sometimes with no credentials and no visible means of support. They had little except the joy of the Lord and a great sense of God's providential care. These were the Pentecostal pioneers.

It is noteworthy that Parham attempted to give leadership to the Azusa Street revival. He was rebuffed in Los Angeles, and his role in the formation of the Pentecostal movement diminished from this point on. In a real sense, the American Pentecostal revival can claim no single father. Beyond American shores, it appears that with the most tenuous of connections, Pentecostal revivals sprang up in various parts of Europe, Asia, and Latin America at this time. Most lines of communication point to the influence of Azusa Street, but one is hard-pressed to certify much beyond the role of the Azusa Street revival serving as a catalyst for the outpourings that occurred elsewhere. This was indeed a fullness of time around the world when people hungry for God recognized that the Pentecostal experience filled their expectations.

2. Antecedents to the Modern Pentecostal Revival

2.1. Holiness Roots

In the late nineteenth century, in nations around the world, believers in various settings were seeking God for a deeper or higher life in him. This experiential hunger expressed itself in two quite different settings. The first was a rebirth of interest among Wesleyans for a recovery of the eighteenth-century message of John Wesley and his followers. The Methodist Church had become successful in the United States, but in the process of ascending the ladder of respectability, much of the spiritual fervor of the early Methodists had been lost. By the decade of the 1860s, in reaction to this decline within Methodism, a whole new cluster of Wesleyan-oriented bodies of Christian believers was being born, most of which were an expression of a hunger for the sanctification experience promulgated by earlier Methodist leaders. This constellation of churches forms the single most significant seedbed for the modern Pentecostal movement.

Donald Dayton has described the emphases common in these circles, emphases that easily passed into the life of the Pentecostal movement. These included a belief in a second blessing, an expectation of an experience of empowerment, a belief in the validity of divine healing, and an affirmation of premillennial eschatology.[2] Many of these believers were committed to a two-stage soteriology, believing that believers should seek a crisis experience subsequent to salvation that was commonly called "entire sanctification." When the Pentecostal revival dawned, these Holiness believers tended to adopt a three-stage view, in which "entire sanctification" was perceived to be the "cleansing," a necessary prelude to the third stage, or "filling," understood as the Pentecostal baptism in the Spirit.

Another type of nineteenth-century Holiness yearning appeared in a non-Wesleyan format. Many Presbyterians, Baptists, Anglicans, and other believers who came more or less from a Reformed tradition were seeking God for a "deeper" or "higher" life. By the mid-1870s, the Keswick conferences in the English-speaking world became an important rallying point for teaching on this life. Keswick teaching, unlike Wesleyan teaching, emphasized the Christian life as a process rather than a crisis of "entire sanctification." Advocates of Keswick theology who adopted Pentecostal theology in the early twentieth century dismissed the notion of a crisis experience of sanctification as a necessary precursor to baptism in the Spirit, favoring instead sanctification as a continuing process in the Christian's life before and after baptism in the Spirit. From 1867 on, Holiness camp meetings were important venues for developing solidarity among advocates and for inspiring followers in their quest for holiness. Later, Pentecostals readily adopted the camp meeting as a useful device for providing inspiration, fellowship, and teaching among their people.

The teaching of Charles G. Finney and his colleague, Asa Mahan of Oberlin, Ohio, is significant for understanding how the terminology of baptism in the Spirit became so readily employed by Pentecostals. By 1875, Finney and Mahan had popularized this term. Much of Evangelical Christianity by the turn of the century freely included the expression in their preaching and writing. Holiness advocates used the expression to describe entire sanctification. Keswick types tended to define baptism in the Spirit as an enduement of power for service. A. J. Gordon's book, *The Ministry of the Holy Spirit*, conveyed virtually all the values with which Pentecostals came to resonate except for the connection between tongues and Spirit baptism.[3]

2.2. Fundamentalism

A second major influence that shaped the values of early Pentecostals was Fundamentalism. Fundamentalism arose in the last third of the nineteenth century as a conscious reaction to the alarming takeover of American Christian institutions by ministers and scholars who had adopted liberal theology. The liberalism of that period, known as Modernism, was marked by skepticism regarding biblical miracles, including rejection of the virgin birth of Christ, his bodily resurrection, and his literal second coming. Modernism featured an optimistic view of humankind and the perfectibility of this world. The standard Modernist eschatology, therefore, fit well with postmillennialism. Through education and social action, Modernists were convinced that they could make the world into an earthly paradise.

Modernists rejected the historical accuracy of the Bible and largely limited their interest in the teaching of the Bible to the ethical principles for organizing constructive human behavior. The teachings of Schleiermacher, Hegel, Kant, Ritschl, and Harnack—scholars in nineteenth-century German universities—had a profound impact on the shaping of late nineteenth-century American liberalism. The great struggle for control of American religious institutions began in the generation immediately prior to the birth of the Pentecostal revival. That generation was the crucible in which Fundamentalism was forged. This was the beginning of the era that came to be known in American religion as the great Fundamentalist-Modernist Controversy.[4]

Fundamentalism, like the Holiness movement, had two streams. One stream was Protestant Orthodoxy. This stream of scholastic Protestantism centered in Princeton Seminary and came to be known as the "Princeton School." Here were produced the great intellectual resources for Fundamentalism—the systematic theology of the Hodges and the apologetic works of Warfield, Green, and later, Machen. Princeton, alone among the influential American seminaries, survived the onslaught of Modernism through this period, succumbing to the allure of liberalism at last only in the late 1920s.

The other stream of Fundamentalism was Evangelical Revivalism. From the time of Jonathan Edwards in colonial America, the country was refreshed by a series of profound revivals or awakenings. In the nineteenth century, chiefly through the ministry of Charles G. Finney, a pattern for the conducting of revival meetings was developed, and a whole revivalistic culture developed. This included a modification of the stern classical Calvinism from which most of these revivalists sprang, opening the door to "whosoever will" rather than focusing attention on the sovereignty of God. D. L. Moody, R. A. Torrey, A. B. Simpson, and a host of others held great public meetings, often across denominational lines, calling people to repentance and to the old-fashioned gospel.

The Evangelical Revivalists, recognizing that they were in a great struggle with Modernism for the soul of the nation, developed new institutions to mobilize resources in this holy war. In the 1870s, D. L. Moody and A. B. Simpson launched crash programs for training workers for evangelism and missions. With the advent of Moody's Bible Institute in Chicago and Simpson's Missionary Training Institute in Nyack, New York, the era of the Bible institute was launched. When the Pentecostal revival came, the Bible institute mechanism was readily adopted as a useful instrument for providing a trained leadership for the revival. Fundamentalists employed a variety of publications to spread their message as well.

Among the distinguishing features of American Fundamentalism in the late nineteenth century was the Bible conference. It was in such settings that the Princeton component of Fundamentalism came together with the Evangelical Revivalist component. The scholastics were not at ease in revival meetings, but they shared deeply with revivalists in their approach to Bible study. If the revivalists were the "heart" of Fundamentalism, it might be said that the Princetonians were the "head" of the movement, providing exegetical and apologetic resources widely appreciated.

It is particularly significant that the Bible study method most readily adopted in the conferences and as a basis for curriculum in the Bible institutes was Scofieldian dispensationalism. Fundamentalist dispensationalism advocated a view toward the present world order markedly different from Modernism. Dispensationalism pictured the church as having a mission, not of reforming society, but of rescuing individuals from a sinking ship. Pessimistic about the near term, the hope Fundamentalists had for the future was the cataclysmic return of Jesus Christ to rescue believers from the Great Tribulation. Scofield's dispensational system provided for laypeople an easily understood method of Bible study and by this means made the message of the Bible available to the average person, a message easy to share with neighbors and friends.

It is fashionable today to complain about features of Scofield's hermeneutical system, but put in the context of the times, one must consider that it is likely no other person contributed so much to the serious study of the Bible in the era of the Fundamentalist-Modernist controversy. To be sure, not all Fundamentalists were dispensationalists, but certainly by 1895, the Bible conference forum had largely developed into prophecy conferences, employing wholesale Scofieldian categories. By this time the "Fundamentals" were fairly well established, commonly calling attention to such basic teachings as the virgin birth of Christ, the substitutionary atonement of Christ, the literal death and resurrection of Christ, the bodily, premillennial return of Christ, and the authority of the Bible, defined as "inerrant in the autograph."

We should also observe that although the Holiness and Fundamentalist movements have been reviewed here as separate groups, there was considerable overlapping. This is particularly true of the Keswick wing of the Holiness movement and the Evangelical Revivalists within Fundamentalism. The speakers at the annual Keswick conventions and the speakers at the Fundamentalist Bible conferences were by and large the same people. By the eve of the Pentecostal revival, these people were almost all employing the language of baptism in the Holy Spirit.

When the Pentecostal revival came, the Pentecostals borrowed heavily from both the Holiness and the Fundamentalist camps, from both the methodologies and the theological values of these groups. Even the polity of the Assemblies of God, the largest of the Pentecostal denominations, was drawn wholesale from the Christian and Missionary Alliance, the Holiness association founded by A. B. Simpson. Thus, even though the Pentecostals were spurned by both Fundamentalists and the Holiness people, they adopted many of their ideas and ways.

In summary, one should note that the early Pentecostals were so overwhelmed by the incredible work of the Holy Spirit that they commonly spoke of this revival as being the long-awaited latter rain prophesied in Scripture. Since they saw little precedent for the manifestations of the Spirit they were experiencing, it seemed to many to be a new thing. Most felt that the revival they were experiencing was the harbinger of the imminent return of the Lord. Out of this came a great sense of urgency, since they felt that the time was short. The intense pioneering spirit and missionary zeal that marked that early generation of Pentecostals is doubtless linked to the sense of their times as being truly the "latter day outpouring." In retrospect, we must concede that the revival did not, in fact, come entirely like a bolt of lightning out of the sky, for it had the discernible antecedents discussed above.

An important additional point should be made here. There is one way in which the modern Pentecostal revival is, indeed, unique. From the time of the Apostolic Age, perhaps two dozen renewal episodes having Pentecostal, or at least Charismatic, overtones can be identified.[5] Yet, all of these prior movements ended dismally, dissolving in fanaticism and/or heresy. The uniqueness of the modern Pentecostal revival lies in its very survival—surviving long enough to gain a hearing in the larger church world and to emerge as a significant component of the Christian world.

3. Characteristics of the Early Pentecostalism

As the Pentecostal movement began to take shape in the first decade of the century, a collective character emerged, making it possible to describe a profile of the distinguishing marks of the adherents of the movement. Several characteristics common in virtually all settings where Pentecostals could be found are identifiable. I find at least eight such characteristics.

3.1. Baptism in the Spirit

Early Pentecostals, as might be expected, proclaimed vigorously what they believed they had experienced in the baptism in the Spirit and what they believed the Bible taught about that experience. It was this experience that set them apart from other Christians. Pentecostals were rejected by virtually all dimensions of the Christian world; they paid a great price for this cherished value but willingly accepted the opprobrium of others. For many, it was the fulfillment of biblical prophecy, the coming of the promised "latter rain." The revival was so remarkable that to many it was like nothing that had ever occurred before. It was not until decades later that most Pentecostals were willing to acknowledge that there were, indeed, antecedents in prior years from which they drew and that the revival, remarkable as it was, was therefore not unique.

3.2. Commitment to Evangelism and Missions

From the outset, Pentecostals understood the purpose of the baptism in the Spirit to be an empowering for witness. Although they reveled in the glory of spiritual experience, most readily organized their lives around the principle of reaching out to the lost of this world. From Azusa Street on, Pentecostalism was stamped with a sense of urgency for spreading the gospel of Jesus Christ. This immediate recognition of a need to reach beyond themselves to the lost of this world is one of the marks that distinguishes Pentecostalism from the Charismatic movement that came sixty years later. When Pentecostal denominations came into being (born of necessity), organizing for the support of foreign missions was one of the compelling motivations.

3.3. Strong Faith

Overwhelmed by the sense of God's immediate presence among them, Pentecostals were quick to believe in the fact of divine intervention in the affairs of this life. They prayed for the sick, expecting God to deliver the afflicted from suffering. They were willing to sacrifice the known and the secure for the distant horizons of frontier ministry at home and abroad. Lacing the pages of early Pentecostal literature are testimonies of remarkable answers to prayer and faith-building exhortations. The early Pentecostals believed ardently in intercessory prayer. They taught the principle of "praying through," of continuing a vigil before the Lord until they had the impression that the prayer was being answered. Believers seeking the baptism in the Spirit were brought into "tarrying meetings," where a cluster of Spirit-baptized believers would gather around the candidate, furnishing a supportive context in which the individual could seek God for the blessing.

3.4. Expectancy

These early Pentecostals expected God to intervene, not only in the immediate need situations in which they found themselves, but in a larger sense, in the return of Jesus to wrap up world history. Conspicuous in early Pentecostalism was a strong commitment to a belief in the second coming of Jesus Christ—a premillennial, literal, physical return. Readily adopting Fundamentalist eschatology (albeit tweaked to conform to Pentecostal needs), Pentecostals believed that the present world order was inevitably doomed and that their assignment was to rescue as many individuals from the coming disaster as they could, since time was short.

The gatherings of Pentecostals, although generally following a simple form, nonetheless were punctuated by manifestations of the Spirit. Early Pentecostals were reluctant to miss a single service for fear that something from God tailored specially for their particular need would be missed. Church services were not boring repetitions of prearranged liturgy; rather, each service had the potential for being the occasion of a special outpouring of the Spirit.

3.5. Reality

Proclaiming the imminent coming of the Lord was marked not by gloom and foreboding, but by an intense sense of joyful expectation. Pentecostals had tasted of the glory of God's presence and longed to see him face to face. Some observers of Pentecostalism were inclined to toss this off as an escape mechanism from the harshness of the poverty and deprivation in which most of the Pentecostals found themselves. Nonetheless, the joy and the warmth found in the oft-beleaguered bands of Pentecostals were in striking contrast to the cold formalism characteristic of much of American Protestantism in that era.

A common banner heralding what visitors might expect in a Pentecostal mission hall proclaimed "Come to the church where Jesus is real." "Reality" was a term used to capture what these believers had experienced. Baptism in the Spirit had made Jesus intensely real for them. This sense of God's nearness led naturally to a lifestyle that would not offend the Holy Spirit. Holiness of life was an authentic quest for these ardent believers. When definitions of acceptable behavior were codified and then imposed on younger adherents, this kind of moral rigorism readily descended into austere legalism. Eager not to offend the Holy Spirit, early Pentecostals sought to scour their behavior for any behaviors that might quench the Spirit.

3.6. Enthusiastic Worship

From the beginning, Pentecostals have been known around the world for loud, joyful worship gatherings. Concert prayer, in which the entire gathering of believers collectively and volubly pour out their hearts to God, is well-nigh universal. The raising of hands is another common response to the perception of God's presence and blessing. Loud singing, accompanied by the clapping of hands and occasionally punctuated by "dancing in the Spirit," has been widely experienced from early days. In such intense meetings, it was not uncommon for one—or many—to fall into a trance-like state, sometimes shaking violently. "Falling under the power" was also a widespread phenomenon.

Such behavior caused critics to label Pentecostals as "Holy Rollers." Earnest, often loud, proclamation of deeply held truths marked much of early Pentecostal preaching. Sometimes believers came to equate volume with the "anointing," though wise leadership sought to steer believers into judging the worth of preaching by the content of the message rather than by the style of delivery. At any point in the service—sometimes during the preaching—gifts of the Spirit could be expected as divine interruptions. Church services were always planned with a degree of tentativeness, since no one could be sure of just what to expect.

3.7. Rich Fellowship

Ostracized by the religious world, early Pentecostals appreciated the companionship they could find among their own. Believers, filled with God's love, reached out to those around them to encourage and bless them. For early Pentecostals, the assembly where they gathered for worship was the center of their lives. Meeting together frequently, sometimes in "cottage prayer meetings," strong bonds of mutual support developed. Often these folks would contrive outreach "bands" to conduct street meetings, home prayer meetings, tent meetings, or other kinds of endeavor to take the gospel to communities or neighborhoods where there was no Pentecostal church. Although it is not clear how widespread it was in the early days, certainly some early Pentecostals came to believe that outside the Pentecostal reality, one's salvation was in question. There was spiritual safety within the fellowship.

3.8. Biblical Authority

It is significant that the Pentecostal revival began among Christian believers who were studying the Bible. A hunger for truth, not merely a quest for experience, energized these early seekers. When one ponders why the modern Pentecostal revival survived while predecessor movements did not, it is likely that the single, most important distinction lies in commitment to the authority of the Bible for governing all belief, experience, and practice. Astute leaders from the beginning of the revival emphasized the need for judging the merit of all teachings, manifestations, and behaviors in the light of God's objective, revealed Word, the Bible. An appreciation for the Bible as totally authoritative was a value readily adopted from Fundamentalism. Mainstream orthodox theology was also borrowed wholesale from Fundamentalism.

It would be inaccurate to portray the earliest generations of Pentecostals as so pious as to be above fault, for there were problems in the embryonic years. One stemmed from the tendency of simple followers to gather about strong personalities, which often resulted in cliques and factions. There was lack of uniformity in teaching, causing confusion among Pentecostals. Some leaders fell into immoralit; others impaired the image of Pentecostalism by failure to meet financial obligations. A sense of need for discipline grew because of such disappointments.

Through these early years, the burgeoning Pentecostal revival was marked by complete ostracism from the larger church world. Rejected by Fundamentalists, by Holiness bodies, and by the great denominations of the day, Pentecostals were forced to carve out their own path in isolation. Not only were they isolated from the religious currents of the larger world, but Pentecostal churches were often isolated from one another.

4. The Formation of Pentecostal Denominations

In Los Angeles, the Azusa Street revival eventually led to the formation of a loose federation of believers that came to be known as the Apostolic Faith.

In 1910 William Durham, a Spirit-baptized Baptist preacher from Chicago, went to Los Angeles. He advocated "the finished work," a Keswick-type view of sanctification that conflicted with the Wesleyan Holiness teaching of Parham and Seymour. A split thus developed in the Los Angeles area. The Apostolic Faith component was quickly overshadowed by the more appealing "finished work" teaching of Durham. By 1913, a rising tide of perceived need for a fellowship of like-minded Pentecostals who inclined toward the "finished work" teaching was apparent. This resulted in a call for a "general council," held in Hot Springs, Arkansas, in April 1914.

About two hundred delegates gathered in Hot Springs for the meeting at which the General Council of the Assemblies was formed. Although this was not the first Pentecostal denomination, it reflected the widest constituency of that early period and quickly emerged as the largest and most representative of the American Pentecostal denominations, a microcosm of Pentecostalism. Some of the reasons given for forming the Assemblies of God were the needs for facilitating the task of world missions, for providing schools to train future leaders, for coordinating publishing endeavors, and for standardizing doctrinal teaching and providing for ministerial discipline.

Eschewing the trappings of contemporary ecclesiastical structures, the people who formed the Assemblies of God resisted the establishing of a formal denomination, preferring to identify the organization as a "cooperative fellowship" of believers and autonomous local churches. The adoption of a constitution was resisted until 1927, when it became apparent that such a document was essential. Not until 1916 was a "Statement of Fundamental Truths" adopted, these sixteen points being a reflection of the theological crisis of that time. The original intent to have no creed was an ideal that was not possible to sustain.

In 1895 the Church of God in Christ denomination was formed, one of the many Wesleyan denominations that had been spawned in the wake of the perceived departure of Methodism from its Wesleyan roots. This group, largely comprised of African-Americans, readily adopted the Pentecostal message in 1906 following the visit of Elder C. H. Mason, their leader, to Azusa Street. He brought the Pentecostal message back to Tennessee with him and urged his followers to add baptism in the Spirit as a third work of grace to their doctrine. This denomination grew to more than 2 million members in the 1990s, rivaling the Assemblies of God for sheer numerical strength.

The complex roots of the Church of God (Cleveland, Tennessee) reach at least as far back as 1902, with the formation of a nucleus of believers in what is considered to be the first church in the present denomination. Church of God historians point to a remarkable revival in Camp Creek, North Carolina, not far from Cleveland, Tennessee, even earlier. Here, in 1896, a great move of God, including speaking in tongues, swept the area. The participants did not fully understand what this meant, but the episode conditioned believers in the area to accept the Pentecostal teaching when it came to the South from Los Angeles.

A fellowship of kindred churches formally organized in 1906 to form the Church of God. Two years later, through the ministry of G. B. Cashwell, who had brought to the American South the message of Pentecost, the Church of God General Overseer, A. J. Tomlinson, received the Pentecostal experience. Already many Church of God pastors had received the baptism in the Spirit, so it was relatively easy for the Church of God to move into the family of Holiness Pentecostal denominations. In time, the Church of God became the most influential of the Wesleyan Pentecostal bodies.[6]

Through the ministry of G. B. Cashwell of Dunn, North Carolina, not only did the Church of God become a Pentecostal body, but other groups in the South followed a similar path. Notable among these is the story of the Pentecostal Holiness Church. In 1908, this small Holiness sect adopted the Pentecostal message and joined sister Wesleyan bodies in the South in adding the Pentecostal experience to their doctrine as a third work of grace. In more recent years, distinguished members of the Pentecostal Holiness Church have been the evangelist Oral Roberts and historian Vinson Synan.

It should be noted that in the brief window of 1906–1909, several significant Holiness denominations were swept into the Pentecostal movement, all from the American South. By 1910, the reaction from the Holiness movement had hardened into the most bitter antagonism against the Pentecostal movement, a position that has been ameliorated only in recent years.

5. The Development of the Modern Pentecostal Movement

Although the Pentecostal churches came into being reluctantly, not wishing to form new denominations, the need for the services provided by formal organization required the early believers to develop new structures. The Assemblies of God, as one major representative group, adopted a creedal statement in 1916, born of necessity because of a major doctrinal crisis.[7] In 1927, with the adoption of a constitution, the Assemblies of God had fully evolved into a denomination.

In the years prior to World War II, Pentecostals grew at home and abroad. During much of this period, the Assemblies of God was considered to be the fastest growing American denomination. Much of this growth was the result of numerous independent Pentecostal congregations choosing to affiliate with the Assemblies of God, since it was becoming evident that organization was not causing God's disfavor, as some had feared, and that the blessings inherent in fellowshiping with a disciplined body had many advantages. It was also during these years that the mechanism of the Sunday school proved to be a good means for mobilizing Spirit-filled laypeople in the enterprise of evangelism and teaching of new converts. As a result, during the era of the Great Depression, in which the mainstream denominations were losing members, vibrant groups like the Pentecostals were gleaning numerous converts.

If the domestic American growth during these years was noteworthy, the overseas expansion of Pentecostal churches was even more spectacular. The passionate missionary impulse that marked the revival from its beginnings found expression in pioneer church planting in many countries. The typical pattern was for individuals to experience a sense of missionary call and to begin forthwith to set out for a chosen foreign field. At first, no formal organizational structure was available to facilitate the sending and supporting of missionaries. But in groups like the Assemblies of God, a department for endorsing candidates and supervising the funding and distribution of personnel rapidly matured.

Missionary philosophy evolved over the years, easily assimilating the principles of indigenous endeavor, so that by mid-century the strategy of Assemblies of God missions centered in the cultivation of self-governing, self-supporting, and self-propagating autonomous national church bodies. Strong belief in the principle of "not by might, nor by power, but by my Spirit" energized pioneers to believe that God would fashion strong national church bodies out of virtually nothing. Although American domestic church statistics experienced one or more plateau periods in which growth was fairly minimal, the statistics for the overseas growth of sister Assemblies of God church organizations grew steadily through the century, so that by the end of the century worldwide membership of Assemblies of God churches approached thirty million.[8]

A principle instrument employed with great effectiveness in the rapid development of indigenous churches has been the Bible institute. The Assemblies of God around the world directs more than three hundred Bible schools, most under local leadership. These schools channel trained young people into the life of the church to fill posts of leadership. Increasingly, churches that were just a generation ago "receiving" churches are now joining hands with Western counterparts in sending missionaries to new frontiers.

The decade of the 1940s is important in the history of the modern Pentecostal movement because this was the period when Pentecostalism moved beyond the isolation in which it had lived from the days of Azusa Street. During World War II, American Evangelical leaders were charting a course for concerted action, desiring to form a collective voice to speak for their interests and not being content to be represented to the public by the World Council of Churches and its American counterpart, an entity that came to be known as the National Council of Churches. One hundred and fifty leaders gathered in St. Louis in a constitutional convention for the formation of the National Association of Evangelicals (NAE) in April 1942.

Leaders from the Assemblies of God were invited to be part of this historic meeting. Evangelicals, many of whom had been led to believe that Pentecostals should be classified as a cult, had come to recognize that apart from the Pentecostal teaching about baptism in the Spirit with the accompanying sign of speaking in tongues, Pentecostal teaching was squarely in line with orthodox Christian theology. Association with Pentecostals during the course of World War II had brought Evangelicals into proximity with Pentecostals, and it was largely out of this encounter that a sense of spiritual solidarity emerged. This is the first evidence that the Pentecostal revival of the twentieth century had survived long enough to gain a hearing by the larger church world. This, in fact, is what makes the modern revival unique in church history.

We should note a distinction developing in American Evangelicalism during this period, one that made the invitation for Pentecostal participation possible. What might be termed "early Fundamentalism" is that amalgam of values that coalesced by about 1895, featuring the core values that Fundamentalists felt were threatened by Modernism. The evidence seems to suggest that the Modernists swept the field in the great denominations, taking over seminaries, publishing houses, and positions of ecclesiastical influence, not by successful argumentation, but by subterfuge.

In fact, the Fundamentalists were not done in by Modernist persuasion at all. The level of debate in that earlier era was on a sophisticated level. The great works of the early Fundamentalist apologists were brilliantly done and still rank among the best statements for supporting the deity of Christ, his miracles, his sinless death and resurrection, and the absolute authority of the Bible. By 1925, the era of the infamous "monkey trial" that lampooned belief in a literal biblical creation, Fundamentalism had been driven from positions of authority in most of the great denominations. From then on, they engaged in a form of religious guerilla warfare.

These "later Fundamentalists" developed a negative image. Bereft of position, Fundamentalism became an underground movement. The literature produced was in the form of pamphlets, documents that betrayed a spirit of defensiveness and rancor. The Fundamentalists lashed out, sometimes at their own colleagues who differed from one another in various ways. This internecine struggle produced splintering among a people who had already separated from parent bodies they deemed to be apostate. The result of this defensive activity led, finally, to a recognition by key Evangelical leaders in the early 1940s that this was not an adequate platform from which the gospel should be heralded in the post-war era soon to come. Leaders such as Harold J. Ockenga and J. Elwin Wright, later joined by Carl F. H. Henry among others, brought into being what came to be termed the "new Evangelicalism."

The spirit of new Evangelicalism was positive, irenic, and inclusive—yet holding to the same orthodox theology as "later Fundamentalism." They sought, in effect, to recapture the spirit of the early Fundamentalists. The periodical *Christianity Today* and Fuller Theological Seminary are direct products of the spirit of the new Evangelicalism. What is significant for Pentecostals is that it was the new Evangelicals who made room for Pentecostals. The later Fundamentalists split from the NAE over the issue of whether or not to include Pentecostals, forming an organization called the American Council of Christian Churches (ACCC). Over the years the NAE has grown substantially (with the Assemblies of God in time becoming the largest single member organization) while the ACCC has remained a marginal endeavor.

6. The Charismatic Renewal

Until about 1955, any pastor or church member in the great American denominations—Modernist, Fundamentalist, or Holiness—who reported receiving the baptism in the Holy Spirit with speaking in tongues automatically separated from the parent body, either voluntarily or involuntarily. Pentecostal churches had received a substantial number of people who came from other church bodies. However, thoughtful people in many church bodies began to realize they were losing some of their best and brightest people.

As early as 1955, some pastors in the American Episcopal Church received the Pentecostal experience and began to proclaim their experience within their church, usually accompanied by arranging meetings for seekers. Meetings where anointing of the sick and prayer for healing were featured accompanied the seeking sessions. Cautious approval of some local episodes of such renewal was given after careful scrutiny by the respective diocesan leaders. When it was noted that these renewal churches were the most vital in the diocese, the leaders were reluctant to reject what clearly was in their best ecclesiastical interests. A similar series of episodes transpired within the Presbyterian Church.

In 1960, in Van Nuys, California, the Easter Sunday message of the Episcopalian rector of St. Mark's Church, Dennis Bennett, produced a major controversy within his church. He told the story of his own encounter with the

Holy Spirit, an experience into which he had been led through Pentecostal influences. This story was broadcast by the press, bringing the Charismatic issue to national awareness.[9] This event is often seen as the Charismatic equivalent to the 1906 era at Azusa Street in Los Angeles for the Pentecostal movement. It was here that the Charismatic movement took on a life of its own.

Over the next decades, virtually every American denomination was affected by the Charismatic Renewal Movement, so that today there are Charismatic fellowships within virtually all these denominations. Several major denominations made serious studies of the phenomenon, issuing official papers on the subject.[10] These studies make it possible to distinguish the ethos of the Charismatic Renewal from the older traditional Pentecostal Movement. Charismatics should be understood as a *renewal agency* within older churches. As such, these ardent believers brought to the attention of their parent church bodies the possibility of God's empowering presence in the church today—something few really expected.

In this renewal mode, the first door to be opened was an expectation of manifesting gifts of the Spirit. This preoccupation with the gifts (*charismata*, as Paul uses the term in 1 Cor. 12–14), makes the word "Charismatic" highly appropriate. Charismatics usually do not focus attention on the Pentecostal event of Acts 2, as do Pentecostals. They tend not to speak of baptism in the Spirit as an experience separable from new birth. Even if they do, they are not likely to assign speaking in tongues to that experience as a necessary accompaniment.

Conspicuous as well is the difference in attitude toward evangelism and missions. Pentecostals from the beginning saw their reason for being as the evangelization of the world. Charismatics, by contrast, tend to see their role as a revitalizing influence within their own tradition. It is encouraging that in more recent years, Charismatics are discovering the challenge of world missions.

The Charismatic Renewal Movement has three distinct phases. (1) The first phase, begun about 1955, impacted high church Protestantism. Sociologists of religion are baffled by the way this revival developed. It trickled from the top down, not from the bottom up, as do most revivals. The high church wing of the American Episcopal Church was the first impacted. Other denominations, often aligned with the World Council of Churches, followed.

The story of David duPlessis figures prominently in this first phase of the Charismatic Renewal. A South African Pentecostal leader, duPlessis felt as early as the 1930s that God was going to work among the great denominations. His Pentecostal brothers looked askance at this. In a fascinating sequence of events, duPlessis found himself immersed in WCC meetings as early as 1954. Here he found Christian leaders greatly burdened about the divisions within Christendom. They were beginning to seek God for a spiritual solution rather than depending on the passing of resolutions and the making of proclamations. This concern over the spiritual quality of the church opened the door to earnest discussions with duPlessis about the role of the Holy Spirit in the life of the church.

DuPlessis led many of his WCC friends into a Pentecostal experience. This involvement with the WCC proved to be an embarrassment to his Pentecostal friends, and he was subsequently dismissed from his adopted denomination, the American Assemblies of God. (Later, before he died, he was quietly reinstated.) The newfound acceptance of groups like the Assemblies of God by the NAE resulted in Evangelicals placing great pressure on their Pentecostal friends to distance themselves from activities in the WCC. That there had been an important opening to the person and work of the Holy Spirit within WCC leadership placed Pentecostals in the middle of conflict during these years. The story of duPlessis illustrates the ambiguity Pentecostals continue to face. How to relate to the fresh wind of the Spirit among people whose theology is at variance with orthodoxy is an unresolved issue.

(2) The second phase of the Charismatic Renewal began dramatically in 1967, at DuQuesne University in Pittsburgh, Pennsylvania. Roman Catholic laypeople were seeking God earnestly. They experienced a powerful move of the Holy Spirit in a prayer meeting setting. This seemed to touch a responsive chord among faculty and students at Notre Dame University in South Bend, Indiana. The Catholic renewal, commonly known as Catholic Pentecostalism, swept around the world in an astonishingly short time. Today, this Charismatic renewal is virtually everywhere to be found, although some feel it has already peaked in some places. Since the 1970s, a continuing dialogue between Catholics and Pentecostals was jointly sponsored by the Vatican and by Pentecostals and Charismatics in North America.[11] However, uncertainties surrounding relationships with the Catholic Pentecostal movement are underscored by the tensions Pentecostals often face as they attempt to evangelize in predominantly Roman Catholic countries.

A considerable body of biblical and theological literature has been produced by Catholic Charismatic scholars. Although there is some variety in how Catholics understand their experience, most adopt "actualization" teaching. In this, the Catholic insists that the initiation episodes of baptism and confirmation convey the grace of Spirit fullness to the communicant, although this is not generally evident at the initiation moments. It may not be until later, perhaps at a prayer meeting where people are encouraged to pray for the "fullness of the Spirit," that they may burst into praises, which include tongues and other manifestations of the Spirit. In this experience what had been latent from the onset of baptism and confirmation is brought into the conscious level of experience.

In other words, Catholic theologians tend to say that baptism in the Spirit really occurred at initiation but is actualized at a later date. The untrained layperson is likely to report, "Last Friday night I was saved and baptized in the Holy Spirit," to the chagrin of the priest. It should be noted that Roman Catholic Charismatic theologians are earnestly endeavoring to frame an understanding of Pentecostal experience in such a fashion that it can be kept within the fold of acceptable church teaching.[12]

(3) Peter Wagner has coined the term "the Third Wave" to describe another phase of the Charismatic Renewal. By this he means the intrusion of manifestations of the Spirit common among Pentecostals and other Charismatics within the confines of conservative Evangelicalism. This, he believes, can be traced to about the year 1985.[13] Some would dispute Wagner's thesis, contending that there has been an evolution over a lengthy period of time of acceptance of Pentecostal-type themes within Evangelicalism. In any event, it does appear that somewhat more tardily than either liberal Protestants or Roman Catholics, Evangelical bodies have been forced to come to terms with the eruption of Pentecostal phenomena in their midst. Perhaps those who have the most strongly held commitments are the most difficult to persuade to make modifications in beliefs and attitudes. Certainly a definite shift in acceptance of Pentecostal values by Evangelicals has transpired, even if this trend has taken place over a more lengthy time than that marked out by Wagner. Evangelical seminaries feature popular courses in Charismatic matters, including how to incorporate prayer for the sick in pastoral ministry.

If the relationship between Pentecostals and the larger church world (WCC) remains uncertain, the relationship of traditional (classical) Pentecostalism to Evangelicalism is also somewhat ambiguous. Like ships passing in the night, the Evangelicals have moved closer to the values espoused by Pentecostals, although few have registered complete acceptance. On the other hand, Pentecostals have sought to identify strongly with Evangelicalism, since in spirit there is a natural affinity for core values.

This yearning for Evangelical acceptance came, however, at a price, seen most clearly in the area of hermeneutics. Blind adherence to the full panoply of standard Evangelical principles of hermeneutics caused Pentecostals to fall unwittingly into a trap. The reason lies in the restrictive rules that govern the Evangelical hermeneutical enterprise, restrictions that rule out the possibility of a Pentecostal outcome. With the rapprochement between Pentecostals and Evangelicals that emerged in the decades following World War II, Pentecostals largely abdicated their theological agenda to Evangelical academic leadership. Pentecostal Bible schools employed Evangelical textbooks whole-sale. There was apparently little on which they disagreed, save in the matter of the doctrine of the Holy Spirit.

Pentecostals were disappointed, however, that they were not successful in persuading Evangelicals to approve of their understanding of the work of the Holy Spirit. Further, some Pentecostal students who were immersed in Evangelical textbooks began to question the premises of Pentecostal theology. It was becoming apparent that a central reason for the theological chasm lay in the different premises on which the Bible was studied. Evangelicals operated with one set of hermeneutical rules; Pentecostals operated with a different approach. It was not until the 1970s that this problem was clearly understood. It is important to take into account significant changes in Evangelical hermeneutical theory since 1970, changes that make it easier for present-day Evangelicals and Pentecostals to speak similar language.

Since the role of hermeneutics is foundational to theology, and since issues within the field of hermeneutics have proven to be crucial for articulating a coherent Pentecostal theology, the next chapters are devoted to an exploration of Pentecostal hermeneutics.

Study Questions

1. In what way is the modern Pentecostal movement unique, differing from all previous charismatic-like movements since the Apostolic Age? What reasons does the author offer for this distinction?
2. How did early Pentecostals define their unique theological contribution? What gave them an identity?
3. Some early Pentecostals employed terms like the "latter rain" to describe the revival. What did they mean by this term? Do you think this understanding is valid?
4. What influences shaped the theological formation of the modern Pentecostal movement?
5. Why were the early Pentecostals of the modern revival ostracized by other Christians?
6. How would you distinguish Pentecostals from Charismatics theologically?
7. How has the Charismatic Renewal impacted Pentecostalism?

Notes

[1] David Barrett, ed., *World Christian Encyclopedia: A Comprehensive Survey of Churches and Religions in the Modern World A.D. 1900–2000* (Oxford: Oxford Univ. Press, 1982), 792–93.

[2] See Donald Dayton, *Theological Roots of Pentecostalism* (Grand Rapids: Francis Asbury, 1987).

[3] A. J. Gordon, *The Ministry of the Holy Spirit* (Philadelphia: Judson, 1894), 67–96.

[4] See Ernest R. Sandeen, *The Roots of Fundamentalism* (Chicago: Univ. of Chicago Press, 1970); Stewart G. Cole, *The History of Fundamentalism* (Westport, Conn.: Greenwood, 1931) for standard studies of Fundamentalism. An Evangelical critique is provided by George M. Marsden, *Understanding Fundamentalism and Evangelicalism* (Grand Rapids: Eerdmans, 1991).

[5] Bernard Bresson, *Studies in Ecstasy* (New York: Vantage, 1966).

[6] Vinson Synan, *The Holiness-Pentecostal Tradition*, 2d ed. (Grand Rapids: Eerdmans, 1997), is an excellent review of the history of the modern Pentecostal movement from a Wesleyan perspective.

[7] The "Jesus Only" controversy, which erupted within a year of the formation of the Assemblies of God, nearly destroyed the new denomination. The heterodox teaching of the Jesus Only people appealed to many of the leaders, but was successfully challenged by J. Roswell Flower with his report that this was not a new revelation, but an ancient heresy that had been condemned by orthodox Christians in the fourth century. Most of the early defectors to the new teaching were chastened by the findings of Flower and returned to the Assemblies of God fold. However, a significant number of ministers and churches remained loyal to the Jesus Only (or Oneness) doctrine, furnishing the nucleus of an entire family of Pentecostal denominations. See William W. Menzies, *Anointed to Serve* (Springfield, Mo.: Gospel, 1971), 106–21.

[8] Sherry Doty, AOG statistician, ed., "The Assemblies of God: Current Facts, Based on Calendar Year 1998," Office of Public Relations, June 1999.

[9] See Dennis Bennett, *Nine O'Clock in the Morning* (Plainfield, N.J.: Logos International, 1970) for his testimony. See Menzies, *Anointed to Serve*, 177–227, for the story of the emergence of the Assemblies of God from isolation into association with other Christian bodies.

[10] See Kilian McDonnell, *Presence, Power, Praise: Documents on the Charismatic Renewal*, 3 vols. (Collegeville, Minn.: Liturgical Press, 1980), for the best collection of official denominational responses to the Charismatic Renewal.

[11] See *Pneuma* 12 (Fall, 1990). This entire issue is devoted to the Catholic/Pentecostal dialog, which began in 1972 and has been renewed continually since then in five-year periods. This issue contains an excellent editorial by Cecil M. Robeck, "Splinters and Logs, Catholics and Pentecostals" (77–83) and is followed by reports of the first three five-year dialog sessions.

[12] Heribert Muhlen, *A Charismatic Theology*, trans. E. Quinn and T. Linton (New York: Paulist, 1978). See also Donald L. Gelpi, *Pentecostalism: A Theological Viewpoint* (New York: Paulist, 1971).

[13] See Peter Wagner's *The Third Wave of the Holy Spirit* (Ann Arbor, Mich.: Vine), 1988.

Chapter Two

Hermeneutics: The Quiet Revolution

A revolution is taking place in Evangelical hermeneutics. No, I do not refer to the influences of postmodern literary theory. Although we will undoubtedly have to deal with the impact of postmodernism for some time, by and large Evangelicals have responded with clarity and acumen to this new movement. Positive influences have been duly noted and negative elements have been rightly critiqued and discarded.[1]

Rather, I refer to the substantial change in Evangelical attitudes toward the theological significance of biblical narrative. The beginnings of this change may be traced to 1970 for reasons we will outline below. Since this time, Evangelical attitudes have slowly and quietly, yet steadily, changed so that today we can now speak of a virtual consensus on this issue. In the following essay I would like to outline the nature of this transformation, the forces which have produced it, and the significant implications that emerge for contemporary theological reflection. More specifically I will seek to (1) outline the perspective of a previous generation of Evangelical scholars, (2) establish how a new consensus has emerged, and (3) look at some of the significant opportunities this new perspective affords for theological reflection within the Pentecostal tradition as we enter a new millennium.

1. The Past: A Canon Within a Canon

A survey of three influential books when I was student in seminary is instructive. These three books stand out as representing the viewpoint of the early phase of modern Evangelicalism (1945–1970): Bernard Ramm, *Protestant Biblical Interpretation* (1956); John R. W. Stott, *The Baptism and the Fullness of the Spirit* (1964); and Gordon Fee and Douglas Stuart, *How to Read the*

Bible for All Its Worth (1981). The latter work, although written after 1970, reflects the perspective of this earlier generation and comes from a transitional period—a period when the traditional perspective was beginning to be challenged and when the implications of new insights for hermeneutical theory, particularly in the study of the Gospels, were beginning to be examined. These books were widely used in Evangelical Bible schools and seminaries, and collectively they have had a substantial impact on a generation of Evangelical students.

These books represent a trajectory from Ramm to Stott and Fee. Ramm sets the tone when, quoting Horne, he defines the analogy of faith as "the constant and perpetual harmony of Scripture in the fundamental points of faith and practice deduced from those passages in which they were discussed by the inspired penmen either directly or expressly, and in clear, plain, and intelligible language."[2] In other words, Ramm highlights the unity of Scripture and suggests that clearer passages of the Bible should be used to help us understand more ambiguous ones. Exactly how Ramm would apply the analogy of faith to narrative portions of Scripture is not specified. But this matter is picked up and clarified by Stott and Fee.

Stott, in the original 1964 version of his book, states that the "revelation of the purpose of God in Scripture should be sought in its *didactic*, rather than in its *historical* parts."[3] In the second edition published in 1976, he insists that he is not saying that descriptive passages are valueless. Nevertheless he continues by affirming: "What I am saying is that what is descriptive is valuable only in so far as it is interpreted by what is didactic."

In his widely influential book (penned together with Douglas Stuart), *How to Read the Bible For All Its Worth*, Gordon Fee echoes this basic line. In a chapter entitled, "Acts—The Problem of Historical Precedent," Fee articulates a now-famous principle: "Our assumption, along with many others, is that *unless Scripture explicitly tell us we must do something, what is merely narrated or described can never function in a normative way.*"[4]

Today, for many it is difficult to imagine how such a restrictive approach came to be axiomatic for Evangelical interpretation. After all, doesn't this principle sound very much like a canon within a canon? Doesn't much of the theology in the Old Testament come to us in the form of narrative? Didn't Jesus himself often teach by relating stories or parables? Doesn't such a theory tend to reduce the Gospels and Acts (as well as other narrative portions of Scripture) to a mere appendage to didactic portions of Scripture, particularly Paul's letters? (Perhaps this explains the overwhelmingly Pauline character of much of Evangelical theology. When all is said and done, has not Evangelical theology tended to be Pauline theology?) In any event, even the most casual reader cannot help feeling the tension with 2 Timothy 3:16, "All Scripture is God-breathed and is useful for teaching, rebuking, correcting and training in righteousness."

However, before we judge our Evangelical precursors too harshly, let us acknowledge that they were addressing a real problem and that they did so in a unique context. Stott and Fee, for example, were seeking to deal with the problem of discerning what exactly we can glean from a narrative. Although they would acknowledge the possibility of doctrine flowing from narrative, the problem is how to pinpoint exactly what doctrine this might be. Which elements of a story are understood to be the basis for normative theology and which are not? As Fee notes, unless we are prepared to choose church leaders by the casting of lots or willing to encourage church members to sell all of their possessions, we cannot simply assume that a particular historical narrative provides a basis for normative theology.

This, of course, is a legitimate concern, a real question. As we have seen, the previous generation offered a straightforward answer: Doctrine cannot be rooted in narrative alone for narrative is simply too slippery, too elastic, too imprecise. We will examine this question more fully below, but for now it is sufficient to remind ourselves that the concerns that gave rise to this rather restrictive stance cannot be avoided.

Additionally, we must be sensitive to the context, the unique set of historical events, that impacted the outlook of this earlier generation. Perhaps we should look as far back as the mid-1800s and the rise of the Tübingen school under the influence of Ferdinand Christian Baur, where we see the seeds of a controversy that has largely given shape to the Evangelical "restrictive" posture. Baur, who taught at the University of Tübingen, applied the Hegelian dialectic (thesis, antithesis, synthesis) to the history of early Christianity, which resulted in a portrayal extremely critical of the historical reliability of Acts. Baur maintained that Acts was essentially a product of revisionist history—a synthesis of Jewish Christianity (thesis) and Gentile Christianity (antithesis).[5]

In short, Baur suggested that Acts gives us little by way of historical facts, but a lot of wishful thinking and theologizing from a later generation. Although his thesis has been largely rejected as yet another illustration of Hegelianism gone mad,[6] his views set the stage for other developments that would shake Evangelical sensibilities. I speak on the one hand of the influential commentary on Acts penned by Ernst Haenchen;[7] on the other, of the rise of redaction criticism.

Haenchen, following in Baur's wake, also stressed the theological character of Acts. According to him, Luke virtually fabricated large sections of Acts in order to make the homiletical points he felt his church needed to hear. Luke had little concern for history; he was essentially a preacher, a theologian. If the facts interfered with the story he wanted to tell, so much the worse for the facts.

At approximately the same time new currents in the study of the Gospels were also developing in Germany. These currents crystallized into a new methodology called "redaction criticism." Günther Bornkamm first applied the method to Matthew.[8] He was soon followed by Hans Conzelmann and Willi Marxsen, who offered redaction-critical readings of Luke and Mark respectively.[9] The key thrust of each of these works was this: Each Gospel writer writes with his own distinctive theological motives in view, and this perspective can be uncovered through careful examination of the manner in which the author selects and shapes his source material (be it Mark, Q, or other sources). The early practitioners of redaction criticism, like Baur and Haenchen in relation to Acts, highlighted the theological character of the Gospels and drastically downplayed the historical concern of the Evangelists. According to the redaction critics, the Gospels tell us much about the theological concerns of Matthew, Mark, and Luke; they tell us far less about the historical events surrounding the ministry of Jesus.

The Evangelical reaction was understandably negative. Any attack on the historical reliability of the Gospels and Acts was an attack on the very foundations of Christianity. Evangelicals countered seeking an eye for an eye: The Gospel writers were *not* theologians; they were historians. In Evangelical circles any discussion of the theological motivation of the Gospel writers, and thus the theological purpose of their narrative, was muted. The Gospels and Acts were viewed as historical records, not accounts reflecting self-conscious theological concerns.

This reaction to the early and more radical expressions of redaction criticism had a significant impact, I would suggest, on Evangelical hermeneutics. Since the theological character of the Gospels and Acts had been largely dismissed, there was little reason to suggest that theology might flow, in and of itself, from the pages of these historical documents. This perspective, coupled with the problem of how one might locate the theological purpose(s) of a narrative, led to the restrictive principle enunciated by Stott and Fee. New winds, however, were blowing within Evangelicalism. They were destined to be winds of change.

2. The Present: Affirming the Theological Significance of Narrative

In 1970, I. Howard Marshall's influential book *Luke: Historian and Theologian* appeared on the scene.[10] The title of the work itself suggests why it is so important for our present discussion. Here was a book written by a leading Evangelical New Testament scholar that argued that Luke was simultaneously a reliable historian *and* a clear-minded theologian. Marshall suggested that Luke wrote history, accurate and careful history; but not bare, objective, detached history. Luke–Acts represents history with a purpose—history written with a theological agenda in view. Marshall's book signaled an important watershed in Evangelical thought. Although in 1970 many had not yet perceived the full implications of Marshall's position, the reappraisal of the theological character of biblical narrative, particularly the Gospels and Acts, was underway.

At the same time, a new generation of Evangelical scholars and seminary instructors, many of whom had studied under Marshall, began to reappropriate and utilize the tools of redaction criticism. These scholars—e.g., Grant Osborne, Robert Stein, Joel Green, Darrell Bock, Craig Blomberg—began to judiciously use the positive insights of this method of analysis while at the same time discarding some of the more radical presuppositions. This resulted in an impressive array of scholarly studies that showed the value of the method and its compatibility—if employed properly—with a high view of Scripture.[11] The impact upon Evangelical hermeneutics was inevitable, if not immediate. Here were Evangelical scholars highlighting the distinctive theological perspectives of the various Gospel writers. Additionally, they stressed not only the fact that the Gospel writers were indeed theologians, but they demonstrated with considerable skill how their distinctive message could and should be heard.

In short, the revolution marked by the emergence of *Luke: Historian and Theologian* offered a fresh response to the questions that had impacted, consciously or otherwise, an earlier generation of Evangelical scholars. The overstated response to Baur, Haenchen, Conzelmann, and company—that the Gospel writers were historians, *not* theologians—was modified. A more sober response, one that more accurately matched the data of the biblical texts themselves, was offered: The Gospels present accurate history, but history with a purpose. Indeed, they were inspired by theological concerns and contain theological lessons directed toward their readers. Furthermore, the question concerning how we might uncover the theological message of the biblical narratives began to receive concrete answers. The tools of redaction criticism, aided by more wide-ranging developments in literary analysis, were employed with considerable success.

These developments converged to produce what is today a clear consensus. There is now widespread recognition in the Evangelical world that biblical narratives, particularly those found in the Gospels and Acts, were shaped with theological concerns in mind and thus they convey a theological message. The crucial question is no longer whether Luke and the others were theologians; the central question now is what is the specific shape or content of their theology.

These conclusions have led to a significant revolution in Evangelical hermeneutics. The older position, which gave theological pride of place to didactic portions of Scripture, has been largely, if not universally, rejected. An excellent example of this shift in thinking is found in the new textbook on hermeneutics produced by William Klein, Craig Blomberg, and Robert Hubbard, entitled *Introduction to Biblical Interpretation*. The authors, addressing the matter head-on, state:

> We have already stated that narrative often teaches more indirectly than didactic literature without becoming any less normative. Thus, we reject Fee and Stuart's highlighted maxim that "unless Scripture explicitly tells us we must do something, what is merely narrated or described can never function in a normative way."[12]

Grant Osborne expresses similar views in his book on hermeneutics. In a section entitled "Narrative," he writes:

> Moreover, I also oppose the current tendency to deny the theological dimension on the grounds that narrative is indirect rather than direct. This ignores the results of redaction criticism, which has demonstrated that biblical narrative is indeed theological at the core and seeks to guide the reader to relive the truth encapsulated in the story. Narrative is not as direct as didactic material, but it does have a theological point and expects the reader to interact with that message. My argument is that biblical narrative is in some ways even better than the teaching applied to similar situations in the lives of the people.[13]

So, the revolution has taken place. It has come gradually, over a period of many years, almost without notice: a quiet revolution. Nevertheless, the changes are real and cannot be missed. As a result, the Gospels, the book of Acts, and other biblical narratives have new life and meaning. They, in turn, are breathing new life into Evangelical theology. The implications of this revolution in hermeneutics are just beginning to be felt, but the potential contributions to our theological understanding should not be underestimated.

3. The Future: Retaining the Full Canon

The most far-reaching implication of this hermeneutical shift is that it opens up the possibility in a fresh way of producing a holistic biblical theology. In the past, as I have noted, Evangelical theology has been largely Pauline theology. The prevailing attitude, shaped by and enshrined in the hermeneutic of the past, was that we go to Paul for theology (since his letters are didactic in character); the Gospels and Acts simply provide the raw historical data for this theological reflection. This inevitably flattened the canon for us, and while perhaps it made talk of the unity of Scripture a bit easier, it also blinded us to the full breadth and richness of the biblical witness.

The more recent emphasis on the role of narrative has opened new windows for us and enabled us to experience fresh winds of theological reflection. In this book, my father and I would like to draw on our own Pentecostal tradition in order to show how Evangelical theology might be enriched by a more holistic approach, one that gives full voice to those inspired by the Spirit to write biblical narrative.

From its inception the Pentecostal movement has emphasized the narrative of Luke–Acts. It is evident that the distinctive features of Pentecostal theology—particularly its emphasis on a baptism in the Spirit distinct from conversion—are rooted in Luke–Acts. Without Luke's writings there could be no Pentecostal theology, for we would not know of the Pentecostal gift (Acts 1–2). Because Luke–Acts is so pivotal for Pentecostal theology and experience, the recent hermeneutical shift within the larger Evangelical world has had a special impact on Pentecostals. Pentecostals, often chided in the past for simplistic arguments from historical precedent, have entered into a new era of creative theological reflection. Pentecostal scholars have seized the opportunity afforded by the new hermeneutical context and raised important questions concerning the nature of Luke's pneumatology (doctrine of the Holy Spirit) and its relationship to that of Paul. This in turn has stimulated discussions within the wider Evangelical world concerning the nature of a fully-orbed biblical pneumatology and how this might impact contemporary church life.

Currently, a lively debate concerning the nature of Lukan pneumatology and its contemporary significance continues.[14] Indeed, the present book seeks to contribute to this ongoing discussion. At this point, however, it is sufficient to note that the key issues in the debate now center on exegesis and the shape of Luke's theology. Gone are the days when we might discuss whether or not Luke should be viewed as a significant theologian with a distinctive message. This new context is a result of the quiet revolution—a revolution that has stressed the significance of biblical narratives and the richness of the biblical witness.

4. Conclusion

The quiet revolution has indeed significantly impacted Evangelical attitudes toward the Gospels and Acts, and the hermeneutical enterprise in general. It has opened up new questions, new fruitful points of discussions. Above all, it is enabling us to acknowledge the wonderful diversity we find in Scripture and to appropriate a more holistic biblical theology.

The revolution has also challenged older, well-established principles of interpretation. No longer can we as a matter of principle give priority to didactic portions of Scripture. No longer can we engage in theological reflection without giving due place to all of the evidence from an author's hand. Indeed, we are just beginning to assess the implications of this far-reaching revolution. Although the authors of this book hope to develop one line of inquiry opened up by recent Pentecostal scholars, we recognize that a number of scholars from a wide range of traditions have contributed to this revolution and undoubtedly will continue to explore its possibilities. It is our hope that the revolution outlined above will help us all more fully grasp the richness of the biblical witness.

Study Questions

1. What historical influences encouraged early Evangelicals to minimize the theological significance of narrative portions of the Bible?
2. Contemporary Evangelical scholars have largely rejected the "restrictive" hermeneutic of the past and highlighted the importance of biblical narrative. What influences have helped bring about this change in perspective?
3. Why is this new appraisal of biblical narrative by Evangelical scholars especially significant for Pentecostals? How does it create fresh opportunities for Pentecostals as they seek to articulate their theology in a fresh and relevant way?

Notes

[1] Positive influences include an emphasis on the significance of our preunderstanding for the interpretive enterprise, and negative influences rightly critiqued include the radical ahistoricism and relativism inherent in many postmodern approaches.

[2] Bernard Ramm, *Protestant Biblical Interpretation*, 3d ed. (Grand Rapids: Baker, 1970), 107. Note that Ramm's first edition was published in 1956.

[3] John R. W. Stott, *The Baptism and Fullness of the Holy Spirit* (Downers Grove, Ill.: InterVarsity, 1964), 7.

[4] Gordon D. Fee and Douglas Stuart, *How to Read the Bible For All Its Worth* (Grand Rapids: Zondervan, 1981), 97 (Fee wrote this chapter; italics his). In the second edition, published in 1993, note how Fee qualifies this principle by tacking on the phrase, "unless it can be demonstrated on other grounds that the author intended it to function in this way." For comments on Fee and his role in both Evangelicalism and Pentecostalism, see chapter 7 of the present book.

⁵ Baur wrote a number of books, but an article written in 1831 first expressed his views.

⁶ Examples of an overly strident application of Hegelianism in other fields of thought include Darwin's views in the field of biology and the political theory of Karl Marx.

⁷ Ernst Haenchen, *The Acts of the Apostles: A Commentary* (Philadelphia: Westminster, 1971; German orig. published in 1955).

⁸ Günther Bornkamm, G. Barth, and H. J. Held, *Tradition and Interpretation in Matthew* (Philadelphia: Westminster, 1963; this incorporated a pivotal article first published in 1948).

⁹ Hans Conzelmann, *The Theology of St. Luke* (Philadelphia: Fortress, 1982; German orig. first published in 1954); W. Marxsen, *Mark the Evangelist* (New York: Abingdon, 1965; German orig. first published in 1956).

¹⁰ I. Howard Marshall, *Luke: Historian and Theologian* (Grand Rapids: Zondervan, 1970).

¹¹ See, e.g., Grant R. Osborne, *The Resurrection Narratives: A Redactional Study* (Grand Rapids: Baker, 1984); Robert H. Stein, *The Synoptic Problem: An Introduction* (Downers Grove, Ill.: InterVarsity, 1987); Joel Green, *The Theology of the Gospel of Luke* (Cambridge: Cambridge Univ. Press, 1995); Darrell L. Bock, *Luke* (2 vols.; Grand Rapids: Baker, 1994); Craig Blomberg, *Interpreting the Parables* (Downers Grove, Ill.: InterVarsity, 1990).

¹² William W. Klein, Craig L. Blomberg, and Robert L. Hubbard, *Introduction to Biblical Interpretation* (Dallas: Word, 1993), 349–50.

¹³ Grant R. Osborne, *The Hermeneutical Spiral: A Comprehensive Introduction to Biblical Interpretation* (Downers Grove: InterVarsity, 1991), 172.

¹⁴ See, for example, Max Turner's recent responses to Pentecostal scholarship: *The Holy Spirit and Spiritual Gifts: Then and Now* (Carlisle: Paternoster, 1996), and *Power from On High* (Sheffield: Sheffield Academic, 1996).

Chapter Three

Hermeneutics: Luke's Distinctive Contribution

In the past two decades the theological chasm that once separated Pentecostals from other Evangelicals has been partially bridged. Spurred on by the scholarly writings of James Dunn and the pragmatic-oriented analyses of Pentecostal church growth by Peter Wagner, Evangelicals have reexamined their theological positions. The results have been impressive. Evangelicals who once consigned a variety of manifestations of the Spirit exclusively to the apostolic age are today claiming these same gifts as contemporary blessings. A "Third Wave" of Evangelicals now celebrate with Pentecostals God's gracious gifts of prophecy, healing, and tongues.

Pentecostals can only applaud the openness of our Evangelical brothers and sisters to new dimensions of the Spirit's work. Yet this recent theological rapprochement presents Pentecostals with a sobering challenge. It is pushing us to define more clearly what it means to be Pentecostal. Indeed, new questions are being asked and, in light of the developments outlined above, they cannot be ignored: How are we Pentecostals different from our Evangelical fellow believers who are open to the gifts? If there are important differences in our theology and practice, can we provide a solid biblical basis for our distinctive positions? It appears to this writer that the answers—or perhaps lack of answers—Pentecostals give to these questions will influence the shape of the Evangelical, as well as the Pentecostal, movement for generations to come.

This chapter is written with the conviction that Pentecostals have much yet to contribute to the larger Evangelical community. The theological chasm has not been closed, for an important difference still separates us. The issue of contention centers on a question that touches the very heart of our Pentecostal theology and heritage: What is the nature of the Pentecostal gift (Acts

2:4)? For the Evangelical the answer to this question has been shaped largely by James Dunn's influential book, *Baptism in the Holy Spirit*. Dunn asserts that the Pentecostal bestowal of the Spirit is the means by which the disciples enter into the new age and experience the blessings of the new covenant.[1]

In other words, for the Evangelical, Spirit-baptism is equated with conversion. It is that which makes a person truly a Christian. By way of contrast, most Pentecostals insist that the Spirit came on the disciples at Pentecost not as the source of new covenant existence, but rather as the source of power for effective witness. Thus Pentecostals generally describe Spirit-baptism as an experience (at least logically, if not chronologically) distinct from conversion, which unleashes a new dimension of the Spirit's power; it is an enduement of power for service.

The differences outlined above cannot be simply dismissed as semantic games played by theologians, ivory-tower stuff with no bearing on the life of the church. While "one baptism, many fillings" may be affirmed by Evangelical and Pentecostal alike, our different understandings of the nature of this baptism (and subsequent fillings) dramatically impact the contours of our faith and practice. Consider this: If the Evangelical is right, then Pentecostals can no longer proclaim an enduement of the Spirit that is distinct from conversion and available to every believer—at least not with the same sense of expectation. For this expectation is rooted in the universality of the Pentecostal promise (Acts 2:8, 17–18, 38). Furthermore, if the Evangelical is right, Pentecostals can no longer maintain that the principal purpose of the Pentecostal gift is to grant power for the task of mission. In short, a Pentecostal perspective on Spirit-baptism is integral to our continued sense of expectation and effectiveness in mission.

Thus we find ourselves as Pentecostals in an exciting, yet precarious situation. The tide of Third Wavers is coming in, challenging us to provide convincing biblical support for our distinctive position on Spirit-baptism. If we meet the challenge, we will continue to influence the theology and practice of the larger Evangelical community. If we fail, we run the risk of being submerged by the wave and losing our identity.

The following chapter is an attempt to suggest how this challenge might be met. We will argue that (1) recognition of the distinctive character of Luke's pneumatology is essential if we Pentecostals are to provide convincing biblical support for our position on Spirit-baptism; (2) evidence from Acts points to the distinctive character of Luke's pneumatology; and (3) although Evangelicals may be inclined to reject descriptions of Luke's pneumatology as "distinctive" on the basis of certain theological and historical presuppositions, this judgment is unwarranted.

1. The Biblical Basis for Pentecostal Theology

If Pentecostals are to communicate effectively to the broader Evangelical community, we cannot simply rely on the answers offered by a past generation of Pentecostal exegetes. Although our Pentecostal forefathers intuitively grasped the correlation between the reality they experienced and the promise of Acts 1:8, they did not always articulate their theology in a manner that was entirely consistent or convincing to other believers committed to the authority of Scripture. Of course writing theology was not their major concern, though many fine contributions were made. Yet the theological legacy of the past is not adequate for the demands of the present.

This judgment is reflected in a paper presented by Roland Wessels at the 1990 gathering of the Society for Pentecostal Studies. Wessels chronicled some of the difficulties with past attempts to distinguish (1) between "He [The Spirit] dwells with you" (conversion) and "will be in you" (Spirit-baptism) in John 14:16–17, (2) between a baptism into the body of Christ in which the Spirit is the agent (1 Cor. 12:13) and a baptism into the Spirit in which Christ is the agent (Luke 3:16), and (3) between receiving the Spirit "within" (John 20:19–20) and having the Spirit come "upon" (Acts 2:4).[2] This critique represents the perception that many have. Indeed, over twenty years ago James Dunn pointed out the methodological flaw characteristic of these positions.

Dunn's critique was specifically aimed at arguments for subsequence based on a conflation of John 20:22 with Luke's narrative in Acts, but it is equally valid for the positions outlined above:

> The common error ... is to treat the NT (and even the Bible) as a homogeneous whole, from any part of which texts can be drawn on a chosen subject and fitted into a framework and system which is often basically extra-biblical.[3]

In accordance with the prevailing scholarly consensus, Dunn suggested there was a better approach. We should

> take each author and book separately and ... outline his or its particular theological emphases; only when he has set a text in the context of its author's thought and intention ... only then can the biblical-theologian feel free to let that text interact with other texts from other books.

Dunn maintained that this method "is always liable to give the truer picture of the biblical thought than the former." He is undoubtedly correct. The irony is that Dunn did not consistently apply his own method. He has been criticized, and appropriately so, for reading Luke–Acts through the lenses of Pauline theology. In spite of the shortcomings of his own work, however,

Dunn has provided a valuable service. He has challenged us to recognize an important truth: Pentecostals cannot continue to rely on the interpretative methods of the nineteenth century Holiness movement and expect to speak to the contemporary Evangelical world.[4] Furthermore, by insisting that we take seriously the theological perspective of each biblical author, Dunn pointed to a positive alternative.

Dunn's methodological challenge was timely, for developments were taking place in Lukan studies that would significantly impact the shape of Evangelical and Pentecostal theology. As we have noted, the publication in 1970 of I. Howard Marshall's *Luke: Historian and Theologian* marked an important shift in Evangelical thinking. In the past Evangelicals had viewed the book of Acts as a historical text with little theological significance. This perspective was a reaction to the radical historical skepticism that marked many of the early works depicting Luke as a theologian.[5] Luke was presented as either a historian with little interest in theology or a theologian with little interest in history. However, Evangelicals slowly began to recognize that Luke was in fact both a historian and a theologian: He wrote a historical account, but with a theological purpose in view. The title of Marshall's book reflects this important change in the Evangelical perspective.

This shift in Evangelical attitudes toward Luke marked the beginning of an exciting era for Pentecostals. Study of Luke's two-volume work received fresh impetus from the new awareness that Luke does indeed have a theological contribution to make to the church. As a result, questions concerning the character of Luke's theology have been given new prominence in recent years. This is particularly significant for Pentecostals, who point to Luke–Acts for much of their distinctive theology. The new emphasis on Lukan theology, coupled with the rigorous application of the interpretative method outlined by Dunn, created a fertile climate for Pentecostal theologizing. Pentecostals now had (and continue to have) a unique opportunity to articulate a biblical theology of the Spirit that is persuasive to both Evangelicals and Pentecostals.

The "firstfruits" from this fertile theological context came from the pen of Roger Stronstad. In his seminal work, *The Charismatic Theology of St. Luke*, Stronstad argued that Luke was a theologian as well as an historian, and therefore Luke–Acts is "a legitimate data base for the doctrine of the Holy Spirit."[6] Furthermore, Stronstad argued that Luke was a theologian *in his own right* and that his perspective on the Spirit was different from—although complementary to—that of Paul.[7] Unlike Paul, who frequently speaks of the soteriological dimension of the Spirit's work, Luke consistently portrays the Spirit as the source of power for service. Thus, Stronstad concludes, Luke has "a charismatic rather than a soteriological theology of the Spirit."[8]

Stronstad's thesis represents a direct challenge to traditional Evangelical perspectives on the Spirit. If Stronstad is correct, the charismatic dimension of the Spirit to which Luke bears witness must be placed alongside the soteriological dimension so prominent in the writings of Paul. For a theology of the Spirit that is truly biblical must do justice to the pneumatology of *each* biblical author.

More specifically, by placing the Pentecost account within the framework of Luke's distinctive theology of the Spirit, Stronstad demonstrates that the Spirit came upon the disciples at Pentecost, not as the source of new covenant existence, but rather as the source of power for effective witness. Since the Pentecostal gift is charismatic rather than soteriological in character, it must be distinguished from the gift of the Spirit that Paul associates with conversion-initiation. Stronstad thus provides a strong argument for a doctrine of subsequence—that is, that Spirit-baptism (in the Pentecostal or Lukan sense) is logically distinct from conversion. This distinction is a reflection of Luke's distinctive theology of the Spirit.

The real significance of Stronstad's thesis, at least from a Pentecostal perspective, can be traced to his claim that Luke's theology of the Spirit is *different* from that of Paul. Most Evangelicals maintain that Luke, in a manner similar to Paul, relates the gift of the Spirit to salvation; he simply chooses to *emphasize* the Spirit's role in equipping the church for its mission. This "same theology, different emphasis" approach undermines the biblical basis for Pentecostal theology. It enables Evangelicals to describe the gift of the Spirit received at Pentecost (in Pauline terms) as the chief element in conversion-initiation, the means whereby the disciples experience the blessings of the new covenant (i.e., cleansing, justification, moral transformation), even though they would acknowledge that divine enabling is prominent in Luke's narrative. Stronstad challenges this approach by arguing that Luke views the gift of the Spirit *exclusively* in charismatic terms. His narrative reflects more than a special emphasis; it bears witness to a distinctive theology of the Spirit. Consequently, the charismatic character of the Pentecostal gift cannot be questioned, and Luke's unique (and Pentecostal) contribution to biblical pneumatology must be given its due.

Stronstad will undoubtedly be criticized by some for reading his own Pentecostal experience into Luke–Acts. Yet he was not the first to emphasize the distinctive character of Luke's theology of the Spirit. Over a century ago Herman Gunkel reached similar conclusions; and he has been followed in more recent years by E. Schweizer, David Hill, and Gonzalo Haya-Prats, all of whom have written works that highlight the distinctive character of Luke's pneumatology.[9] Furthermore, might it not be that Stronstad's Pentecostal experience has actually enabled him to read Luke–Acts more accurately? An analysis of Luke–Acts reveals this to be the case.

Luke's theology of the Spirit is indeed *different* from that of Paul. Luke not only fails to refer to soteriological aspects of the Spirit's work, his narrative presupposes a pneumatology that does not include this dimension (e.g., Luke 11:13; Acts 8:4–25; 18:24–19:7). Of course a detailed examination of Luke's two-volume work would be required to defend this assertion. Chapters 5 and 6 of this book will attempt to provide detailed exegesis of the relevant passages.[10] At this point, however, it may be possible for us to make our point by focusing on one of the passages that bear witness to Luke's distinctive perspective: Acts 8:4–25.

2. Evidence from Acts 8:4–25

Acts 8:4–25 provides a real problem for those who argue that for Luke, as for Paul, reception of the Spirit is a necessary element in Christian initiation. The narrative indicates that the Samaritans believed the preaching of Philip and were thus baptized (v. 12), yet they did not receive the Spirit until some time later (vv. 15–17). Since Luke considered the Samaritans to be Christians (i.e., converted) before they received the Spirit, it can hardly be maintained that he understood the Spirit to be the "one thing that makes a man a Christian."[11]

Those advocating a necessary link between reception of the Spirit and baptism/Christian initiation have attempted to mitigate the force of this text in a variety of ways. Some have sought to ease the tension by describing the course of events narrated in Acts 8:4–25 as a unique exception, necessitated by a new and decisive turning point in the mission of the church: The Spirit was withheld until the coming of the apostles from Jerusalem in order to demonstrate to the Samaritans "that they had really become members of the Church, in fellowship with its original 'pillars.'"[12]

This view faces a number of serious objections. (1) There is little reason to assume that this instance represents a unique exception, either historically or for Luke. Nothing in the text itself supports such a view, and Luke regularly separates the gift of the Spirit from the baptismal rite (Acts 2:4; 8:15–16; 9:17–18;10:44–45).[13] (2) This explanation is highly improbable. That is, it is unlikely that the Samaritans would need any further assurance of their incorporation into the church after baptism. In similar decisive turning points, the assurance of incorporation into the church (as well as the reality itself) is not dependent on contact with representatives of Jerusalem (Acts 8:26–27; 9:17–18; 18:24–25) or their bestowal of the Spirit to the newly converted (Acts 11:22–24).[14]

Even if this explanation for Acts 8:4–25 is accepted, the problem posed by the text is not eradicated. For however exceptional the event may have been (historically and for Luke), we must still account for Luke's carefully crafted interpretation of this event. Indeed, Luke's account betrays a pneumatology decidedly different from Paul or John, neither of whom could conceive of baptized believers being without the Spirit.[15] Fully aware that the implications for Luke's pneumatology that emerge from the position outlined above are incompatible with their respective attempts to tie reception of the Spirit to conversion-initiation (Dunn) and baptism (Beasley-Murray) in Luke–Acts, Dunn and Beasley-Murray offer alternative interpretations of Acts 8:4–25.

Beasley-Murray argues that Luke "regarded these Christians as not without the Spirit but without the spiritual gifts that characterized the common life of the Christian communities."[16] According to Beasley-Murray the "great joy" (*pollē chara*) of Acts 8:8 implies that the Samaritans received the Spirit when they were baptized, and the use of "Holy Spirit" (*pneuma hagion*) without the definite article in Acts 8:15–16 suggests that apostles imparted spiritual gifts, not the Spirit himself. Neither of these arguments commend themselves. The "great joy" of Acts 8:8 results from the exorcisms and healings performed by Philip; it does not imply possession of the Spirit.[17] Nor can a neat distinction be made between the Holy Spirit with the article and without the article; they are equivalent titles.[18] But the decisive objection against Beasley-Murray's thesis is Luke's explicit statement in verse 16: "the Holy Spirit had not yet come [lit., fallen] upon any of them."[19]

Dunn seeks to establish that the Samaritans were not really Christians before they received the Spirit. He maintains that their "initial response and commitment was defective" and that Luke "intended his readers to know this."[20] A number of arguments are produced in support of this claim, but the most significant are: (1) Luke's description of Philip as simply preaching "the Christ" (*ton Christon*, v. 5) and "the kingdom of God" (*tēs basileias tou theou*, v. 12) suggests that the Samaritans understood Philip's message in terms of their own nationalistic expectations of the Messiah and the kingdom he was to bring—expectations already "roused to near fever-pitch" by the magician Simon. For the former phrase "is always used in Acts of the Messiah of pre-Christian expectation" and the latter, when preached to non-Christians, always refers to the "Kingdom of Jewish expectations."[21] (2) Since "to believe" (*pisteuō*) with the dative object usually signifies intellectual assent, Luke's use of the phrase "they believed Philip" rather than "they believed on [*eis* or *epi*] the Lord" (v. 12) suggests that the Samaritan response was simply an assent of the mind and not reflective of genuine faith.

Dunn's hypothesis has been subjected to intense criticism and must be rejected.[22] Indeed, neither of the arguments outlined above can be sustained. (1) There is nothing in Luke's account which would suggest that Philip's message was either deficient or misunderstood. On the contrary, Philip is presented as one of the group alluded to in Acts 8:4 who went about "preaching the word" (*euangelizomenoi ton logon*). Since "the word" (*ton logon*) embodies the content of the kerygma (cf. 2:41; 6:2; 8:14),[23] it is evident that Luke understood Philip's preaching, variously described (vv. 5, 12) to be "kerygmatic in the full sense."[24]

Moreover, there is nothing in the phrases "[he] proclaimed the Christ there" (v. 5) and "he preached the good news of the kingdom of God and the name of Jesus Christ" (v. 12) that would suggest that the Samaritans misunderstood Philip's message. The phrase "the Christ" (*ton Christon*), standing alone, appears frequently in Christian proclamation in Acts and with reference to the central elements of the kerygma: Christ's death (e.g., 3:18) and resurrection (e.g., 2:31).[25] In verse 5, as elsewhere in Acts (9:22; 17:3; 26:23; cf. 18:5, 28), it serves as a summary of the kerygma.[26] Similarly, the phrase "the kingdom of God and the name of Jesus Christ" can scarcely mean less since it parallels the content of Paul's preaching in Rome (28:31).[27] If the Samaritans had misunderstood Philip, we would expect the apostles to correct the deficiency through additional teaching (cf. 18:26), yet any reference to such activity is conspicuously absent.[28]

(2) Dunn's attempt to derive significance from the fact that the object of the verb "believed" is the preaching of Philip rather than "Lord" or "God" is without warrant. In his description of Lydia's conversion in 16:14, for example, Luke equates belief in the message of an evangelist with belief in God.[29] Moreover, Luke uses the verb "to believe" with a dative object elsewhere to describe genuine faith in God (16:34; 18:8).[30] Nor does Luke distinguish between "to believe" with a dative object (cf. 18:8) or with the prepositions *eis* (cf. 14:23) or *epi* (cf. 9:42); all three constructions appear with "Lord" in descriptions of genuine faith.[31] That "they believed Philip as he preached" does indeed refer to genuine faith is confirmed by the report that reached the apostles in Jerusalem: "that Samaria had accepted the word of God" (8:14). A similar report heralds the conversion of Cornelius and his household (11:1; cf. 2:41; 17:11). Since this latter report is not questioned, "we should therefore find no reason to question the former."[32]

It has become apparent that the separation of Spirit-reception from baptism/Christian initiation in Acts 8:4–25 cannot be disregarded as a unique exception. This position is based on a hypothetical reconstruction of the event and ignores the significance of the existing narrative for Luke's pneumatology. Nor is it possible to eliminate the contradiction by postulating a "silent" bestowal of the Spirit at baptism or impugning the faith of the Samaritans; the evidence speaks decisively against both views. Acts 8:4–25 poses an insoluble problem for those who maintain that Luke, in a manner similar to Paul, establishes a necessary link between baptism/Christian initiation and the gift of the Spirit.

This problem is resolved, however, when we recognize the distinctive character of Luke's pneumatology. Luke can speak of baptized believers being without the Spirit because his theology of the Spirit is not the same as that of Paul. It is charismatic rather than soteriological. Luke evidently viewed the gift of the Spirit received by the Samaritans in Acts 8:17 as of the same character as the Pentecostal gift, that is, as a prophetic endowment granted to the converted that enabled them to participate effectively in the mission of the church.

3. A Response to Evangelical Objections

In spite of the evidence from Luke's own hand, two commonly held presuppositions have inhibited many Evangelicals from recognizing the distinctive character of Luke's pneumatology. The first presupposition is associated with the inspiration of Scripture, the second stems from the conviction held by most Evangelicals that Luke traveled with Paul. We will address the theological objection first and then move to the historical one.

3.1. Distinctive Pneumatology and the Inspiration of Scripture

It is often assumed that since the Holy Spirit inspired each of the various New Testament authors, they must all speak with one voice. That is to say, each biblical author must share the same theological perspective. Thus, to speak of Luke's distinctive pneumatology is to question the divine and authoritative character of Scripture.

Yet does an Evangelical or conservative view of Scripture demand such a view? In his helpful article, "An Evangelical Approach to 'Theological Criticism,'" I. Howard Marshall points out that a conservative doctrine of Scripture assumes that "Scripture as a whole is harmonious."[33] However, he notes that this assumption does not rule out theological differences among biblical authors. Rather, it suggests that the differences that do exist are "differences in harmonious development rather than irreconcilable contradictions."[34] We suggest, therefore, that a high view of Scripture demands not that Luke and Paul have the same pneumatological perspective, but rather that Luke's distinctive pneumatology is ultimately reconcilable with that of Paul, and that both perspectives can be seen as contributing to a process of harmonious development.

It is imperative to note that when we speak of Luke's distinctive pneumatology, we are not asserting that Luke's perspective is irreconcilable with that of Paul.[35] On the contrary, we suggest that the pneumatologies of Luke and

Paul are *different but compatible*, and that the differences should not be blurred, for both perspectives offer us valuable insight into the dynamic work of the Holy Spirit. Clearly Paul has the more developed view, for he sees the full richness of the Spirit's work. He helps us understand that the Spirit is the source of the Christian's cleansing (Rom. 15:16; 1 Cor. 6:11), righteousness (Rom. 2:29; 8:1–17; 14:17; Gal. 5:5, 16–26), and intimate fellowship with God (Rom. 8:14–17; Gal. 4:6), as well as the source of power for mission (Rom. 15:18–19; Phil. 1:18–19). Paul attests to both the soteriological and the charismatic dimensions of the Spirit's work.

Luke's perspective, by contrast, is less developed and more limited. He bears witness solely to the charismatic dimension of the Spirit's work and thus gives us a glimpse of only a part of Paul's fuller view. Nevertheless, like Paul, Luke has an important contribution to make. He calls us to recognize that the church, by virtue of its reception of the Pentecostal gift, is a prophetic community empowered for a missionary task. In short, not only are the pneumatological perspectives of Luke and Paul compatible, they are complementary: Both represent important contributions to a holistic and harmonious biblical theology of the Spirit.

This leads us to another important observation: If the differences between the perspectives of Luke and Paul are not recognized, the full richness of the biblical testimony cannot be grasped. This is why it is tragic when, in the name of biblical inspiration, legitimate theological diversity within the canon is repudiated. We must examine the biblical texts and be sensitive to the theological diversity that exists, for harmonization, when foisted on the text, exacts a heavy price. In the case of Luke and Paul, that price is biblical support for a Pentecostal position on Spirit-baptism.

3.2. Luke's Interaction with Paul

Evangelicals usually identify Luke as someone who traveled with Paul. This being the case, it is understandable that some might be inclined to question whether Luke's pneumatology really could be different from Paul's. Would it have been possible for Luke to remain uninfluenced by the apostle's soteriological perspective on the Spirit?[36]

We suggest that a thorough examination of Luke–Acts reveals this is precisely what happened. Several factors indicate that this conclusion should not surprise us even though Luke, as the traveling companion of Paul, probably spent a considerable amount of time with the apostle. (1) It is generally recognized that Luke was not acquainted with any of Paul's letters,[37] so that Luke's contact with Paul's theology was probably limited to personal conversation or secondary (oral or written) sources. It is probable that Luke did not know Paul's letters because they were not yet widely accessible or recognized in non-Pauline sectors of the church. Thus, Paul's perspective had not yet significantly influenced these broader, non-Pauline elements of the early church.

(2) Since other aspects of Paul's theology have not significantly influenced Luke, our suggestion is all the more credible. One example of Luke's theological independence from Paul (i.e., that he does not slavishly imitate Paul) may be found in his rationale for salvation. While Luke emphasizes that salvation is found in Jesus because he is Lord and Messiah, he does not develop in a manner like Paul the full implications of the cross as the means of salvation.[38] Again we see that the perspectives of Luke and Paul complement one another: Together they lead us into a deeper and fuller understanding of truth.

(3) Luke's summaries of Paul's preaching—generally viewed as accurate representations of Paul's gospel by those who affirm that Luke traveled with Paul—do not contain any traces of Paul's soteriological pneumatology. This indicates that if, as is most likely the case, Luke heard Paul preach or entered into discussions with him and thereby came to an accurate understanding of his gospel, it is probable that he did so without coming to terms with Paul's fuller pneumatological perspective.[39]

These points are offered as a challenge to let the text of Luke–Acts speak for itself. Whatever we think of these specific points, one fact is undeniable: Assumptions concerning the extent to which Luke was influenced by Paul must be judged in light of the evidence we have available to us, not on speculation of what might have been.

4. Conclusion

Back in 1918, Roland Allen wrote these perceptive words to a church that had lost sight of the missiological nature and purpose of the Pentecostal gift:

> We often complain that Christian people at home have little zeal for the spread of the gospel. How can it be otherwise when our people are taught that the Holy Spirit is given, when they are taught to recognize him in their own souls, almost entirely as the sanctifier, the truth revealer, the strengthener, and in the church as the organizer and the director of counsels, whilst they are not taught in anything like the same degree that [the Spirit] is the spirit of redeeming love, active in them towards others, moving every individual soul to whom [the Spirit] comes and the church in which [the Spirit] dwells to desire and to labour for the bringing of all men everywhere to God in Jesus Christ?[40]

Today Pentecostals have an unprecedented opportunity to encourage the broader Evangelical community to recognize the Spirit of Pentecost as the Spirit "active in them towards others." If we are to make the most of this opportunity, we must highlight the distinctive character of Luke's pneumatology, and we must work toward a holistic biblical theology of the Spirit that does justice to this perspective. Such a theology will be Pentecostal in nature. In the following pages we will attempt to demonstrate what such a theology might look like. By way of introduction to this enterprise, we have argued that evidence from Acts 8:4–25 supports the thesis that Luke's pneumatology is *different* from that of Paul and that this thesis is both consistent with a high view of Scripture and historically credible.

Study Questions

1. The theological proximity of non-Pentecostal Evangelicals, especially Third Wavers, to Pentecostals poses new challenges for Pentecostals. What are these challenges?
2. According to the author, a recognition of the distinctive character of Luke's pneumatology provides an important foundation for Pentecostal theology. Why is this the case?
3. The author suggests that Luke's pneumatology is different from, but complementary to, that of Paul. How should we evaluate this claim?
4. Does a high view of Scripture demand that all of the biblical authors have the same perspective? Is it possible for biblical authors to have different theologies but ultimately be compatible or even complementary?
5. The New Testament bears witness to a process of theological development in the early church, one that was superintended by the Holy Spirit and thus invested with unique authority. How would you respond to this statement?

Notes

[1] See J. D. G. Dunn, *Baptism in the Holy Spirit* (London: SCM, 1970), 38–54. See also G. W. H. Lampe, "The Holy Spirit in the Writings of Saint Luke," in *Studies in the Gospels*, ed. D. D. Nineham (Oxford: Blackwell, 1957), 162; cf. Lampe, *God as Spirit: The Bampton Lectures, 1976* (Oxford: Clarendon, 1977), 65; F. Büchsel, *Der Geist Gottes im Neuen Testament* (Gütersloh: C. Bertelsmann, 1926), 234–35; F. F. Bruce, "The Holy Spirit in the Acts of the Apostles," *Int* 27 (1973): 170–72; F. D. Bruner, *A Theology of the Holy Spirit: The Pentecostal Experience and the New Testament Witness* (Grand Rapids: Eerdmans, 1970), 214.

[2] Roland Wessels, "How Is the Baptism in the Holy Spirit to be Distinguished from Receiving the Spirit at Conversion?" (paper delivered at the 20th Annual Meeting of the Society for Pentecostal Studies, Nov. 9, 1990).

[3] This and the following quotations are from Dunn, *Baptism*, 39.

[4] Both Dunn (*Baptism*, 39) and Wessels ("How Is the Baptism," I–23, n. 69) note the influence the Holiness Movement has exerted upon Pentecostal methods of interpretation.

[5] See the previous chapter and its description of the historical skepticism in Ernst Haenchen's *The Acts of the Apostles*.

⁶ Roger Stronstad, *The Charismatic Theology of St. Luke* (Peabody, Mass.: Hendrickson, 1984), 11.

⁷ Stronstad (ibid., 11) quotes Marshall (*Luke: Historian and Theologian*, 75) with approval: "Luke was entitled to his own views, and the fact that they differ in some respects from those of Paul should not be held against him at this point. On the contrary, he is a theologian in his own right and must be treated as such."

⁸ Stronstad, *Charismatic Theology*, 12.

⁹ H. Gunkel, *The Influence of the Holy Spirit* (Philadelphia: Fortress, 1979; original German ed., 1888); E. Schweizer, "πνεῦμα," *TDNT*, 6:389–455; D. Hill, *Greek Words and Hebrew Meanings* (Cambridge: University Press, 1967); G. Haya-Prats, *L'Esprit force de l'église* (Paris: Cerf, 1975). It is unfortunate that Schweizer's position has been obscured by a mistranslation. The English summary statement mistakenly includes a negative: "Luke thus shares with Judaism the view that the Spirit is essentially the Spirit of prophecy. This does *not* prevent him from directly attributing to the πνεῦμα both the χαρίσματα ἰαμάτων on the one side and strongly ethical effects like the common life of the primitive community on the other" ("πνεῦμα," *TDNT*, 6:409; italics mine). Compare this reading with the original German ("πνεῦμα," *TWNT*, 6:407).

¹⁰ See also Robert P. Menzies, *Empowered for Witness: The Spirit in Luke–Acts* (JPTSup 6; Sheffield: Sheffield Academic, 1994).

¹¹ Dunn, *Baptism*, 93.

¹² G. W. H. Lampe, *The Seal of the Spirit* (London: Longmans, Green & Co., 1951), 70. Similar views are espoused by M. A. Chevallier, *Souffle de Dieu* (Paris: Éditions Beauchesne, 1978), 201–2; Bruner, *Holy Spirit*, 175–76; D. Ewert, *The Holy Spirit in the New Testament* (Kitchener, Ont.: Herald, 1983), 119–20; M. Green, *I Believe in the Holy Spirit* (Grand Rapids: Eerdmans, 1975), 138–39; I. H. Marshall, *The Acts of the Apostles* (Leicester: InterVarsity, 1980), 153, 157; R. F. O'Toole, "Christian Baptism in Luke," *RevRel* 39 (1980): 861–62.

¹³ S. Brown, "'Water-Baptism' and 'Spirit-Baptism' in Luke–Acts," *ATR* 59 (1977): 143–44; J. D. M. Derrett, "Simon Magus (Acts 8:9–24)," *ZNW* 73 (1982): 53. The responses offered by Haenchen ("the few cases in Acts when reception of the Spirit is separated from baptism are justified exceptions," *Acts*, 184), J. H. E. Hull ("exceptions only prove the rule," *The Holy Spirit in the Acts of the Apostles* [London: Lutterworth, 1967], 119), and Bruner ("the Spirit is temporarily suspended from baptism here 'only' and precisely to teach . . . that suspension cannot occur," *Holy Spirit*, 178) are hardly compelling.

¹⁴ See Dunn, *Baptism*, 62–63, and G. R. Beasley-Murray, *Baptism in the New Testament* (Exeter: Paternoster, 1962), 117–18. Lampe also acknowledges that the hypothesis outlined above does not adequately account for all of the evidence and therefore modifies his thesis (*Seal*, 70).

¹⁵ J. Coppens, "L'imposition des mains deans les Actes des Apôtres" in *Les Actes des Apôtres*, ed. J. Kremer (Gembloux: Leuven Univ. Press, 1979), 430; Hull, *Acts*, 107–8; A. Weiser, *Die Apostelgeschichte* (OTKNT 5; Gütersloh: Gütersloher Verlagshaus, 1981), 1:203; M. Turner, "Luke and the Spirit" (Ph.D. diss.; University of Cambridge, 1980), 169; Lampe, *Seal*, 53, 65, 70–78.

¹⁶ Beasley-Murray, *Baptism*, 119; see 118–20 for his argument. Similar views are espoused by J. E. L. Oulton, "The Holy Spirit, Baptism, and Laying on of Hands in Acts," *ExpTim* 66 (1955): 236–40; M. Gourges, "Esprit des commencements et Esprit des prolongements dans les Actes: Note sur la 'Pentecôte des Samaritains' (Act., VIII,

5–25)," *RB* 93 (1986): 376–85; and many others from the Reformed school who follow the lead of J. Calvin, *The Acts of the Apostles 1–13* (Torrance ed., 1965), 235–36.

[17] Turner, "Luke and the Spirit," 168. Turner, citing as examples Luke 13:17 and 19:37, notes that "such joy is frequently mentioned as the response to God's various saving acts throughout Luke–Acts."

[18] See Dunn, *Baptism*, 56, 68–70; Turner, "Luke and the Spirit," 167–68. As Dunn aptly puts it: "The true formula is not πνεῦμα ἅγιον = charismata (alone), but πνεῦμα ἅγιον = Holy Spirit + charismata, or more precisely, the Holy Spirit bringing and manifesting his coming and presence by charismata" (56).

[19] Dunn, *Baptism*, 56; Marshall, *Acts*, 157; F. Bovon, *Luc le théologien* (Paris: Delachaux & Niestlé, 1978), 247, 249–50, 252.

[20] Dunn, *Baptism*, 63; for his argument see pp. 63–68.

[21] Quotations from ibid., 64.

[22] See, e.g., the critiques offered by E. A. Russell, "'They Believed Philip Preaching' (Acts 8.12)," *IBS* 1 (1979): 169–76; Turner, "Luke and the Spirit, 163–67; H. Ervin, *Conversion-Initiation and the Baptism in the Holy Spirit* (Peabody, Mass.: Hendrickson, 1984), 25–40; Marshall, *Acts*, 156; Ewert, *Holy Spirit*, 118–19; H. D. Hunter, *Spirit-Baptism: A Pentecostal Alternative* (Lanham, Md.: Univ. Press of America, 1983), 83–84; K. Giles, "Is Luke an Exponent of 'Early Protestantism'? Church Order in the Lukan Writings (Part 1)," *EvQ* 54 (1982): 197; O'Toole, "Christian Baptism," 861; Green, *Holy Spirit*, 138; D. Carson, *Showing the Spirit: A Theological Exposition of 1 Corinthians 12–14* (Grand Rapids: Baker, 1987), 144; W. Russell, "The Anointing with the Holy Spirit in Luke–Acts," *TJ*, n.s., 7 (1986): 60–61; Stronstad, *Charismatic Theology*, 64–65.

[23] J. Roloff, *Die Apostelgeschichte* (Göttingen: Vandenhoeck & Ruprecht, 1981), 133.

[24] Russell, "They Believed," 170.

[25] Ibid.

[26] Roloff, *Die Apostelgeschichte*, 133; Turner, "Luke and the Spirit," 163.

[27] Russell, "They Believed," 170. G. Schneider notes that this phrase is a Lukan description of the content of the proclamation (*Die Apostelgeschichte*, vol. 1 [Freiburg: Herder, 1980], 490).

[28] Marshall, *Acts*, 158; Turner, "Luke and the Spirit," 164.

[29] Turner, "Luke and the Spirit," 165. For the use of *pisteuō* in a similar context see Acts 4:4.

[30] Ervin, *Conversion-Initiation*, 31; Marshall, *Acts*, 156.

[31] Russell, "They Believed," 173. Russell also points out that *pisteuō* is used in relation to the Scriptures with both the simple dative (Acts 24:14; 26:27) and the preposition *epi* (Luke 24:45).

[32] Giles, "Church Order (Part 1)," 197. See also Turner, "Luke and the Spirit," 165.

[33] I. H. Marshall, "An Evangelical Approach to 'Theological Criticism,'" *Them* 13 (1988): 81.

[34] Ibid., 83.

[35] Nor is this the position espoused by Stronstad, although D. A. Carson's unfortunate misrepresentation of Stronstad's position (*Showing the Spirit*, 151) has fostered this misguided notion. Had Carson read Stronstad's work more carefully, he would not have implied that Stronstad characterizes the theologies of Luke and Paul as contradictory. Furthermore, he would not have been able to glibly dismiss Stronstad's thesis as generating "more problems than it solves" (151).

[36] There is a prior question: Was Paul's perspective on the Spirit influenced by pre-Pauline Christian tradition (hymns, liturgical formulations, etc.)? It is often assumed that the soteriological aspect of the Spirit's work so prominent in Paul's writings was universally recognized and acknowledged in the early church. Thus many scholars maintain that Paul's pneumatology was shaped by pre-Pauline tradition and that Luke's perspective must also have been influenced by similar traditions. In my book, *The Development of Early Christian Pneumatology with Special Reference to Luke–Acts* (JSNTSup 54; Sheffield: Sheffield Academic, 1991), I have attempted to show that this assumption is erroneous by demonstrating that the Christian tradition taken up by Paul does not attribute soteriological functions to the Spirit. I argue that Paul was the first Christian to attribute soteriological functions to the Spirit and that this original element of Paul's pneumatology did not influence wider (non-Pauline) sectors of the early church until after the writing of Luke–Acts.

[37] M. Hengel, *Acts and the History of Earliest Christianity*, trans. J. Bowden (London: SCM, 1979), 66–67; J. C. O'Neill, *The Theology of Acts in Its Historical Setting*, 2d ed. (London: SPCK, 1970), 135; C. K. Barrett, "Acts and the Pauline Corpus," *ExpTim* 88 (1976): 2–5; R. Maddox, *The Purpose of Luke–Acts* (Göttingen: Vandenhoeck & Ruprecht, 1982), 68: "It is today generally recognized that Luke did not know the Pauline letters." A. Lindemann however suggests that Luke did know a few of Paul's letters (Romans, 2 Corinthians, and perhaps Galatians), but that Luke, like Matthew and Mark, was not significantly influenced by Paul's theology (*Paulus im ältesten Christentum* [Tübingen: J.C.B. Mohr, 1979], 171–73). Of course Paul mentions Luke in three of his letters (Col. 4:14; 2 Tim. 4:11; Philem. 24), all of which were probably written from Rome. While this suggests that Luke knew that Paul wrote these letters, it does not indicate that Luke saw or read them. And since Luke–Acts does not reveal any contact with the letters (quotations, allusions, etc.), it is unlikely that Luke had read them.

[38] Marshall, *Luke: Historian and Theologian*, 175: "He [Luke] demonstrates quite clearly that salvation is bestowed by Jesus in virtue of His position as the Lord and Messiah. What is lacking is a rather full understanding of the significance of the cross as the means of salvation."

[39] Since the Johannine writings originate from a geographical environment in which Paul was active (Ephesus) and an era considerably later than the writing of Luke–Acts, we are justified in assuming that the soteriological elements of John's pneumatology reflect Pauline influence. In view of the similarities in the theological perspectives of Paul and John (e.g., the Spirit as the controlling factor of the new life), U. Schnelle argues that the Pauline tradition reached John's school through oral tradition and that this transmission of tradition reflects a dominant geographical environment, probably Ephesus ("Paulus und Johannes," *EvT* 47 [1987]: 212–28).

[40] Roland Allen, "The Revelation of the Holy Spirit in the Acts of the Apostles," *IRM* 7 (1918): 167.

Chapter Four

Hermeneutics: Jumping Off the Postmodern Bandwagon

The postmodern bandwagon is racing into the future. And so, Timothy Cargal explains, if we do not want to be rendered "irrelevant" and left behind, we had better jump on.[1] In this chapter, I would like to explain why I disagree with Cargal's triumphalistic assessment of postmodernism, especially as it pertains to biblical hermeneutics, and why my counsel concerning this bandwagon is: If already on, "jump off."

I have chosen to respond to Cargal's essay because it was lucid, insightful, and ultimately disturbing. After reading volumes laden with Ricoeurian rhetoric, I found it refreshing to read an article with so little jargon. Cargal's skills are evident and I commend him for communicating his postmodern vision of the future in such a clear and compelling way. Cargal's article is significant for our task because it speaks directly to the issue of biblical hermeneutics.

Building upon three characteristics of Pentecostal hermeneutics as described by French Arrington (an emphasis on pneumatic illumination, the dialogical role of experience, and biblical narratives), Cargal seeks to show affinities between the hermeneutic of traditional Pentecostalism and that of postmodernism. In his view, all that is needed for Pentecostals to enter into the postmodern age is for us to throw off our Fundamentalist and Evangelical shackles. More specifically, Cargal challenges us to reject our concern to root meaning in history in favor of the more dynamic and reader-oriented postmodern approach. We are called to recognize the subjectivity inherent in all interpretation and use this insight to our advantage, to revel in the multiple meanings of the text that the Spirit may illuminate. Indeed, this path is not only open to us; it is a path which we must take if we expect to communicate to our postmodern world.

What shall we make of Cargal's brave new world? I will answer this question with reference to Cargal's perception of the past, present, and future.

1. The Past and the Quest for Meaning

Cargal's article represents a critique of Evangelical approaches to Scripture and a call to embrace the postmodern interpretative paradigm. Specifically, Cargal chides Pentecostal scholars for working "within a philosopical paradigm dominated by historical concerns."[2] He calls for Pentecostals to follow postmodernism in its rejection of the notion that "only what is historically and objectively true is meaningful."[3] Cargal's call directly impinges on two significant Evangelical concerns.

Evangelicals have generally insisted that ascertaining the historical meaning of a text is the central goal of hermeneutics. This concern for historical meaning is evident in the excellent textbook on hermeneutics recently penned by three faculty members of Denver Seminary. The authors define textual meaning as "that which the words and grammatical structures of that text disclose about the probable intention of its author/editor and the probable understanding of that text by its intended readers."[4] Here, reconstructing the past is a crucial dimension in the quest for meaning.

Postmodernists are quick to criticize this historical focus. Attempted reconstructions of the past are deemed illusionary and ultimately irrelevant because they are never objective, always colored by the interpreter's preunderstanding. Intellectual honesty demands that we move away from this epistemologically flawed emphasis on the past. Cargal notes that in practice Pentecostals have never been overly concerned about historical meaning. Thus the move to postmodernism should not be too difficult.

My own fear is that Cargal's analysis of Pentecostalism and its potential for being significantly influenced by the postmodern paradigm is correct. Certainly postmodernism has much to contribute to those who will listen. As a result of recent trends, Evangelicals are more aware of their lack of objectivity, the nature of their preunderstanding, and the need to listen to those with whom we may disagree. Yet the ahistorical stance and epistemological skepticism of postmodernism is extreme and leads to relativism. While we cannot achieve certainty concerning authorial intent of historical texts, we can gain knowledge. The hermeneutical circle is not entirely vicious; it is in reality a spiral.[5] And it is the concern for historical meaning that allows the text to confront and transform our preunderstanding, thereby making the spiral (or development in understanding) possible. If we loose the meaning of a text from its historical moorings, how shall we evaluate various and even contradictory interpretations? How shall we keep our own ideologies and prejudices from obliterating the text?[6]

Cargal is silent here, for in the postmodern paradigm he describes there is no criterion by which to evaluate an interpretation. His call to embrace multiple meanings reflects this reality: All readings are valid.[7] A philosophical paradigm and a hermeneutical method that cannot distinguish between truth and falsehood, valid and invalid interpretations, will hold little attraction for most Christians. As Allan Bloom notes, "Historicism [the view that all thought is essentially related to and cannot transcend its own time] and cultural relativism actually are a means to avoid testing our own prejudices."[8]

The postmodern paradigm challenges a second Evangelical perspective: Evangelicals believe that the Christian faith is intimately connected to the key redemptive events of salvation history recorded in Scripture. Therefore, Evangelicals are concerned with Scripture's record of past events (i.e., the historicity of the text). This is not to affirm that only that which is historical is true or meaningful. The parables, for example, though not records of historical events, are meaningful and convey truth. Rather, it is to affirm that we must take seriously the biblical authors' intentions concerning how their texts should be read, whether as history, fiction, or some blending of the two. Furthermore, the meaning and truthfulness of those texts purporting to be historical cannot be divorced from their historicity. It mattered to Paul whether the resurrection actually happened (1 Cor. 15:12–19)! How can it be different for us?

In short, Cargal is probably right: Pentecostalism, because of its pragmatic and experiential focus, may be easily attracted to the ahistorical vision inherent in postmodern thought. This, however, is a weakness, not a strength. Although, as Cargal notes, postmodernism "provides philosophical space in which it is meaningful to speak of an encounter with transcendent reality,"[9] we must ask at what price. Postmodernism may allow Christians to speak about such encounters, but not with authority; we are but one voice in a cacophony of unintelligible sounds.

2. The Present and the Quest for Relevance

Cargal's postmodernism not only diminishes the place of historical investigation in the interpretative enterprise; it also minimizes the role of the text itself. The locus of meaning shifts from the author/text to the reader. This shift is evident in the way Cargal emphasizes the "shaping influence of [the interpreter's] experience" and the multiple meanings that it yields.[10]

This focus on the reader reflects an admirable concern for contemporary life. Indeed, this concern for relevance has led to the rise of numerous reader-oriented approaches to biblical interpretation. Yet in spite of noble aspirations, there is cause for concern. While many forms of the new literary criticism, when used in conjunction with more traditional methods, have much to offer, the extreme subjectivity of some reader-oriented methodologies (such as reader-response criticism and deconstructionism) is disturbing. These approaches strike me as the logical successors of a sterile biblical criticism that had so emasculated the text that it had nothing of significance to communicate. At some point, the question had to be asked: Why bother with all of this? The solution to this dilemma was obvious: If significance cannot be found in the meaning of the text, then it must be imported from outside the text.

Perhaps this is why many postmodernists so vehemently attack traditional approaches: These critical methods are vestiges of a dark and meaningless past. Cargal is more restrained than most, though he too lampoons the quest for "'kernels' discovered by critical, objective historical reconstruction."[11] Yet this critique of the historical-critical method, at least as employed by Evangelicals, appears to be misguided. For example, source and redaction criticism are employed not to get behind the text to some pristine and authoritative "kernel"; rather, we use them so that we may better understand the text itself (in its final form, no less). For the Evangelical, critical methods help uncover textual meaning. This is important and relevant because it is God's Word to us.

Of course, a focus on the original meaning of the text does not solve all of our interpretative problems. We still have to appropriate the message for our culture and age in a way that is faithful and relevant. As a missionary, I am all too aware of the complexity of this task. However, the distinction between the meaning of the text and the numerous applications (or significances) it may have for various situations and cultures is necessary if we are to restrain ourselves from distorting the text. Unfortunately, this distinction is lost in the postmodern paradigm. Clark Pinnock speaks forthrightly: "I repudiate the idea so prevalent today that the human standpoint acts as a sort of lens or grid on the basis of which we can understand the Bible. When this happens, one is not interpreting the Bible but judging and rewriting it."[12]

3. The Future and the Quest for Pentecostal Identity

Cargal's brave new world has little space for modern Evangelicalism, mired as it is in Enlightenment thinking. No, Evangelicalism will be left behind. But what of Pentecostalism? According to Cargal, if we can free ourselves from those who seek to enslave us—those promoting the Evangelicalization of Pentecostalism—there may be hope. We must also recognize that not all of our interpretations are mediated by the Spirit and thus free ourselves from "the insidious influences of sexism, racism, and classism."[13] Of course, how we are to make such judgments and achieve this liberation is never articulated.

My vision of the future is quite different. I see the assimilation of the modern Pentecostal movement into the broader Evangelical world as an exciting and positive event. Looking back over the past fifty years, we can affirm the strength we have found in our Evangelical heritage. This is especially true with respect to biblical interpretation. We can also rejoice in our own positive contributions to the larger body. Twenty years ago, who would have thought that today we would find such openness concerning gifts of the Spirit? Looking forward, I see the potential for additional theological contributions to the larger body.

Our understanding of the Pentecostal gift is important in this regard. Indeed, today we find ourselves with many opportunities. As we have noted in the previous chapters, the hermeneutical climate within Evangelicalism is more conducive now than ever before to our theological contributions.[14] And by virtue of our experiential focus, we can serve as an important bridge between other Evangelicals and the non-Evangelical world.

True, as Cargal notes, we may be rendered irrelevant if we do not hop on the postmodern bandwagon. But in view of the waning interest in structuralism and the vigor of Evangelical scholarship, particularly in the field of hermeneutics, I would argue that the opposite is true.

Study Questions

1. What is central to the postmodern perspective?
2. The author suggests that key elements of postmodernism are not compatible with the values of the Pentecostal movement. Why is this the case?
3. How have postmodern thinkers helped to sharpen our own theological perspective?
4. The author suggests that the postmodern approach to historical meaning is too pessimistic and that the hermeneutical process is best described as a spiral rather than a circle. What does he mean by this?
5. What core values tie Pentecostals together with Evangelicals? According to the author, why should Pentecostals identify with the larger Evangelical world and seek to work together with and influence this group?

Notes

[1] Timothy B. Cargal, "Beyond the Fundamentalist-Modernist Controversy: Pentecostals and Hermeneutics in a Postmodern Age," *Pneuma* 15 (Fall 1993): 163–87 (p. 187).

[2] Ibid., 164.

[3] Ibid., 171.

[4] Klein, Blomberg, and Hubbard, *Introduction to Biblical Interpretation*, 133.

[5] See G. R. Osborne, *The Hermeneutical Spiral*, 379–80, 397–415 and Klein, Blomberg, and Hubbard, *Introduction*, 114.

[6] Klein, Blomberg, and Hubbard, *Introduction*, 135: "We can apply interpretative controls only if we seek as our primary goal the meaning that would have made sense to the original writer and readers."

[7] Cargal might object to our use of "all," but it is not clear how he would judge any reading invalid.

[8] Allan Bloom, *The Closing of the American Mind* (New York: Simon & Schuster, 1987), 40.

[9] Cargal, "Postmodern Age," 179.

[10] Ibid., 181–82.

[11] Ibid., 168.

[12] Clark H. Pinnock, "The Work of the Holy Spirit in Hermeneutics," *JPT* 2 (1993): 15–16.

[13] Cargal, "Postmodern Age," 187.

[14] See Klein, Blomberg, and Hubbard, *Introduction*, 349–50. Note also their comments concerning the different ways in which Luke and Paul describe the activity of the Spirit: "These descriptions are complementary rather than contradictory. A proper doctrine of Scripture will not allow Acts to be subordinated to Paul" (351).

Chapter Five

Exegesis: A Reply to James Dunn

James Dunn has significantly shaped the context in which current discussion on the work of the Holy Spirit is being carried out. As questions generated by the rise of the Pentecostal and Charismatic movements became especially prominent, Dunn's *Baptism in the Holy Spirit* provided answers for many. Although Dunn affirmed the charismatic character of the early church, he challenged the classical Pentecostal understanding of Spirit-baptism. Thus, while Dunn encouraged many to take seriously the charismatic dimension of the Christian life, his views also supported non-Pentecostals in their reluctance to accept and to seek a Spirit-baptism distinct from conversion. Dunn quickly became a champion of the non-Pentecostal Evangelical community.

Yet, Dunn's contribution to the Pentecostal movement has also been enormous. He demonstrated that Pentecostals could no longer continue to rely on the interpretative methods of the nineteenth-century Holiness Movement and expect to speak to the contemporary church world. Dunn not only challenged the hermeneutical foundation of traditional Pentecostal positions (a hermeneutic that treated the Bible as "a homogenous whole"), he also pointed the way forward by stressing the theological integrity of each biblical author. A truly biblical theology, Dunn rightly urged, could be developed only when we "take each author and book separately.... Only then can the biblical-theologian feel free to let that text interact with other texts from other books."[1]

Dunn's critique stimulated a burst of creative theological reflection by Pentecostal scholars. Following the methodology he outlined, Pentecostals have sought to interpret Luke on his own terms and, in this way, to highlight Luke's distinctive contribution to a biblical theology of the Spirit. Although many of these efforts have been critical of Dunn's treatment of Luke–Acts, his influence is apparent. Indeed, one can hardly discuss early Christian pneumatology without interacting with his views.

Because of Dunn's influence and his role as a critical protagonist, Pentecostal scholars wondered how he might respond to their recent efforts. All eagerly waited for his response. The wondering and waiting ended with Dunn's 1993 article, "Baptism in the Spirit in Luke–Acts: A Response to Pentecostal Scholarship on Luke–Acts."[2] Dunn's article serves as an excellent point of departure for analyzing a number of the key exegetical points in the current debate concerning the character of Luke's pneumatology. Therefore, in this chapter I will summarize Dunn's article, evaluate the major arguments he presents, and assess its significant implications.

1. A Summary of Dunn's Response

In his earlier work, *Baptism in the Holy Spirit*, Dunn argued that the authors of the New Testament uniformly present the gift of the Spirit as "the most fundamental aspect of the event or process of becoming a Christian, the climax of conversion-initiation."[3] The pneumatological perspective of Luke, according to Dunn, is thus similar to that of Paul and John: The Spirit initiates believers into the new age and mediates to them the life of the new covenant. Recent Pentecostal scholarship has challenged this position, asserting that Luke is a theologian *in his own right* and that his perspective on the Spirit is different from, although complementary to, that of Paul. Unlike Paul, who frequently speaks of the soteriological dimension of the Spirit's work,[4] Luke *consistently* portrays the Spirit as the source of power for service. This line of thought has affinities with earlier writings produced by H. Gunkel, E. Schweizer, and G. Haya-Prats, but has been developed more recently by Roger Stronstad, James Shelton (more tentatively), and myself.[5]

My contribution to this discussion came in the form of a monograph that argued that Paul was the first Christian to attribute soteriological functions to the Spirit and that this original element of his pneumatology did not influence wider (non-Pauline) sectors of the early church until after the writing of Luke–Acts. The crucial point of disagreement with Dunn was my insistence that Luke never attributes soteriological functions to the Spirit and that his narrative presupposes a pneumatology excluding this dimension (e.g., Luke 11:13; Acts 8:4–17; 19:1–7). Or, to put it positively, Luke describes the gift of the Spirit *exclusively* in charismatic terms as the source of power for effective witness.

Dunn's article represents his response to this appraisal of Lukan pneumatology. The central question in the current debate is clearly stated at the outset of the article: "Does Luke separate the outpouring of the Spirit on individuals from 'conversion-initiation' and see it as an empowering gift rather than a soteriological gift?"[6] Dunn's answer to this question—an emphatic "no"—comes in four sections entitled, "The Spirit of Prophecy," "The Soteriological Spirit," "The Eschatological Spirit," and "The Spirit and Faith."

In "The Spirit of Prophecy," Dunn asserts that while Luke does indeed feature inspired speech and other visible manifestations of the Spirit, it is not tenable to suggest that this is the *only* function of the Spirit in Luke–Acts. The argument at this point rests largely on a series of rhetorical questions (e.g., "Is there not a danger of confusing the fuller effect of the Spirit's entry into a life with the physical manifestations of that impact?").[7] Dunn does suggest that the evidence from Acts 8:4–17 is meager and ultimately inconclusive. This is, in effect, Dunn's denial of my claim that Luke's narrative presupposes a pneumatology that excludes the soteriological dimension.

Dunn moves to the offensive in "The Soteriological Spirit." He seeks to demonstrate that Luke does indeed attribute soteriological functions to the Spirit. His argument rests largely on an analysis of two texts: Acts 2:38–39 and 10:43–48 (and the parallel texts, 11:14–18 and 15:7–9). According to Dunn, 2:38–39 presents the Spirit as the mediator of "life-giving grace," and the Cornelius passages indicate that the Spirit is the source of cleansing and forgiveness.[8]

In his section "The Eschatological Spirit," Dunn acknowledges that his former view was based on an artificial and overly rigid schematization of epochs in Luke–Acts. Nevertheless, he insists that Luke intended "to accord an unrepeatable eschatological significance to the events at Jordan and Pentecost" and that these events represent much more than simply a Spirit-anointing for witness.[9]

Specifically, Dunn argues that the coming of the Spirit at Jordan and Pentecost inaugurated new stages in God's plan, stages with eschatological significance. While this conclusion is not particularly striking—the events at Jordan and Pentecost clearly inaugurate the ministry of Jesus and the mission of the church (and who would deny their eschatological significance?)—Dunn continues to argue that these events actually initiate Jesus and the disciples into the new age! Thus, in his view, the Spirit comes on the disciples at Pentecost, not primarily to empower them for their mission, but more importantly to usher them into the new age and mediate its blessings.

Dunn claims that the linkage between Pentecost and the Cornelius passages (Acts 10:47 and parallels) confirms this judgment. John the Baptist's prophecy (Luke 3:7–9, 16–17) is cited as providing further evidence for this view. Special significance is again attached to Acts 2:39. According to Dunn, this text indicates that "the promise of the Father" (cf. Luke 24:49; Acts 1:4; 2:33) has soteriological significance. In addition, Dunn maintains that Luke's understanding of the "promise of the Father"—clearly shaped by Joel 2:28–29—was also informed by a number of other Old Testament prophecies regarding the Spirit's eschatological role (e.g., Isa. 32:15; 44:3–5; Ezek. 36:26–27). Although Luke cites none of these texts, Dunn criticizes my "complete disregard" for them.[10]

The final section ("The Spirit and Faith") contains Dunn's argument for an inextricable link between faith and reception of the Spirit. Here Dunn attempts to reconcile the Samaritan (Acts 8:4–17) and Ephesian (19:1–7) narratives with his perspective. This leads to his conclusion, which is a reaffirmation of his older position, that "the pneumatology of Luke is essentially one with the pneumatology of Paul."[11]

Although Dunn's article is largely a restatement of his previous position and offers little that is new, it does reflect the current thinking of a prime mover in the discussion. Perhaps the most significant feature of the article is that it clearly identifies the crucial question that has emerged in the intervening years since the publication of *Baptism in the Holy Spirit*: Does Luke, in a manner analogous to Paul, present the Spirit as a soteriological agent (the source of cleansing, justification, and sanctification)? Or does Luke describe the working of the Spirit *exclusively* in charismatic terms as the source of power for effective witness? Dunn's article also highlights specific texts and exegetical issues that are especially significant for all who attempt to answer these questions. We now turn to an analysis of these specific texts and Dunn's handling of them.

2. Luke's Distinctive Pneumatology: The Evidence For

We will begin by examining Dunn's treatment of two texts that I have suggested indicate that Luke's pneumatological perspective is indeed more limited than that of Paul: Acts 8:4–17 and 19:1–7.

2.1. Acts 8:4–17

The Samaritan narrative (Acts 8:4–17), with its description of the Samaritans as baptized believers without the Spirit, is the most problematic for Dunn. The narrative indicates that the Samaritans believed the preaching of Philip and were thus baptized by him (v. 12), yet they did not receive the Spirit until some time later (vv. 15–17). The implications of this account for Luke's understanding of the Spirit are apparent. Since Luke considered the Samaritans to be Christians (i.e., converted) before they received the Spirit, it can hardly be maintained that he understood the Spirit to be the "one thing that makes a [person] a Christian."[12]

As we have seen, Dunn initially sought to mitigate the force of this text by arguing that, in Luke's view, the Samaritans were not really Christians prior to their reception of the Spirit. He maintained their "initial response and commitment was defective" and that Luke "intended his readers to know this."[13] However, this hypothesis has been subjected to intense criticism and rejected by virtually every scholar who has evaluated it.[14] With his older position effectively discredited, Dunn tries to reconcile the text with his thesis by a position of agnosticism toward the text. Stressing the brevity of the narrative and the sparseness of information it offers, Dunn maintains that "the one fact given us by Luke is that the coming of the Spirit was delayed."[15] Beyond this all is idle speculation. Indeed, Dunn claims that the sparseness of the narrative calls us not to ponder why the Spirit was delayed, but rather the simple fact that it was delayed. The delay serves to stress what is really important, the Spirit's coming. Dunn proceeds to define the impact of this "coming of the Spirit" in a manner consistent with his thesis: The Spirit incorporates the believers into the body of Christ and mediates the blessings of the new age.[16]

What all of this misses is that Luke gives us more than one simple fact. His narrative is actually explicit. He describes the Samaritans, prior to their reception of the Spirit, as people who had "believed" (8:12), "accepted the Word of God" (8:14), and been "baptized" (8:12). And while the reason the reception of the Spirit and faith are separated in the narrative (the "why" that Dunn suggests we need not bother with) may not be self-evident, this simply indicates that for Luke, this sort of language posed no problem. It certainly does not allow us to ignore the clear implications of the narrative for Luke's pneumatology. Indeed, his carefully crafted interpretation of this event tells us much about his understanding of the Spirit.[17] The essential fact that Dunn ignores is this: Luke's account betrays a pneumatology decidedly different from Paul or John, neither of whom could conceive of baptized believers being without the Spirit.

The primary intent of the narrative, as Dunn suggests, may be to stress the importance of receiving the gift of the Spirit (as empowering for mission, I would add[18]). In any event, it is unlikely that Luke consciously sought to teach here that the gift is normally separate from faith. Yet the fact that he *does* separate the two clearly reveals his distinctive pneumatological perspective. As we have noted, Paul would not—indeed, could not—have interpreted and narrated the event in this way.

Furthermore, the separation refutes Dunn's interpretation of the Lukan gift as "the climax of conversion-initiation." This is why originally, against all the evidence, Dunn sought to deny that such separation did in fact occur. Perhaps Dunn's call for us to overlook glaring inconsistencies in the narrative in favor of his version of Luke's message would sound more plausible if Luke proved to be editorially inept. Yet, in view of Luke's obvious ability, it is difficult to believe that he was unable to shape this account without contradicting his own pneumatology. Perhaps if this were the only exception to a uniform pattern, Dunn's call would have some credence. But Luke elsewhere separates conversion from reception of the Spirit (e.g., Luke 11:13; Acts 19:1–7). As it stands, Dunn's recent position sounds strikingly similar to his previous one: a desperate attempt to dodge the obvious implications of the text.

2.2. Acts 19:1–7

Luke's account of the Ephesian disciples' reception of the Spirit is again filled with difficulties for Dunn. First there is Paul's question: "Did you receive the Holy Spirit when you believed?" (19:2). Then there is also the reference to "disciples" (19:1) who have received neither Christian baptism nor the gift of the Spirit.

Dunn's brief treatment of this passage focuses on Paul's question and the temporal relationship of the aorist participle (*pisteusantes*; lit., "having believed") to the action of the principal verb (*elabete*, "did you receive?"). He argues on contextual grounds that the key phrase should be translated "when you believed" rather than "after you believed." Actually, the specific temporal nuance of the participle is ultimately irrelevant, for the potential separation of belief from reception of the Spirit is presupposed by the question itself.

The other crucial question centers on the status of the "disciples" (19:1) without the Spirit: Are they truly disciples of Jesus? When the immediate context, which contains the closely related pericope concerning Apollos (18:24–28), is considered, the evidence demands an affirmative response. Apollos's standing can hardly be questioned, for Luke indicates that "he had been instructed in the way of the Lord" and "taught about Jesus accurately" (18:25). The latter phrase, descriptive of Paul's preaching in 28:31, suggests that Apollos preached the Christian gospel. Since according to Luke the gift of the Spirit is not inextricably bound to the rite of baptism (e.g., 8:17; 10:44), there is no contradiction in his portrait of Apollos as an articulate minister of the gospel who had not received Christian baptism.

Similarly, Apollos's Christian experience does not presuppose an awareness of the Pentecostal event or promise. Thus it does not preclude his contact with the Ephesian disciples, who had not heard of the availability of the Spirit. On the contrary, Luke has carefully constructed the narrative in order to emphasize the relationship between Apollos and the Ephesians (cf. 19:1), all of whom knew only "the baptism of John" (18:25; 19:3). The clear implication is that the twelve from Ephesus were converts of the able preacher active in the same city.[19] We must therefore conclude that in Luke's estimation the Ephesians were, like Apollos, disciples of Jesus. This conclusion is supported by Luke's description of the Ephesians as "disciples" (*mathētai*, 19:1), for when he employs that word without any qualification, it always refers to disciples of Jesus.[20] And since "faith" (*pistis*) is the essence of discipleship,[21] the description of the Ephesians as "believers" (19:2) confirms these findings.[22]

In *Baptism in the Holy Spirit*, Dunn defended his thesis by arguing that Luke uses the indefinite pronoun "certain" (*tinas*) with "disciples" in 19:1 in order to highlight the Ephesians' lack of relation to the church in Ephesus: "They are disciples, but they do not belong to *the* disciples."[23] However, this argument ignores Luke's usage elsewhere: He uses the same pronoun in the singular with "disciple" in order to describe Ananias (9:10) and Timothy (16:1). To his credit, Dunn now acknowledges the weakness of his former position,[24] yet he insists that his argument is not dependent on it. Indeed, he continues to follow his earlier suggestion that Paul's question in 19:2 is "one of suspicion and surprise": The Ephesians claimed to be men of faith, but Paul queries whether or not their claim is valid. According to Dunn, Paul finds the claim to be false.[25]

It is worth noting that Dunn's argument at this point, developed in *Baptism in the Holy Spirit*, is based on the observation that the Paul of the letters could not countenance the idea of "believers" being without the Spirit (Rom. 8:9; 1 Cor. 12:3; Gal. 3:2; 1 Thess. 1:5–6; Tit. 3:5). Of course this objection fails to take into account the fact that the narrative as it currently exists (particularly Acts 19:2–4) has been significantly shaped by Luke. The dialogue between Paul and the Ephesians was penned by Luke[26] in order to highlight the Ephesians' need of the Spirit's enablement and its normal prerequisite, Christian baptism. Paul would undoubtedly have related the story differently, for the potential separation of belief from reception of the Spirit is implicit in the question.[27] Again, in the face of every evidence, Dunn will not let Luke be Luke.

We all come to the text with theological presuppositions. And Dunn has been more forthright than most in this regard. In a previous response to criticisms of his treatment of the Samaritan episode, Dunn readily acknowledged that his interpretation of this incident was influenced by his conviction that "Luke shared the regular view among the major NT writers that it is the gift of the Spirit which constitutes a Christian."[28] This honesty is admirable. However, since our goal is to allow exegesis to inform and, if need be, challenge our theological presuppositions, honesty concerning presuppositions needs to be coupled with openness to the text.

Apart from Dunn's treatment of the texts noted above, one other feature of his response suggests that Dunn's reading of Luke–Acts in general, and these texts in particular, has been largely shaped by questionable presuppositions. The initial section of his article, which is also the section where Dunn first mentions the Samaritan text ("The Spirit of Prophecy"), is essentially a collection of rhetorical questions. Before any evidence is cited or any reasons proffered, we read: "Is there not a danger here of speaking as though . . . in effect, the Spirit of prophecy was a different Spirit from the Spirit of salvation?" Again Dunn queries, "Why should it be assumed that Luke thinks of the Spirit only as the power of inspiration?" And again, this time answering his own question, "There is surely a danger here of being so struck with the visible effects of the Spirit's coming in Luke–Acts that one diminishes Luke's pneumatology to such effects."[29]

Underlying these questions is the controlling presupposition alluded to above: The early church, from its earliest days, uniformly viewed the Spirit as the source of Christian existence. Yet this presupposition is the very point which I, and others before me,[30] have questioned. Dunn virtually ignores the wealth of evidence that indicates first-century Jews identified the gift of the Spirit as the source of prophetic inspiration and not as a soteriological necessity. This view was dominant for the Judaism that gave birth to the early church, with Wisdom of Solomon and the Hymns of Qumran providing the only exceptions.[31]

Furthermore, Dunn ignores the fact that there is no evidence from Paul's letters that his broader view of the Spirit's work, embracing soteriological functions, is based on underlying pre-Pauline tradition. As I have argued in detail elsewhere, the evidence suggests that Paul was the first Christian to attribute soteriological functions to the Spirit.[32] All of this indicates that Dunn's presuppositions, based on a questionable reading of the evidence outside of Luke–Acts, have shaped his reading of the text of Luke–Acts. The evidence from Luke's own hand is compelling, and Dunn has provided nothing new by way of evidence that would refute our claim: Acts 8:4–17, 19:1–7, and other texts that Dunn does not treat,[33] confirm that Luke's pneumatology is not only different from that of Paul, but that it does not embrace the soteriological functions that Paul so frequently attributes to the Spirit. This is no weakness, as Dunn suggests; rather, it is testimony to the richness of the diversity we find in the New Testament and an affirmation of Luke's unique contribution to it.

3. Luke's Distinctive Pneumatology: The Evidence Against

We now examine those texts that Dunn suggests do indicate that Luke attributed soteriological functions to the Spirit. The key texts that appear repeatedly in Dunn's article are Acts 2:38–39 and the Cornelius texts (10:43–

48; 11:14–18; 15:7–9). Dunn also briefly discusses John the Baptist's prophecy (Luke 3:16–17), but we will deal with this text in the following chapter.

3.1. Acts 2:38–39

Acts 2:38–39 represents a key link in Dunn's argument. His treatment of the text may be summarized in three points: (1) The reference to "the promise" in 2:39 links the gift of the Spirit (v. 38) to salvation; (2) Luke's understanding of the "promise of the Father" was informed by a number of Old Testament prophecies regarding the Spirit's eschatological role other than Joel 2:28–32; (3) the collocation of repentance, baptism, and the promise of the Spirit in Acts 2:38 demonstrates that Luke viewed reception of the Spirit as a necessary element in Christian initiation.[34] An examination of the evidence, however, reveals that none of these points is convincing.

(1) At the outset, it should be noted that Luke refers to "the promise" of the Spirit four times in close proximity (Luke 24:49; Acts 1:4; 2:33; 2:39). "The promise" is identified with the Pentecostal gift of the Spirit (2:33) and explicitly defined: Reception of "the promise" will result in the disciples being "clothed with power from on high," enabling them to be effective "witnesses" (Luke 24:48–49; Acts 1:8). Furthermore, for Luke "the promise" with reference to the Spirit refers to the gift of the Spirit of prophecy promised in Joel 2:28–32. This is made clear through Luke's citation of Joel 2:28–32 in Acts 2:17–21, and is further emphasized in his redactional introduction of the citation.

This introduction includes the phrase "God says" and thus identifies the prophecy of Joel as "the promise of the Father"—the full description of "the promise" in three of the four Lukan references (Luke 24:49; Acts 1:4; 2:33). In Joel's prophecy the Spirit comes as the source of prophetic inspiration, a point that again Luke highlights by altering the Greek text of Joel by inserting the phrase "and they will prophesy" (Acts 2:18). Another alteration, Luke's transformation of Joel's "slaves" into "servants of God"—effected by his double insertion of "my" in Acts 2:18 (a fact not reflected in Joel 2:29 in the NIV)—highlights what is implicit in the Joel text: The gift of the Spirit is given only to those who are members of the community of salvation.[35] Thus Luke's explicit definitions (Luke 24:49; Acts 1:4–8) and his use of the Joel citation indicate that "the promise" of the Spirit, initially fulfilled at Pentecost (Acts 2:4), enables the disciples to take up their prophetic vocation to the world.

Although the Lukan "promise" of the Spirit must be interpreted in light of Joel's promise concerning the restoration of the Spirit of prophecy, Acts 2:39 does include an additional element, insofar as Luke extends the range of the promise envisioned to include the promise of salvation offered in Joel

2:32 (as well as the promise of the Spirit of prophecy in Joel 2:28). As Dunn notes, Acts 2:39 echoes the language of Joel 2:32/Acts 2:21: "Everyone who calls on the name of the Lord will be saved." In Acts 2:39 Luke extends the range of "the promise" to include this salvific dimension because the audience addressed is not disciples.

Yet we must not miss the fact that "the promise" of Acts 2:39 embraces more than the experience of conversion. Consistent with Luke 24:49; Acts 1:4; 2:33, the promised gift of the Spirit in Acts 2:39 refers to the promise of Joel 2:28, and thus it is a promise of prophetic enabling granted to the repentant.[36] The promise of Acts 2:39, like the promise of Jesus in 1:8, points beyond "the restoration of the preserved of Israel": Salvation is offered (Joel 2:32), but the promise includes the renewal of Israel's prophetic vocation to be a light to the nations (Joel 2:28).[37]

Dunn criticizes this approach, suggesting that we should read Luke's earlier references to the promise of the Spirit in light of the promise of salvation offered in Acts 2:39.[38] Yet, as we have seen, Acts 2:39 does not indicate that the Spirit comes as the source of new covenant existence. Rather, it simply reminds us that the prophecy of Joel 2:28–32 includes two elements: the gift of the Spirit of prophecy (v. 28) and the offer of salvation to those who call on the name of the Lord (v. 32). Acts 2:39 refers to both, but it does not suggest the two are identical. Indeed, this sort of equation runs counter to Luke's explicit statements (Luke 24:49; Acts 1:4–8), his use and redaction of the Joel citation (cf. Acts 2:17–18), and the broader context of his two-volume work (e.g., Luke 3:16–17; Acts 8:4–17; 19:1–7).

(2) Dunn attempts to support his reading of Acts 2:38–39 by asserting that Luke's understanding of the "promise" of the Spirit—clearly shaped by Joel 2:28–29—was also informed by a number of other Old Testament prophecies regarding the Spirit's eschatological role (e.g., Isa. 32:15; 44:3–5; Ezek. 36:26–27). Indeed, he criticizes my "complete disregard" for these Old Testament texts. Furthermore, he implies that my emphasis on the pneumatological perspectives of intertestamental Judaism is misguided since Luke was not a Palestinian Jew and would have been familiar with the LXX (the Greek version of the OT).[39] Yet Dunn's comments miss a number of important points.

(a) Martin Hengel has established that rigid distinctions between Hellenistic and Palestinian Judaism should not be overemphasized, for "Jewish Palestine was no hermetically sealed island in the sea of Hellenistic oriental syncretism."[40]

(b) Many of the Jewish sources I cite stem from and reflect the thinking of the Hellenistic Judaism Luke supposedly knew so well.

(c) Dunn fails to examine how the Old Testament texts he cites were interpreted in the (first-century) Judaism that gave rise to the Christianity Luke knew. For example, he fails to recognize that the transformation of the heart referred to in Ezekiel 36:26–27 was viewed as a prerequisite for the eschatological bestowal of the Spirit and that the rabbis interpreted Isaiah 44:3 as a reference to the outpouring of the Spirit of prophecy on Israel. Rather than simply reading our own agenda and exegesis into the first-century setting, surely it is better to ask how those Jews closest in time to the early Christians understood the relevant texts and what significance they attached to them.

This is particularly important at this point, for the eschatological outpouring of the Spirit was generally interpreted in light of Joel 2:28–29 as a restoration of the Spirit of prophecy. By way of contrast, Ezekiel 36:26–27 was usually interpreted as a prophecy concerning the end-time removal of the evil "impulse," and most frequently without reference to the activity of the Spirit. Indeed, the eradication of the evil "impulse" was presented as a prerequisite for the end-time bestowal of the Spirit of prophecy.[41] This means that Dunn's call for us to interpret the "promise" of the Spirit in light of a plethora of Old Testament texts conflicts with the evidence from early Jewish sources and Luke's own hand (Luke, as we have noted, cites none of these other Old Testament texts). There simply is no evidence to support the notion that by referring to Joel 2:28–29, Luke intended his readers to think of some commonly expected, all-embracing soteriological bestowal of the Spirit, the details of which were pieced together from a variety of Old Testament texts.

(3) Finally, should the collocation of repentance, baptism, and reception of the Spirit in Acts 2:38 cause us to reconsider these conclusions? No, for it tells us little about the nature of the gift of the Spirit. While the collocation may indicate that for Luke the rite of water baptism is normally accompanied by the bestowal of the Spirit, Luke's usage elsewhere suggests that even this conclusion may be overstating the case. There is certainly nothing in the text that lends credence to Dunn's contention that the Spirit is presented here as the "bearer of salvation."[42]

Dunn's point would be made if we could establish that the text presupposes an inextricable bond between water baptism and forgiveness of sins on the one hand and reception of the Spirit on the other. But this conclusion is unwarranted. Since Luke fails to develop a strong link between water baptism and the bestowal of the Spirit elsewhere and regularly separates the rite from the gift (Luke 3:21–22; Acts 8:12–13; 9:17–18; 10:44; 18:24), the phrase "and you will receive the gift of the Holy Spirit" (2:38) should be interpreted as a promise that the Spirit will be "imparted to those who are already converted and baptized."[43] In any case, the most that can be gleaned from the text is that repentance and water baptism are the normal prerequisites for reception of the Spirit, which is promised to every believer.

In short, Dunn suggests that we interpret the explicit testimony of Luke concerning the significance of the "promise" of the Spirit in Luke 24:49; Acts 1:4; and 2:17–18—all of which describe the pneumatic gift as a prophetic enabling for the missionary task—in light of a questionable reading of Acts 2:38–39, one that conflicts with Luke's usage elsewhere (e.g., Acts 8:4–17; 19:1–7). Moreover, he calls us to interpret the "promise" against the backdrop of a plethora of Old Testament texts—none of which is mentioned by Luke or linked (in the suggested manner) with the Joel text by contemporary Jewish thinkers—rather than in light of the text Luke does cite (Joel 2:28–32) and contemporary Jewish expectations. Some may be persuaded by such arguments, but I do not find them compelling.

3.2. The Cornelius Texts: Acts 10:43–48; 11:14–18; 15:7–9

The Cornelius texts represent another key link in Dunn's argument. Pointing to these texts, Dunn confidently writes: "Here ... it is surely difficult beyond human contrivance to avoid the conclusion that Luke intended his readers to understand the coming of the Spirit in soteriological terms."[44] Dunn finds support for this conclusion in Acts 10:43–48. He notes that the Spirit falls just as Peter announces the promise of forgiveness to those who believe. The most natural conclusion to be drawn from this, we are told, is that the Spirit is the "transmitter of forgiveness."[45]

This ignores two important facts, however. (1) Elsewhere Luke always attributes forgiveness (*aphesis*), which is granted in response to faith/repentance, to Jesus, never to the Spirit.[46] This should caution us against making facile assumptions at this point, particularly in view of the attribution of forgiveness to Jesus' name in 10:43.

(2) Peter also spoke of the testimony of prophets immediately prior to the Spirit's interruption: "All the prophets testify about him" (Acts 10:43). Now the decisive sign of God's favor on the Gentiles is their reception of the gift of the Spirit, manifested in inspired speech (10:46). It is this sign that astonishes Peter's circumcised companions (10:45–46) and results in his command to baptize the Gentile converts (10:47–48). And it is also through reference to this sign that Peter justifies his table fellowship with the uncircumcised (11:3, 15–17) and their admission into the church (15:8–9). This emphasis on the sign-value of Spirit-baptism accords well with Luke's distinctive, prophetic pneumatology. Since according to Luke reception of the Spirit is the exclusive privilege of "the servants" of God and generally results in miraculous and audible speech,[47] by its very nature the gift provides demonstrative proof that

the uncircumcised members of Cornelius's household have been incorporated into the community of salvation. The sign-value of the prophetic gift is also emphasized in the Pentecost account (2:4–5, 17–20). Whether from the lips of a Jew in Jerusalem or a Gentile in Caesarea, the manifestation of inspired speech marks the speaker as a member of the end-time prophetic community.

The evidence suggests that Peter and company (and thus also Luke) viewed the Gentiles' reception of the Spirit as the decisive *sign* of their acceptance by God. Luke's perspective is based on the prophetic nature of the pneumatic gift. Although in this instance (in contrast to 8:17 and 19:6) reception of the Spirit accompanies conversion, the text does not imply that the gift is the means by which the uncircumcised are actually cleansed and forgiven. This unwarranted assumption is based on the summaries of the event recorded in 11:15–17 and 15:8–10.

Pointing to the similarities between Acts 11:17a and 11:18b, J. Dunn declares: "God gave the Spirit (11:17) means God gave repentance unto life (11:18)."[48] However, Dunn's equation must be rejected since elsewhere "repentance" (*metanoia*) is a *prerequisite* for receiving the Spirit (2:38–39) and is clearly distinguished from the gift itself (cf. 5:31–32).[49] The similarities between 11:17a and 18b simply reflect the logic of Peter's argument: Since God has granted the Gentiles the gift of the Spirit, it follows a fortiori that they have been granted "repentance unto life" and are eligible for the baptismal rite.[50]

Dunn treats Acts 15:7–9 in a manner similar to 11:17–18: God's giving of the Sprit (15:8) is equated with his cleansing of their hearts (15:9).[51] But again Peter's argument in 15:7–9 speaks against this equation.[52] Verse 8 is the premise from which the deduction of verse 9 is drawn: God's bestowal of the Spirit bears witness (v. 8) to the reality of his act of cleansing (v. 9). Dunn notes that the grammar suggests both the cleansing and bestowal of the Spirit occur simultaneously, but this is of little consequence. Although in 10:44–45 conversion and Spirit-baptism occur simultaneously, the logical distinction (clearly demanded by the instances of chronological separation cited above) is implicit in the narrative. Peter's argument here is similar to that in 11:16–18. In each instance the distinction between the premise (gift of the Spirit) and deduction (repentance/cleansing) is apparent.

As we have noted, our analysis is supported by Luke's usage of "forgiveness" (*aphesis*) and "repentance" (*metanoia*) elsewhere and by instances of chronological separation in his narrative (Acts 8:17; 19:6). However, the decisive objection against Dunn's interpretation is that Luke equates the gift of the Spirit granted to Cornelius's household not with cleansing and forgiveness, but with the Pentecostal gift of prophetic inspiration.[53] Luke stresses the point through repetition: The Gentiles received the same gift granted to the Jewish disciples on Pentecost (10:47; 11:15, 17; 15:8). The significance Peter attaches to the gift as a sign of God's acceptance is based on the prophetic nature of this gift, explicitly affirmed at Pentecost (2:17–18).

Indeed, the manifestation of the prophetic gift by the Gentiles is the climactic event in a series of divine interventions that serve to initiate and validate the Gentile mission. Since this is Luke's central purpose, he does not pursue further at this point the significance of the gift for the missionary activity of this newly formed Christian community. However, we may presume that the prophetic band in Caesarea, like the communities in Jerusalem and Samaria, by virtue of the pneumatic gift participated effectively in the missionary enterprise (cf. Acts 18:22; 21:8).

4. Conclusion

I have argued, over against Dunn's objections, that Luke describes the gift of the Spirit *exclusively* in charismatic or prophetic terms as the source of power for effective witness. Although Dunn suggests that this conclusion diminishes "the weight and force of Luke's pneumatology,"[54] I would argue that it actually affirms the special contribution Luke has to make to a biblical theology of the Spirit—a contribution that has far-ranging implications for contemporary church life. Indeed, Dunn's attempt to "safeguard the fulness and wholeness of Luke's pneumatology" dulls the sharpness and vigor of Luke's message.[55]

Over twenty years ago, Dunn noted the positive contributions of the Pentecostal movement, especially "their rediscovery of the Spirit in terms of experience." And with wistfulness, he uttered the hope that "some synthesis of Pentecostal experience with older traditions" might "result in a new Christian presence which is both truer to . . . the New Testament and more suited and adaptable to our fast changing world."[56] This hoped-for synthesis, from Dunn's perspective, included the rejection of the Pentecostal understanding of Pentecost and Spirit-baptism. Yet is there not a connection between experience and theology? Is it possible that our "older traditions," at least with reference to Luke's theology and Pentecost, might dull our sense of expectation, understanding, and ultimately, experience of the Pentecostal gift?

Pentecostals, as we have noted, have long affirmed that the purpose of the Pentecostal gift is to empower believers to become effective witnesses. This missiological understanding of Spirit-baptism, rooted in the Pentecost account of Acts 1–2, gives important definition to the experience. In contrast to introverted (e.g., "purifying") or vague ("powerful" or "charismatic") descriptions of Spirit-baptism (in the Lukan sense), Pentecostals have articulated a clear purpose: power for mission. However, when the distinctive character of Luke's pneumatology is blurred and the Pentecostal gift is identified with conversion, this missiological (and I would add, Lukan) focus is lost.

Furthermore, this blurring of focus inevitably diminishes one's sense of expectation. For it is always possible to argue, as most Evangelicals do, that while all experience the soteriological dimension of the Pentecostal gift at conversion, only a select few receive gifts of missiological power. Yet Luke's distinctive voice calls us to remember that the church, by virtue of its reception of the Pentecostal gift, is a prophetic community empowered for a missionary task.

Study Questions

1. How has James Dunn been both a critic of and contributor to Pentecostal theology?
2. James Dunn clearly highlights the continuity between the pneumatologies of Luke and Paul. Why does this lead him to reject Pentecostal theology?
3. According to the author, what is the key issue in the current debate between Evangelicals and Pentecostals?
4. What key texts are cited to support the thesis that Luke's pneumatology is different from that of Paul?
5. What key texts are cited by Dunn to support his thesis that Luke, like Paul, presents the Spirit as a soteriological agent, the chief element in conversion?
6. How would you evaluate Dunn's central thesis? How would you evaluate Menzies' response? What implications emerge from this discussion for Pentecostal theology?

Notes

[1] Dunn, *Baptism in the Holy Spirit*, 39.
[2] Published in *JPT* 3 (1993): 3–27.
[3] Cited in ibid., 5.
[4] Paul describes the Spirit as the source of the Christian's cleansing (1 Cor. 6:11; Rom. 15:16), righteousness (Gal. 5:5; Rom. 2:29, 14:17; cf. Gal. 3:14), and intimate fellowship with God (Gal. 4:6; Rom. 8:14–17). Thus, in this present age the gift of the Spirit is the "initial-installment" or "first-fruit" (2 Cor. 1:22; 5:5; Eph. 1:14; Rom. 8:23) of a more glorious transformation to come.
[5] For the works by Gunkel, Schweizer, and Haya-Prats, see footnote 9 of chapter 3; for Stronstad, see footnote 6 of chapter 3; J. Shelton, *Mighty in Word and Deed* (Peabody, Mass.: Hendrickson, 1991); R. Menzies, *The Development of Early Christian Pneumatology with Special Reference to Luke–Acts*. For an assessment of Shelton's book,

see my "James Shelton's *Mighty in Word and Deed*: A Review Article," *JPT* 2 (1993): 105–15.

[6] Dunn, "Response," 6.

[7] Ibid., 9.

[8] Ibid.,12–16.

[9] Ibid., 17.

[10] Ibid., 21.

[11] Ibid., 27.

[12] Dunn, *Baptism*, 93.

[13] Ibid., 63; see 63–68 for his argument.

[14] See, e.g., the critiques offered by E. A. Russell, "'They Believed Philip Preaching' (Acts 8:12)," 169–76; Turner, "Luke and the Spirit," 163–67; H. Ervin, *Conversion-Initiation and the Baptism in the Holy Spirit*, 25–40; Marshall, *Acts*, 156; D. Ewert, *The Holy Spirit in the New Testament*, 118–19; H. D. Hunter, *Spirit-Baptism: A Pentecostal Alternative*, 83–84; K. Giles, "Is Luke an Exponent of 'Early Protestantism'? Church Order in the Lukan Writings (Part 1)," *EvQ* 54 (1982): 197; O'Toole, "Christian Baptism in Luke," 861; M. Green, *I Believe in the Holy Spirit*, 138; D. Carson, *Showing the Spirit: A Theological Exposition of 1 Corinthians 12–14*, 144; W. Russell, "The Anointing with the Holy Spirit in Luke–Acts," *TJ*, n.s., 7 (1986): 60–61; R. Stronstad, *Charismatic Theology*, 64–65; and Menzies, *Development*, 252–57.

[15] Dunn, "Response," 10; note also his comments on pp. 24–25.

[16] Ibid., 25: "Reception of the Spirit . . . constitutes divine acceptance and Christian identity."

[17] Note that the "problem" passage (vv. 14–17) is filled with themes and language characteristic of Luke.

[18] The following considerations indicate that Acts 8:17 describes the commissioning and empowering of the Samaritan believers for the missionary task that lay before them: (1) Luke's language in 8:15–16 indicates that he considered the pneumatic gift received by the Samaritans to be identical to the Pentecostal gift; (2) the association of the gift of the Spirit with the laying on of hands (8:17) suggests that Luke viewed the gift as an enduement for service in the mission of the church; (3) Luke's summary statement in 9:31 indicates that a new center of missionary activity had been established in Samaria. These points are developed more fully in my *Development*, 258–60.

[19] For the literary connections between 18:24–28 and 19:1–7 see M. Wolter, "Apollos und die ephesinischen Johannesjünger (Acts 18:24–19:7)," *ZNW* 78 (1987): 61–62, 71.

[20] See Luke 9:16, 18, 54; 10:23; 16:1; 17:22; 18:15; 19:29; 19:37; 20:45; 22:39, 45; Acts 6:1, 2, 7; 9:10, 19, 26, 38; 11:26, 29; 13:52; 14:20, 22, 28; 15:10; 16:1; 18:23, 27; 19:1, 9, 30; 20:1, 30; 21:4, 16. K. Haacker, "Einige Fälle von 'erlebter Rede' im Neuen Testament," *NovT* 12 (1970): 75: "Der absolut Gebrauch von μαθητής wird von allen Auslegern als eine Bezeichnung für Christen erkannt."

[21] See K. H. Rengstorf, "μαθητής," *TDNT*, 4:447.

[22] See, e.g., F. F. Bruce, *Commentary on the Book of Acts* (NICNT; Grand Rapids: Eerdmans, 1984), 385: "Paul's question, 'Did ye receive the Holy Spirit when ye believed?' suggests strongly that he regarded them as true believers in Christ."

[23] Dunn, *Baptism*, 85.

[24] Dunn, "Response," 24 n. 1.

[25] Dunn, *Baptism*, 86.

[26] A. Weiser, *Die Apostelgeschichte*, 2:513: "Die Formung von Dialogen ist ein von Lukas oft angewandtes Gestaltungsmittel." Cf. Luke 1:34–35; Acts 1:6–8; 4:7–12; 8:34–36; 16:30–32.

[27] Luke appears to have compressed a more lengthy traditional account of the event. In any event, we need not question the essential features of Luke's account; he simply tells the story from his own theological perspective.

[28] James Dunn, "'They Believed Philip Preaching (Acts 8:12)': A Reply," *IBS* 1 (1979): 178.

[29] Dunn, "Response," 10.

[30] Note especially the works of H. Gunkel, *The Influence of the Holy Spirit*; E. Schweizer, "πνεῦμα," *TDNT*, 6:389–455; G. Haya-Prats, *L'Esprit force de l'église*.

[31] See Menzies, *Development*, 52–112.

[32] Ibid., 282–315.

[33] See, e.g., my discussion of Luke 11:13 and Luke's adaptation of the Joel text in Acts 2:18 in ibid., 180–85 and 218–21, respectively.

[34] For Dunn's discussion of these points see "Response," 12, 21–22 (cf. Dunn, *Baptism*, 47–48, 90–93).

[35] As Dunn notes, "in Joel's prophecy the outpouring of the Spirit is antecedent to the survivors in Jerusalem calling upon the Lord for salvation" ("Response," 12). It is antecedent because it is understood to be a sign—and, certainly for Luke, the means by which the message is proclaimed (cf. Luke 24:49; Acts 1:4–8)—that the "last days," that period (of opportunity for those would repent) immediately preceding the Day of the Lord, have arrived.

[36] K. Lake and H. J. Cadbury, *The Beginnings of Christianity* (London: Macmillan, 1933), 4:26.

[37] D. L. Tiede, "The Exaltation of Jesus and the Restoration of Israel in Acts 1," *HTR* 79 (1986): 278–86.

[38] Dunn, "Response," 12, 21.

[39] Ibid., 21–22.

[40] Martin Hengel, *Judaism and Hellenism: Studies in Their Encounter in Palestine During the Early Hellenistic Period* (London: SCM, 1974), 1:312.

[41] For further discussion of these points and the relevant Jewish texts see Menzies, *Development*, 52–112, esp. 104–11.

[42] Dunn, *Baptism*, 92.

[43] E. Schweizer, "πνεῦμα," 6:412. The judgment offered by S. Brown is compelling: "Surely it is preferable to interpret the passage in accordance with all the other texts which we have considered and to understand the words 'you shall receive' to point to an event subsequent to baptism" ("'Water-Baptism' and 'Spirit-Baptism' in Luke–Acts," *ATR* 59 [1977]: 144).

[44] Dunn, "Response," 12. For Dunn's discussion of these texts, see 12–14, 22–23.

[45] Ibid., 13.

[46] *Aphesis* is attributed to Jesus (Acts 5:31; 13:38), to the name of Jesus (Luke 24:47; Acts 2:38; 10:43), and to faith in Jesus (Acts 26:18). See also Luke 1:77; 3:3; 4:18(2x). Note the conclusions reached by G. Haya-Prats: "Nous n'avons trouvé aucun indice nous permettant de dire que les Actes attribuent à l'Esprit Saint le pardon des péchés ou une purification progressive" (*L'Esprit*, 123); "Luc attribue à Jésus toute l'œuvre du salut" (125).

[47] Of the eight instances where Luke describes the initial reception of the Spirit by a person or group, five specifically allude to some form of inspired speech as an immediate result (Luke 1:41; 1:67; Acts 2:4; 10:46; 19:6) and one implies the occurrence

of such activity (Acts 8:15, 18). In the remaining two instances, although inspired speech is absent from Luke's account (Luke 3:22; Acts 9:17), it is a prominent feature in the pericopes that follow (Luke 4:14, 18–19; Acts 9:20).

[48] Dunn, "Response," 14 (cf. *Baptism*, 81).

[49] M. Turner, "Luke and the Spirit," 172; G. Haya-Prats, *L'Esprit*, 122–25. Acts 5:31–32 is instructive: repentance (*metanoia*) and forgiveness (*aphesis*) are attributed directly to Jesus, whom God has exalted to his right hand as Savior; the Spirit, given to the obedient, bears witness to Jesus' true identity.

[50] See I. H. Marshall, *Acts*, 197. Marshall notes that the saying in Acts 11:16 probably means: "John baptized (merely) with water, but you shall be baptized (not only with water but also) with the Holy Spirit." Thus Peter considered water-baptism to be the normal prerequisite for the gift of the Spirit and the a fortiori argument is made. Water baptism implies that the recipient has received "repentance unto life."

[51] Dunn, "Response," 14 (cf. *Baptism*, 81–82).

[52] J. Taeger, *Der Mensch und sein Heil* (SNT 14; Gütersloh: Gütersloher V., 1982), 108.

[53] D. Hill, *New Testament Prophecy* (London: Marshall, Morgan & Scott, 1979), 96–97: "That Luke is so careful to record the same signs of Spirit-possession on these two great occasions [Acts 2:4–5; 10:44–45] demonstrates clearly that for him the 'prophetic' character of the gift is central: it is the equipment for Gospel proclamation."

[54] Dunn, "Response," 26.

[55] Ibid., 26.

[56] James Dunn, "Spirit-Baptism and Pentecostalism," *SJT* 23 (1970): 406–7.

Chapter Six

Exegesis: A Reply to Max Turner

Max Turner has recently penned two substantial monographs. The first volume, rather lengthy and technical, focuses specifically on Lukan pneumatology.[1] The second work, more concise and oriented toward the non-specialist, is wide-ranging in its scope.[2] It discusses the shape of New Testament pneumatology more generally and addresses related questions of interest for the church today. Both books are what we have come to expect from Prof. Turner. They are marked by an impressive knowledge of the secondary literature, careful analysis of competing viewpoints, and a logical and detailed presentation of his own case.

The major thesis that emerges in both books is that all of the writings of the New Testament reflect a common understanding of the Spirit as the Spirit of prophecy. To be sure, this theological foundation is picked up and developed in diverse ways by the various authors, but an essential unity can be traced throughout the New Testament. The Spirit, as the Spirit of prophecy, grants wisdom and revelation as well as prophetic speech and praise. The wisdom afforded by the Spirit comes with transforming and sanctifying power and thus is essential for authentic faith and Christian existence. This essential core is reflected in the major contributions of Luke, John, and Paul, all of whom portray the gift of the Spirit as a soteriological necessity and central to conversion. For this reason, Prof. Turner rejects "the classical Pentecostal two-stage view of Spirit-reception" in favor of "a more broadly charismatic one-stage conversion-initiation paradigm."[3]

In this chapter I will evaluate this thesis. My goal is not to offer a detailed and comprehensive critique of these substantial works.[4] Rather, I would like to point out what I believe to be key areas of weakness in Turner's overall thesis, particularly as it relates to Luke–Acts. In this way I trust that the on-going discussion concerning the work of the Spirit in the New Testament and today might, in some small way, be pushed forward.

I would like to preface my critique with a word of appreciation for Prof. Turner's work. I first met Prof. Turner at the University of Aberdeen in Scotland. I was a young Ph.D. student; he had just arrived as a new member of the divinity faculty. I have vivid memories of our early discussions, sometimes quite animated and always stimulating. Our conversation did not end with my departure (and later his) from Aberdeen;[5] rather, we have carried on the discussion both in various academic forums as well as through private correspondence. While we hold many points in common, our public dialogue has inevitably featured areas of disagreement. I have always viewed Prof. Turner's proddings, critiques, and queries as a blessing rather than a curse. It is precisely through this sort of dialogue that we grow to understand one another and the issues before us more clearly. I greatly appreciate Prof. Turner as a friend, former instructor, and gifted colleague.

There is certainly much in these two books that I would want to affirm. I find myself in general agreement with the notion that, at least in one sense, all Christians, by virtue of their reception of the Spirit at conversion, are charismatic and should be increasingly so. The transforming and sanctifying work of the Spirit often does come in the form of charismatic wisdom. Thus, Turner rightly highlights the charismatic nature of our life in the Spirit. I found his discussion of the gifts of the Spirit particularly helpful. In my opinion, he builds a devastating case against cessationist claims.

There are, however, a number of points that require further consideration. (1) I would like to help clarify my own position regarding the nature of the Spirit's work in Luke–Acts. (2) I intend to challenge Turner's suggestion that the writings of intertestamental Judaism (frequently) and Luke (even occasionally) describe the Spirit as the source of wisdom necessary to live in right relationship to God. (3) I will respond to Turner's critique of my theological method and his rejection of the Pentecostal two-stage paradigm.

1. The Spirit in Luke–Acts: My Position Clarified

It appears that Turner and at least one of his students have at times failed to grasp nuances in my argument and thus presented a caricature of my position. Thus, under the heading, "The Spirit Exclusively as Empowerment for Mission?" Turner evaluates my thesis with these words:

> This interpretation is certainly too narrow to be sustained. . . . this view needs to turn a blind eye to a whole series of pneumatological texts in Acts that clearly have little or nothing to do with missionary empowering, but serve the spiritual life of the church (or individuals within it).[6]

This, of course, implies that I deny that the Spirit is active, in any sense, in the community life of the church. This misunderstanding is perhaps due to shortcomings in my attempts to present my position to a broader audience. It is always difficult to capture the essence of one's thought in a short phrase, although at times this is required. In my book *Empowered for Witness*, I described Luke's pneumatology as "prophetic" and provided detailed argumentation and explanation of this position. In subsequent articles, often directed to a broader audience, I have described Luke's pneumatology as "charismatic," "prophetic," and "missiological." I believe that each of these terms, if understood properly, highlights important aspects of Luke's understanding of the Spirit. Perhaps my occasional use of the term "exclusive" in relation to these terms has caused some confusion. In any event, I am thankful for this opportunity to help clarify a few important nuances in my own position.

My concise definition of Luke's understanding of the gift of the Spirit reads as follows: "a prophetic enabling that empowers one for participation in the mission of God." This definition, as understood in the larger context of my book, actually has three main thrusts. I maintain that the gift of the Spirit in Luke–Acts is nonsoteriological (or charismatic), prophetic, and missiological.

1.1. Nonsoteriological (or Charismatic)

Luke does *not* present reception of the Spirit as necessary for one to enter into and remain within the community of salvation: the source of cleansing, righteousness, intimate fellowship with and knowledge of God.[7] Of course in Acts the Spirit, as the source of prophetic wisdom and speech, does indeed occasionally impact the ethical or moral life of the church (e.g., Acts 5:1–11). This sort of *indirect* influence on the larger community, mediated as it is through the prophet, is entirely consistent with the judgment voiced above: In Luke–Acts the gift of the Spirit is never presented as the source of moral transformation for its recipient.

It is one thing to assert that the Spirit influences, in an indirect manner (i.e., through the prophetic gift), the ethical life of the Christian community; it is quite another to assert that the Spirit transforms in a direct way the ethical life of each *individual* within the community.[8] This latter notion, although clearly articulated by Paul (e.g., 1 Cor. 6:11), is not a dimension of Luke's pneumatology. Thus I maintain that for Luke, the gift of the Spirit is not a soteriological necessity; rather, it is a *donum superadditum* (or a charismatic gift). When I use the term "exclusive" (e.g., "exclusively prophetic" or "exclusively missiological"), it should be understood in this context: The Spirit in Luke–Acts is *never* presented as a soteriological agent.

1.2. Prophetic

I have also argued that the Spirit in Luke–Acts is presented almost exclusively as the source of inspired speech and special revelation. Miracles (healing, exorcism, feats of strength) are also associated with the Spirit, but only in an indirect and cautious way. According to Luke, the primary manifestation of the Spirit is prophetic inspiration, which results in charismatic wisdom and/or inspired speech. Thus I prefer to characterize Luke's pneumatology as "prophetic" rather than "charismatic."

1.3. Missiological

For Luke, the Spirit is "the Spirit for others," and the impact of the Spirit's inspiration is primarily associated with the missionary enterprise of the church. (a) The Spirit in Luke–Acts is not given principally for the benefit of its recipient; rather, it is directed toward others. Roland Allen describes this Lukan emphasis beautifully when he speaks of the Spirit as "the Spirit of [God's] redeeming love, active in [us] toward others."[9]

(b) The Spirit in Luke–Acts is also the Spirit of mission.[10] While it is true that prophecy within the community (i.e., directed to believers) is associated with the Spirit, this is not Luke's focus. Even here, Luke links the inspiration of the Spirit to the mission or outward expansion of the church (Acts 9:31; 11:24). Again, praise is not highlighted as a manifestation of the Spirit of prophecy.[11] Although this would not be incompatible with Luke's theology (I would see it as a form of inspired speech), this is not his focus. And joy and other psychological or emotional effects of the Spirit's presence are at times related to the mission of the church, but they are not seen as significant in themselves or a focus of the Spirit's work.

In short, I do not deny that in Luke–Acts that the Spirit is associated with prophetic phenomena within the community of believers; rather, I simply maintain that this needs to be recognized as an expression of "the Spirit for others" and as secondary to the principal product of the Spirit of prophecy's inspiration: the witness of the church to the unbelieving world.

I trust that this clarification, brief though it may be, will help others form a clearer understanding of my position. One always hopes that the various nuances of arguments presented in a lengthy book are understood, but this is not always the case. And perhaps the occasional need to describe one's position in a concise manner heightens the potential for misunderstanding. In any event, I do feel that dismissals of my position on the grounds that I make no room for the work of the Spirit in the community are unfounded. A more careful reading of my writings is required.

2. Turner: The Spirit of Prophecy as a Soteriological Agent

As I have noted, Turner stresses the fundamental unity that unites the pneumatologies of the various authors of the New Testament. Luke, John, and Paul are all described as attributing four central functions to the Spirit. The Spirit as the Spirit of prophecy inspires charismatic revelation or guidance, charismatic wisdom, invasive prophetic speech, and invasive charismatic praise or worship.[12]

Turner's understanding of the charismatic wisdom afforded by the Spirit is of special importance, for here he maintains that the Spirit acts as a soteriological agent: The Spirit grants that wisdom necessary for one to enter into and remain within the community of salvation. The Spirit as the source of charismatic wisdom is the essential bond that links the believer to Christ. Without this Spirit-inspired wisdom, authentic Christian existence is unthinkable. Turner maintains that this concept of the Spirit as the dispenser of life-giving wisdom is central to the pneumatologies of Luke, John, and Paul. It is therefore fundamental to his larger thesis, for it is the chief means by which he ties together at a fundamental or soteriological level the pneumatologies of the various New Testament writers.

However, the question must be asked: Does this accurately represent Luke's perspective? Few, if any, would deny that Paul (1 Cor. 2:6–16) and John (John 16:12–15) present the Spirit as the source of life-giving wisdom—that wisdom essential for Christian existence. But can it be maintained that this is Luke's understanding as well? I suggest that Turner's thesis is inaccurate at this crucial point. With his four prototypical gifts (cited above), Turner has created a construct that he then foists on Luke.[13] The relevant texts (intertestamental Jewish texts and Luke–Acts) frequently describe the Spirit as the source of esoteric wisdom, but rarely do the Jewish sources, and never does Luke, present the Spirit as the source of wisdom at the more fundamental level of life-giving wisdom. An examination of Turner's argument reveals a number of weaknesses.

2.1. The Jewish Background

Turner begins his study with an examination of Jewish attitudes toward the Spirit. Here is where we first encounter the four prototypical gifts, including his assessment of the Spirit as the source of life-giving wisdom. Turner's judgment that the Spirit provides wisdom "essential for fully authentic human existence before God"[14] is supported with several citations from the Qumran literature, which Turner notes appear to draw on Ezekiel 36:26–27. He also suggests that rabbinical traditions on Ezekiel 36 and Jewish conceptions of the Spirit on the Messiah strengthen his case. Yet none of these points is as significant as Turner maintains. They certainly do not support the notion that first-century Jews associated the Spirit with life-giving wisdom. Let us examine the various strands of evidence.

(1) Turner makes much of the messianic traditions related to Isaiah 11:1–4, such as the *Targum of Isaiah*, which speaks of the Messiah as possessing "a spirit of wisdom and understanding, a spirit of counsel and might, a spirit of knowledge and the fear of the Lord."[15] He concludes that these traditions associate the Spirit of prophecy with ethical vitality and implies that they thus support his characterization of the Spirit as a soteriological agent, the source of life-giving wisdom.

Yet it is all but certain that first-century Jews would not have understood these texts to mean that the Spirit granted the Messiah life-giving wisdom or that wisdom necessary for the Messiah to live in right relationship with God. What is described in these traditions instead is the bestowal of *Amtscharisma*, the ability to rule with wisdom and power. While in these texts the Spirit is associated with wisdom or ethical insight, it is still esoteric wisdom (a special and heightened form of wisdom) rather than life-giving wisdom. In view of those Jewish traditions that speak of the withdrawal of the Spirit as a result of Israel's sin (e.g., *MHG Gen*. 135, 139–40), is it really credible to think of the Spirit as granting the righteousness and wisdom "necessary for authentic existence before God" to the Messiah? Surely, it is more plausible to understand these texts as referring to a special, charismatic endowment to rule that is given to the Messiah *because* he is worthy and righteous.

It is interesting to note that Turner understands Jesus' anointing purely in terms of empowering for mission and not as somehow bringing to him "new covenant life" or "eschatological sonship."[16] This suggests the connection between these messianic texts and life-giving wisdom is motivated by Turner's desire to build his case rather than by the evidence itself.

(2) Turner points to the rabbinic traditions related to Ezekiel 36 as supporting his case. However, as I have noted elsewhere, most of these traditions interpret Ezekiel 36:26 as a reference to the end-time removal of the evil impulse (*yetzer*) and, in this regard, almost always without reference to the activity of the Spirit. The rabbis generally present the transformation of the heart alluded to in Ezekiel 36 as a prerequisite for the eschatological outpouring of the Spirit, which is understood as a restoration of the Spirit of prophecy (Joel 2:28–32).[17] While it is possible to read some of these texts differently, the most that Turner can say is that the evidence is mixed, ambiguous, and late.

(3) Finally, Turner points to the literature from Qumran. Here, as I have noted elsewhere, we do find texts that describe the Spirit as the source of life-

giving wisdom.[18] Yet this line of evidence from one sectarian group (see also Wisd. Sol. 9:17) needs to be seen in relation to the vast amount of literature that describes the Spirit as the source of esoteric wisdom alone. The more dominant perspective, illustrated clearly in Sirach and *4 Maccabees*, is that life-giving wisdom is associated with the law and that it can be attained by purely rational means—study unaided by the illumination of the Spirit. In short, while some texts do indeed attribute esoteric (or higher levels of) wisdom to the inspiration of the Spirit (e.g., Sir. 39:1–8), they also affirm that sapiential achievement at a more fundamental level is available simply through the study of the law.

All of this indicates that it is inappropriate to assume that most first-century Jews would identify the Spirit as the source of life-giving wisdom—that wisdom necessary for "authentic existence before God." The evidence suggests that this pneumatological perspective was actually rare in first-century Jewish circles. When it comes to the New Testament and particularly Luke–Acts, we should demand clear evidence for similar claims. However, this is exactly what Turner fails to produce.

2.2. Luke–Acts

What texts support Turner's claim that Luke presents the Spirit as the source of life-giving wisdom? Turner adduces four major lines of evidence: (1) John the Baptist's prophecy (Luke 3:16–17) is cited as a reference to the cleansing and restoring work of the Spirit-inspired Messiah; (2) Jesus overcomes the temptations in the desert (Luke 4:1–13) through the "charismatic wisdom" granted by the Spirit; (3) the summary of community life in Acts 2:42–47 implies that the Spirit is the operative force in the moral and religious life of the Christian community; and (4) Luke's description of the Pentecostal gift in Acts 2 suggests that it is central to Israel's restoration, the manner in which Jesus exercises his cleansing and transforming rule over Israel. We will look at each of these points.[19]

(1) John the Baptist's prophecy. There can be little doubt as to the importance of John the Baptist's prophecy (Luke 3:16–17) for our present discussion. Craig Keener illustrates this point when he states:

> Whereas John the Baptist, Paul, John the apostle, and others in the New Testament usually spoke of baptism in the Spirit as the whole sphere of the Spirit's work (including rebirth and prophetic inspiration), Luke focuses almost exclusively on the prophetic empowerment dimension of the Spirit. As many of us have argued elsewhere, Luke emphasizes particularly the Spirit's role in inspired speech.... By retaining John's contrast between Spirit and fire, *Luke 3:16 may constitute the one clear exception to this emphasis.*[20]

But when John the Baptist's prophecy is correctly understood, this "one clear exception" vanishes. The Jewish background is particularly instructive. There are no pre-Christian references to a messianic bestowal of the Spirit that purifies and transforms *the individual*. However, there are a wealth of passages that describe the Messiah as charismatically endowed with the Spirit of God so that he may rule and judge (e.g., *1 En.* 49:3; 62:2). And Isaiah 4:4 refers to the Spirit of God as the means by which the nation of Israel (not individuals!) will be sifted and the righteous separated from the wicked and thus cleansed.

Several texts tie these two concepts together. Perhaps most striking is Psalms of Solomon 17:26–37, a passage that describes how the Messiah, "powerful in the Holy Spirit" (17:37), will purify Israel by ejecting all aliens and sinners from the nation. Isaiah 11:2, 4, which is echoed in *1 Enoch* 62:2 and 1QSb 5:24–25, declares that the Spirit-empowered Messiah will slay the wicked "with the breath [*ruach*] of his lips." Against this background it is not difficult to envision the Spirit of God as an instrument employed by the Messiah to sift and cleanse the nation. Indeed, these texts suggest that when John the Baptist referred in metaphorical language to the messianic deluge of the Spirit, he had in mind Spirit-inspired oracles of judgment uttered by the Messiah (cf. Isa. 11:4), blasts of the Spirit that would separate the wheat from the chaff.

Luke, writing in light of Pentecost, sees the fuller picture and applies the prophecy to the Spirit-inspired witness of the early church (Acts 1:4–5). Through their witness, the wheat is separated from the chaff (Luke 3:17; cf. 2:34). In short, John the Baptist described the Spirit's work not as cleansing repentant individuals, but rather as a blast of the "breath" of God that would sift the nation. Luke sees the prophecy, at least with reference to the sifting work of the Spirit, fulfilled in the Spirit-inspired mission of the church. The essential point is that Luke presents the Spirit here not as the source of cleansing for the individual, but rather as the animating force behind the witness of the church.

Turner's reading of this crucial text is actually similar to my own. He too recognizes the importance of the Jewish background material and affirms, "We have no need to posit that John went beyond the traditional expectation of a messianic figure powerfully fulfilling Isaiah 11:1–4."[21] But Turner does not highlight the significance of this fact: The Spirit is then viewed not as cleansing repentant individuals and giving them a heart for God, but rather as a force that sifts the nation, separating the repentant from the unrepentant. This is undoubtedly due to the fact that Turner accepts the thesis advanced by Robert Webb that the Coming One's instrument is a spade, and thus he comes to cleanse or clear the threshing floor rather than to sift the wheat from the chaff in Israel.[22] Turner states the matter clearly:

From the Baptist's perspective, the task of the coming one is not to sift the wheat from the chaff in Israel, nor is the instrument in his hand a threshing fork (as is usually maintained). John understood himself largely already to have accomplished the sifting process through his preaching and baptismal ministry. From his point of view what remains is for the Coming One to *"cleanse the threshing floor"* (17b), and deal with the already-separated wheat and chaff: so, appropriately, he comes with a *spade (ptuon)* in hand.[23]

There are, however, several weighty objections to the view that John's prophecy deals with cleansing (usually associated with the repentant individual) rather than sifting (which is how Isa. 4:4 suggests the nation will be cleansed). (a) The significance of Webb's contention that the term *ptuon* refers to a spade rather than a winnowing fork should not be overestimated. I suspect this is a classic example of over-exegesis. I have lived in China for the past six years. In the rural parts of our province one can still see the winnowing process carried out much as it has been for thousands of years. The actual separation of the wheat from the chaff is accomplished with a variety of instruments, including baskets, shovels, and forks. Would it have been any different in Palestine? After all, both a spade and a fork can be used to winnow wheat. I suggest then that it is unreasonable to assume that if Luke's audience read "spade" rather than "fork," they would have immediately understood the entire metaphor (Luke 3:17) to refer simply to the clearing of the threshing floor and not sifting as well.

(b) A second criticism of this reading is that it is clearly out of touch with Luke's understanding of John's prophecy. Note Simeon's prophetic words uttered over the Christ child, which are clear on this point: "This child is destined to cause the falling and rising of many in Israel" (Luke 2:34). Above all, it is Jesus, not John the Baptist, who will sift and separate (cf. 12:49–53). As we have noted, this sifting work is carried on by the disciples through their Spirit-inspired witness (Acts 1:4–5). In short, to suggest that the Coming One simply deals "with the already-separated wheat and chaff" is to misread Luke–Acts.

(c) Finally, the Jewish background strongly suggests that we understand the cleansing of the nation anticipated by John the Baptist to be accomplished through the separation of the wicked from the righteous (Isa. 4:4; Ps. Sol. 17:26–37; *1 En.* 62:2; 1QSb 5:24–25). These key passages all highlight this sifting aspect of the Spirit's work: They do not describe the Spirit as transforming repentant individuals; rather, they describe the Spirit-empowered Messiah as sifting the nation.

Thus, John's prophecy should not be understood as "the one clear exception" to Luke's prophetic pneumatology. Rather, the prophecy is entirely consistent with it, and it offers no support for Turner's thesis that the Spirit of prophecy in Luke–Acts acts as a soteriological agent, dispensing life-giving wisdom. As we have noted, the Spirit is presented here as the animating force behind the prophetic ministry of Jesus (cf. Luke 4:18–19) and the witness of the church (Acts 1:4–8).

(2) The temptation account. Turner suggests that with the temptation account (Luke 4:1–13), Luke implicitly presents the Spirit as the source of "new depths of charismatic wisdom and insight," which in turn enables Jesus to overcome the temptations of the Evil One.[24] Yet this is not stated by Luke, and two observations suggest that this is not how Luke or his audience would have understood the text. (a) The Scriptures rather than the Spirit are presented as the source of Jesus' moral power (Luke 4:4, 8, 12).

(b) While the references to the Spirit that appear at the beginning (Luke 4:1) and end (4:14) of the account highlight the fact that Jesus is indeed the Anointed One and thus empowered by the Spirit, they do not present the Spirit as the source of Jesus' moral determination. Rather, Luke has precisely the opposite in mind: By remaining faithful to his calling in the face of Satan's temptations, Jesus demonstrates that he is indeed worthy to be the bearer of the Spirit, and thus he emerges from the desert as he entered, full of the Holy Spirit (4:1, 14). In short, Luke's point is not that Jesus is faithful and upright because the Spirit enables him to be so; rather, Luke declares that because Jesus is faithful and upright, he is the bearer of the Spirit.

This conclusion is confirmed by the parallels between Jesus' being tempted in the desert and that of the children of Israel. Turner himself notes that "the final 'temptations' echo Israel's in the wilderness, but while they 'rebelled and grieved his Holy Spirit' there (Isa. 63:10), the new representative of Israel remains faithful and overcomes the tempter."[25] The point is clear: Unlike Israel of old, Jesus demonstrates that he is worthy to be the bearer of the Spirit. Against this conceptual backdrop, it is difficult to imagine the text proclaiming any other message.

(3) Summaries of community life. Turner is well aware that a host of scholars, from H. Gunkel to G. Haya-Prats, have noted that "nothing in the summaries of the church's new life (Acts 2:42–47; 4:32–37) is directly attributable to the Spirit."[26] Nevertheless, he attempts to make his own case:

> The narrative tension of expectation of an "Israel of the Spirit" is carefully built up from Acts 2:1 to 2:38, 39. Yet the summary of conversions and the life of this community (2:40–47) *has not a single mention of the Spirit.* This device requires the reader to resolve the tension with the assumption that it is the unmentioned advent and charismata of the promised Spirit that is responsible for the overall dynamic of the new community.[27]

By way of response we might simply point out that the "tension" Turner feels is generated by his own theological presuppositions. It is a tension that would not have been felt by Luke's first-century readers. Luke himself is clearly quite oblivious to it. Elsewhere he does not hesitate to describe baptized believers who have not yet received the Spirit (Acts 8:16). Why should he feel compelled to present the Spirit as the source of the ethical life of the church?

Luke does, however, continually speak of the Spirit as the impetus behind the witness of the early church. Indeed, he is clear concerning the nature and impact of the Spirit of Pentecost: "You will receive power when the Holy Spirit comes on you; and you will be my witnesses" (Acts 1:8). The "Israel of the Spirit" is called and empowered to take up the prophetic vocation of Isaiah 49:6: They are to be a "light for the Gentiles" and bring salvation "to the ends of the earth" (cf. Acts 1:8; 13:47).

The narrative highlights this fact in a variety of ways. The repetition of the promise of power (Luke 24:49; Acts 1:8), the catalogue of peoples present and the dramatic language miracle (Acts 2:4–11), and the quotation from Joel 2:28–32 with its references to prophetic power (Acts 2:17–21) all highlight the missiological significance of this event. Actually, Luke states the matter clearly. We need not posit subtle literary devices, nor do we need to make unwarranted assumptions in order to make sense of the text.

(4) The restoration of Israel. In spite of Luke's explicit statements that define the purpose of the Spirit's coming in terms of power for witness (Luke 24:48–49; Acts 1:4–8), Turner suggests that in reality there is more. At Pentecost the Spirit comes, not simply to enable the disciples to be a light to the nations (Isa. 49:6), but also to raise up and restore the preserved of Israel. The Spirit who inspires the disciples' witness also cleanses and transforms their hearts. Turner argues that this broader understanding of the Spirit's work is developed by Luke in three ways: The life of the community described in Luke's summaries (Acts 2:42–47; 4:32–35) associates the Spirit with the salvation hoped for in Luke 1–2; John the Baptist's promise of cleansing for Israel is realized in the life of the early church (cf. Acts 5:3, 9; 11:16); and the Pentecost account (2:1–3) echoes Jewish accounts of the Sinai theophany and thus presents the gift of the Spirit as "a gift of foundational importance which [Jesus] gives to his people" at a decisive new phase of their existence.[28]

We have already noted that Luke does not associate the Spirit with the summaries of community life in Acts 2:42–47 and 4:32–35, a striking omission that casts serious doubts on Turner's thesis. We have also seen that Turner's understanding of John the Baptist's prophecy is faulty: John does not anticipate a bestowal of the Spirit that will cleanse and transform *individuals* within Israel. But what of the alleged parallels to the Sinai theophany? Did Luke consciously craft his Pentecost account in order to highlight parallels between Moses' giving of the law at Sinai and Jesus' bestowal of a superior gift (the Spirit) at Pentecost? Two observations suggest that this is highly unlikely.

(a) An examination of the purported parallels (the most prominent parallels are found in Philo, *Dec.* 46–47; *Spec. Leg.* 2.188–89, and *Targ. Ps.-J.* on Ex. 20:2) reveals that the terms shared by Luke, Philo, and Jonathan Ben Uzziel are not unique to Sinai traditions but characteristic of theophanic language in general. This fact and the notable differences between Acts 2:1–13 and the texts of Philo and *Targum Pseudo-Jonathan* suggest that Luke's Pentecost account was not influenced by these or similar Sinai traditions. Rather, the similarities are best explained by their common acquaintance with the language of Jewish theophany.[29]

(b) The absence of any reference to Moses, the law, or the covenant in Acts 2 speaks decisively against Turner's proposal. While Acts 2:33 clearly signifies that the Pentecostal outpouring of the Spirit constitutes irrefutable proof that Jesus has been exalted to the right hand of God, this proof does not consist of a powerful pneumatic transformation of the recipient's ethical life. Rather, the proof is an irruption of Spirit-inspired prophetic activity that is visible to all.[30]

Turner's attempt to associate the Spirit with the cleansing and moral transformation of individual believers in Luke–Acts fails at each point. His one-size-fits-all approach to the pneumatology of the New Testament does not match the reality. We need to be more sensitive to the theological diversity reflected in the writings of the New Testament, and, with respect to pneumatology, we especially need to hear Luke's distinctive voice. This leads us to the question of theological method.

3. Theological Method: In Defense of a Two-Stage Model of Spirit Reception

As we have seen, Turner highlights what he considers an essential unity that ties together the prophetic pneumatologies of Luke, Paul, and John, all of whom portray the gift of the Spirit as a soteriological necessity and central to conversion. It should not surprise us, then, to learn that Turner also advocates a one-stage model for reception of the Spirit. According to Turner, there is one gift of the Spirit that is granted as part of the conversion-initiation complex, and this gift is the fount of all Christian experience. Subsequent charismatic experiences are to be understood as renewing experiences of this one gift given to every Christian in conversion-initiation.[31]

Of course this leaves little room for classical Pentecostal theology, with its two-stage model of reception of the Spirit. But, according to Turner, we should not overly trouble ourselves concerning this matter, for the two-stage model fails to integrate the insights of Luke and Paul in a coherent manner. Turner characterizes my own approach as involving simple addition:

> Believers first, at conversion, receive the Spirit as the regenerating soteriological Spirit of sonship, and new covenant life (as Paul and John agree), then at some point subsequently they receive the Lucan 'Spirit of prophecy' as an experientially distinct empowering for mission.[32]

Turner suggests that this approach would work if Luke associated "the gift of the Spirit" with activities distinct from those that mark Paul's "gift of the Spirit." Yet Turner asserts that this is not the case: "Paul's conception of the gift of the Spirit is simply *broader* than Luke's, *while nevertheless containing everything that Luke implies.*"[33] Thus, "Paul's comprehensive understanding of the gift of the Spirit granted to Christians at conversion does not leave anything for Luke to add."

Turner acknowledges that Paul does not envision believers receiving all they will ever receive from the Spirit at conversion, but the crucial point is that these subsequent experiences or giftings flow from the same Spirit received in conversion: Paul *"does not suggest they should seek some second giving of the Spirit before they might be granted such charismata."*[34] In other words, Turner asserts that Paul's pneumatology embraces all that really matters (the soteriological and prophetic dimensions), and since he doesn't speak of a normative, second gift of the Spirit, neither should we.

Turner thus offers a thoughtful restatement of the traditional Evangelical approach to pneumatology, albeit one that is open to the full range of the Pauline gifts. Of course, any attempt at systematization is based on the raw data of the text (exegesis). And although Turner maintains that we must listen to each individual author and not prematurely fuse their horizons, we have found reason to question whether Turner has succeeded in this endeavor. Has he really heard Luke's distinctive voice?

This leads to the first problem with Turner's approach. He misses this fundamental fact: *Luke does indeed have something distinctive to offer.* Although Paul is aware of both the soteriological and prophetic dimensions of the Spirit's work, he never alludes to Pentecost or the Pentecostal gift. But Luke does. This may not seem significant if we identify the Pentecostal gift with conversion as Turner does. But if our reading of Luke–Acts is correct, the significance of Luke's contribution at this point cannot be missed. In a unique way, Luke calls us to recognize the richness of the Spirit's resources, which are available to us. Luke alone speaks of the Pentecostal gift—a prophetic empowering available to every believer that enables them to participate effectively in the divine mission. This promise of Pentecostal power offers the church a solid basis for a focused and aggressive sense of expectation with respect to spiritual power. This sense of purpose and expectation is greatly diminished if the Pentecostal dimension of the Sprit is simply fused together with the soteriological.

Luke declares that we should *expect* to be a community of witnesses, empowered by the Spirit of Pentecost. This expectation is missiological rather than soteriological in nature, for it is defined by the character of the Pentecostal gift. This expectation embraces every believer, for it is rooted in the universality of the Pentecostal promise (Acts 2:8, 17–18, 38). Turner's theology, rooted as it is in Pauline theology, fails to provide a solid theological foundation for such an expectation. The crucial question is, after all, what happened at Pentecost? According to Turner, one may still describe the gift of the Spirit received at Pentecost (in Pauline terms) as the chief element in conversion-initiation. In this way, the universality (and specific nature) of our expectation for "*subsequent* empowerings"—rooted in the Pentecostal promise—is undermined: All experience the soteriological dimension of the Pentecostal gift at conversion, but perhaps only a few will receive missiological power.

Some might argue that Paul's gift language offers the same sort of promise for divine empowerment. But this is clearly not the case, as a review of Evangelical attitudes toward spiritual gifts indicates. The attitude of many Evangelical Christians may be described as follows: All of the gifts of the Spirit are valid for the church today, but since God sovereignly bestows his gifts on selected individuals, we must wait and watch what God chooses to do. Certainly God gives gifts to every believer, but we cannot presume to know which gift or gifts he desires to bestow on us. While we may receive gifts of missiological power, there is always the chance we will not.

While this approach captures an important aspect of Paul's teaching, it is not the final word concerning God's promise of power. Yet this limited Pauline perspective shapes the theology and expectation of many Evangelicals, including that of Turner.[35] It is instructive to note that theologically there is little that would distinguish Turner from many of his Evangelical brothers and sisters who have remained rather passive in their approach to divine enabling. Note, for example, M. Erickson's comments concerning Pauline gifts:

> Whether the Bible teaches that the Spirit dispenses special gifts today is not an issue of great practical consequence. For even if he does, we are not to set our lives to seeking them. He bestows them sovereignly; he alone determines the recipients (1 Cor. 12:11). If he chooses to give us a special gift, he will do so regardless of whether we expect it or seek it.[36]

In short, Turner has failed to articulate a theology that provides a fully biblical sense of purpose and expectation with reference to the Spirit's empowering. Luke's Pentecost account provides what is needed, a promise of missiological power for every believer.[37]

A second problem with Turner's approach is his insistence that Paul makes no room for a second gift of the Spirit—a gift that is distinct from conversion and that serves as a gateway to a new dimension of the Spirit's power. It is true that Paul does not allude to Pentecost or the Pentecostal gift. Yet this should not surprise us since he does not set out to write a comprehensive systematic theology, but rather letters that address specific situations and needs. Although Paul shows an awareness of the full range of the Spirit's work, he does not chronicle every stage or experience in the life of a Christian. Surely Turner does not mean to suggest that outside the Pauline corpus, there can be no further contributions to or impetus for refinement of our theological understanding. Yet he seems to come close to this canon-within-a-canon position when he writes:

> One certainly cannot use Luke to *impose* such a distinction [between charismatic and soteriological pneumatology] on a reading of Paul, as though Luke's effort might bring theological nuance to Paul, and clarify for us that Paul must really have "meant" to teach something like a doctrine of subsequence, even if he never expressed it quite clearly enough.[38]

If we are to hear the multifaceted contributions of the various New Testament authors, we will inevitably need to allow them to bring their unique insights that, at times, will help clarify the incomplete views of their biblical colleagues. For example, Paul helps us understand that the Spirit is active from the very beginning of the believer's Christian life: affording intimate communion with God, bestowing gifts that enhance the life of the community, and shaping our lives into conformity with Christ. Much of this would be lost if Paul were not able to inform the more limited contributions of Luke and the other New Testament writers.

Yet, as we have seen, the same is true for Luke. He too offers an important insight into the dynamic life of the Spirit of God. Although Luke's overall pneumatological framework is more limited than that of Paul, this does not mean that he has nothing to contribute. As Turner notes, Paul himself clearly envisions that various gifts, various aspects of the Spirit's work, will become active in our lives subsequent to our conversion experience (e.g., 1 Cor. 12:31; 14:1). Paul does not tell us precisely how this all happens, how these gifts of the Spirit are actualized in our lives. Thus, there is room here for the contributions of Luke to be integrated together with those of Paul.

Later, in chapter 14, I will argue that the Pentecostal gift overlaps with a special cluster of the Pauline gifts—gifts I describe as prophetic-type gifts. These include a word of wisdom, a word of knowledge, prophecy, the ability to distinguish between spirits, the ability to speak in different kinds of tongues, and the interpretation of tongues (1 Cor. 12:8–12). Although I acknowledge that it cannot be maintained that Spirit-baptism (i.e., the Pentecostal gift) is the gateway to every spiritual gift, I will assert that Spirit-baptism is the gateway to a special cluster of gifts described by Paul, the prophetic-type gifts noted above.

Here the perspectives of Paul and Luke can be constructively integrated. Paul tells us that in one sense, every Christian "is, and should be increasingly, charismatic."[39] He highlights this fact by insisting that every believer has something to offer, that everyone is enabled by the Spirit to contribute to the common good (1 Cor. 12:11). Yet Luke also tells us that there is a dimension of the Spirit's enabling that one enters by virtue of a baptism in the Spirit distinct from conversion. This dimension can be properly called the prophetic dimension.[40] In Luke's perspective, the community of faith is potentially a community of prophets, and it is by reception of the Pentecostal gift (Spirit-baptism) that this potential is realized. Here Luke helps bring clarity to aspects of Christian experience that Paul did not definitively address.

Certainly there is no compelling reason to suggest that because Paul doesn't specifically speak of a gateway experience distinct from conversion, neither should we. Our Christian canon is, after all, rather larger than Paul's letters. Although undoubtedly Turner's reading of Luke–Acts (and the New Testament in general) has colored his approach at this point, he comes dangerously close to asserting that New Testament pneumatology is indeed Pauline pneumatology. This is an approach that Pentecostals have correctly resisted.

4. Conclusion

Over the last fifteen years we have witnessed the emergence of a new wave of Pentecostal scholarship. These scholarly writings have challenged long-standing Evangelical assumptions concerning the shape of New Testament pneumatology, particularly the nature of Luke's theology of the Spirit. It has now been almost thirty years since James Dunn wrote his influential work, *Baptism in the Holy Spirit*. Now, just at a time when Dunn's arguments are beginning to lose their persuasive power, Max Turner provides an updated approach, fully conversant with recent scholarship, which once again bolsters the traditional Evangelical position.

Turner has indeed produced two notable books, and anyone discussing pneumatology will need to deal with them. *The Holy Spirit and Spiritual Gifts: Then and Now*, more accessible and comprehensive in scope than *Power From On High*, is destined to be influential for the many Evangelicals seeking to address the questions of this new generation. Apart from its comforting conclusions, the book has many others strengths that will not go unnoticed by the Evangelical community (and those beyond). Turner interacts with an amazing array of scholarship, including more recent Pentecostal contributions, and he puts forward a crisp thesis that provides a united and coherent assessment of New Testament pneumatology. He also fleshes out the implications of his conclusions for the life of the church in a clear and thoughtful manner.

Turner's approach, however, also has its limitations. His central thesis—that all of the writings of the New Testament reflect a common understanding of the Spirit as the Spirit of prophecy: the source of life-giving wisdom, charismatic revelation, prophetic speech, and praise—is not flexible enough to do justice to Luke's distinctive perspective, and it is probably too narrow for Paul and John as well. It appears that Turner, with his four prototypical gifts (cited above), has created a construct that he then foists on Luke–Acts and the entire New Testament.

Specifically, we have challenged Turner's claim that Luke presents the Spirit as the source of life-giving wisdom. The relevant texts frequently describe the Spirit as the source of esoteric wisdom, but rarely do the Jewish sources, and never does Luke, present the Spirit as the source of wisdom at a more fundamental level—life-giving wisdom. Turner's attempt at theological synthesis, based as it is on a narrow reading of the data, also fails to convince. He seems to equate biblical pneumatology with Pauline pneumatology and thus fails to acknowledge Luke's unique contribution. The result is perhaps a coherent system, but one that fails to grasp the full richness and power of the New Testament witness concerning the work of the Spirit.

Study Questions

1. Turner maintains that Luke portrays the Spirit as the source of life-giving wisdom. In light of the Jewish background, is this something we would expect? Is the evidence Turner offers from Luke–Acts compelling?

2. In what way are the positions of Max Turner and James Dunn similar?

3. In contrast to Turner, Menzies argues that Luke does have something unique and important to offer to a holistic biblical theology of the Spirit. What is that contribution?

4. Turner suggests that Paul allows no room for a second gift of the Spirit, one that is distinct from conversion. How would you evaluate this claim?

5. What are the implications of Turner's reconstruction of New Testament pneumatology for our understanding of the Pentecostal gift?

Notes

¹ Max Turner, *Power from On High*.

² Max Turner, *The Holy Spirit and Spiritual Gifts: Then and Now*. Our review will feature this book, which is broader in its scope and more accessible to the general reader.

³ Ibid., xii.

⁴ For a broader perspective, see John Christopher Thomas' engaging review, which discusses Turner's analysis of Paul and John as well as Luke (J. C. Thomas, "Max Turner's *The Holy Spirit and Spiritual Gifts: Then and Now* [Carlisle: Paternoster, 1996]: An Appreciation and Critique," *JPT* 12 [1998]: 3–21). Note also Turner's response in the same issue (M. Turner, "Readings and Paradigms: A Response to John Christopher Thomas," *JPT* 12 [1998]: 23–38).

⁵ Prof. Turner is now Vice-Principal for Academic Affairs at London Bible College.

⁶ Turner, *The Holy Spirit*, 47–48. Note also the cavalier dismissal found in W. Atkinson, "Pentecostal Responses to Dunn's *Baptism in the Holy Spirit*: Luke–Acts," *JPT* 6 (1995): 120–24. For example, after stating that my prophetic empowering thesis is too limited, Atkinson notes that there "is evidence that Luke also thinks of the Spirit as the church's guide in the conduct of its own affairs" (123). These statements ignore the larger context of my work, and particularly the Appendix found in *Empowered for Witness* (258–59; see also 187 n. 4).

⁷ By way of contrast, Paul clearly presents the Spirit as the source of cleansing (Rom. 15:16; 1 Cor. 6:11), righteousness (Rom. 2:29; 8:1–17; 14:17; Gal. 5:5, 16–26), intimate fellowship with God (Rom. 8:14–17; Gal. 4:6), and knowledge of God (1 Cor. 2:6–16; 2 Cor. 3:3–18).

⁸ See my related comments in *Empowered*, 258.

⁹ Roland Allen, "The Revelation of the Holy Spirit in the Acts of the Apostles," 160–67.

¹⁰ See John Michael Penney, *The Missionary Emphasis of Lukan Pneumatology* (JPTSup 12; Sheffield: Sheffield Academic, 1997).

¹¹ The inspired speech described in Acts 2:11 should not be understood simply as praise directed to God. It is, above all, proclamation. See my discussion of this text in *Empowered*, 177.

¹² For a description of these "prototypical gifts" see Turner, *The Holy Spirit*, 6–12. For Turner, the term *invasive* means "that as the Spirit comes upon the person they are caught up and inspired to speak." This "invasive" form of prophetic speech is differentiated from "the usual form of prophecy, which was not immediately inspired, but involved the relating to a target audience of some revelation given (perhaps days or weeks) beforehand" (ibid., 10).

¹³ It is also doubtful whether Paul's concept of the Spirit can be adequately understood simply as a developed form of the Spirit of prophecy. Craig Keener's suggestion that the Spirit is the source of purity and prophecy points to an additional and important strand in Paul's usage (1 Cor. 6:11), one that is lacking in Luke–Acts (see C. Keener, *The Spirit in the Gospels and Acts: Divine Purity and Power* [Peabody, Mass.: Hendrickson, 1997]). And the transforming work of the Spirit (Rom. 8), as well as references to the Spirit as the source of the resurrection (Rom. 1:4; cf. 1 Cor. 15:42–49), seem to transcend the categories of the Spirit as the Spirit of prophecy as well. This discussion, however, takes us well beyond the bounds of this study.

¹⁴ Turner, *The Holy Spirit*, 15.

¹⁵ Ibid., 17.

[16] Ibid., 34.

[17] See Menzies, *Empowered*, 94–98, and the rabbinic texts cited there.

[18] Ibid., 71–82.

[19] Turner also suggests that the close association between conversion and reception of the Spirit in Acts indicates that the Spirit is essential for authentic Christian existence. Since we dealt with this objection in the previous chapter, we will not discuss it here.

[20] Craig S. Keener, *3 Crucial Questions About the Holy Spirit* (Grand Rapids: Baker, 1996), 35 (italics mine).

[21] Turner, *The Holy Spirit*, 26.

[22] R. L. Webb, "The Activity of John the Baptist's Expected Figure at the Threshing Floor (Matthew 3.12 = Luke 3.17)," *JSNT* 43 (1991): 103–11.

[23] Turner, *The Holy Spirit*, 26 (italics his).

[24] Ibid., 29.

[25] Ibid.

[26] Ibid., 49.

[27] Ibid. (italics are his).

[28] Ibid., 53; see 52–55 for Turner's discussion of the restoration of Israel.

[29] For an examination of the evidence see Menzies, *Empowered*, 189–201.

[30] It is instructive to note that Ezek. 36:26–27 is significant for the development of new covenant themes in the writings of Paul (e.g., 2 Cor. 3) and John (e.g., John 3:1–21); yet Luke is strikingly silent at this point. Turner, speaking of Paul, writes: "From the beginning he evinces awareness of the Spirit as the Spirit of prophecy, but connects this with Ezekiel 36–37 in such a way as to make the Spirit of prophecy a soteriological necessity" (Turner, *The Holy Spirit*, 113). Luke does not make this connection.

[31] Ibid., 157–68.

[32] Ibid., 152.

[33] Ibid., 154 (italics his).

[34] Ibid., 155 (italics his).

[35] Note especially Turner, *The Holy Spirit*, 162: Luke's "account fails to give the impression that all Christians are empowered as missionaries." If we understand "missionaries" in the broader sense of witnesses, I would whole-heartedly disagree (e.g., Acts 1:8; 2:17–18; 4:31).

[36] M. Erickson, *Christian Theology* (Grand Rapids: Baker, 1983–1985), 881.

[37] Turner correctly notes that there can be "dead formalism in the post-'baptism in the Spirit' sector of the Pentecostal and Charismatic church too. An experience of the Spirit and glossolalia alone can easily lead to the complacency of 'having arrived'" (Turner, *The Holy Spirit*, 167). This fact, however, calls for a clearer articulation of Luke's theology and the Pentecostal gift, not its abandonment. We need to recognize that Luke speaks of the Pentecostal gift as an initiation into a dimension of the Spirit's power, and this calls for an ongoing openness toward and apprehension of the Spirit's power. This is why I especially like G. Haya-Prats' understanding of the Pentecostal gift: It is the promise that the Spirit will be there in our time of need (*L'Esprit force de l'eglise*, 198).

[38] Turner, *The Holy Spirit*, 155 (italics his). Turner also states: "It is clear that Paul anticipated a lively 'charismatic' church, in which every area of Christian life and ministry was deeply shaped by experiential awareness of the Spirit. Yet apparently he felt no need to elucidate any second-blessing theology in order to undergird and strengthen

this.... There is no reason to tie missionary orientation and zeal to a second-blessing theology. Paul's churches appear to have grown rapidly without his expressing the view that the Spirit is granted to each as an empowering for witness" (ibid., 166–67). These comments assume that Paul's ad hoc letters give us a comprehensive picture of the theology and practice of the Pauline churches. They also reflect Turner's tendency to see Paul's perspective as definitive.

[39] H. I. Lederle, *Treasures Old and New: Interpretations of "Spirit-Baptism" in the Charismatic Renewal Movement* (Peabody: Hendrickson, 1988), 228.

[40] The prophetic dimension in Luke–Acts is much broader than Paul's understanding of the gift of prophecy. In addition to prophecy within the congregation, it also embraces activities such as inspired proclamation, charismatic guidance, glossolalia, and, above all, bold witness and perseverance in the face of opposition ("staying power"). The nature of this prophetic dimension is developed more fully in chapters 7, 8, 10, 14, and 15, below.

Part Two

Theological Affirmations

Chapter Seven

The Issue of Subsequence

From the earliest days of the modern Pentecostal Movement, Pentecostals have proclaimed that all Christians may, and indeed should, experience a baptism in the Holy Spirit "distinct from and subsequent to the experience of new birth."[1] This doctrine of subsequence flowed naturally from the conviction that the Spirit came upon the disciples at Pentecost (Acts 2), not as the source of new covenant existence but as the source of power for effective witness. Although early Evangelical thinkers such as R. A. Torrey and A. J. Gordon also advocated a baptism in the Spirit subsequent to conversion, more recent Evangelical theologians have largely rejected the doctrine of subsequence, particularly in its Pentecostal form. Influenced largely by James Dunn's seminal work, *Baptism in the Holy Spirit*, Evangelicals have commonly equated the baptism of the Holy Spirit with conversion. Evangelicals thus view Spirit-baptism as the sine qua non of Christian existence, the essential element in conversion-initiation.

Although for years Pentecostals and Evangelicals were entrenched in their respective positions and seldom entered into dialogue, after 1970 this situation changed dramatically. James Dunn's sympathetic but critical assessment of Pentecostal doctrine marks a watershed in Pentecostal thinking, for it stimulated a burst of creative theological reflection by Pentecostals. As a result, the theological terrain today is considerably different from that of thirty years ago. Yet, in spite of significant changes, the issue of subsequence still remains high on today's theological agenda.

This fact is reflected in Gordon Fee's book *Gospel and Spirit*, which contains two previously published but updated articles on this issue.[2] A Pentecostal minister and noted Evangelical scholar, Fee has been an active and influential participant in the post-Dunn Pentecostal-Evangelical dialogue. While he speaks from inside the Pentecostal tradition, his viewpoint generally reflects

prevailing Evangelical attitudes. I offer the following evaluation of Fee's position on the doctrine of subsequence with the hope that it might highlight the
major issues in the discussion. Specifically, I will argue that Fee's discussion
ignores important developments in New Testament and Pentecostal scholarship and that when these developments are taken into consideration, Luke's
intention to teach a baptism in the Spirit distinct from (at least logically if not
chronologically) conversion for every believer—the essence of the doctrine of
subsequence—is easily demonstrated.

1. Fee's Critique of the Pentecostal Position

Fee has established a reputation for acumen in the area of hermeneutics,
and his sympathetic critique of the Pentecostal doctrine of subsequence
focuses on shortcomings in this area. He notes that Pentecostals generally
support their claim that Spirit-baptism is distinct from conversion by appealing to various episodes recorded in the book of Acts. This approach, in its
most common form, appeals to the experience of the Samaritans (Acts 8), Paul
(ch. 9), and the Ephesians (ch. 19) as a normative model for all Christians. But
Fee, following the lead of many Evangelicals, maintains that this line of argumentation rests on a shaky hermeneutical foundation. Its fundamental flaw is
its failure to appreciate the genre of the book of Acts: This book is a description of historical events. Unless we are prepared to choose church leaders by
the casting of lots or are willing to encourage church members to sell all of
their possessions, we cannot simply assume that a particular historical narrative provides a basis for normative theology.

Fee's concern is a legitimate one: How do we distinguish between those
aspects of Luke's narrative that are normative and those that are not? His
answer is that historical precedent, if it is "to have normative value, must be
related to intent."[3] That is to say, Pentecostals must demonstrate that Luke
intended the oft-cited episodes in Acts to establish a precedent for future
Christians. Otherwise, Pentecostals may not legitimately speak of a Spirit-
baptism distinct from conversion that is in any sense normative for the
church. According to Fee, this is exactly where the Pentecostal position fails.

Fee describes two kinds of arguments offered by Pentecostals: arguments
from biblical analogy and arguments from biblical precedent. (1) Arguments
from biblical analogy point to Jesus' experience at the Jordan (subsequent to
his miraculous birth by the Spirit) and the disciples' experience at Pentecost
(subsequent to John 20:22) as normative models of Christian experience. Yet
these arguments, as all arguments from biblical analogy, are problematic
because, to Fee, "it can seldom be demonstrated that our analogies are inten-

tional in the biblical text itself."[4] These purported analogies are particularly problematic because the experiences of Jesus and the apostles—coming as they do prior to "the great line of demarcation," the day of Pentecost—"are of such a different kind from succeeding Christian experience that they can scarcely have normative value."[5]

(2) Arguments from biblical precedent seek to find a normative pattern of Christian experience in the experience of the Samaritans, Paul, and the Ephesians. Fee asserts that these arguments also fail to convince because it cannot be demonstrated that Luke intended to present in these narratives a normative model. The problem here is twofold. (a) The evidence is not uniform: However we view the experience of the Samaritans and the Ephesians, Cornelius and his household (Acts 10) appear to receive the Spirit as they are converted. (b) Even when subsequence can be demonstrated, as with the Samaritans in Acts 8, it is doubtful whether this can be linked to Luke's intent. Fee suggests that Luke's primary intent was to validate the experience of the Christians as the gospel spread beyond Jerusalem.[6]

This leads Fee to reject the traditional Pentecostal position. He concludes that a baptism in the Spirit distinct from conversion and intended for empowering is "neither clearly taught in the New Testament nor necessarily to be seen as a normative pattern (let alone the only pattern) for Christian experience."[7] Yet this rejection of subsequence is, according to Fee, really of little consequence, for the central truth that marks Pentecostalism is its emphasis on the dynamic, powerful character of experience of the Spirit. Whether the Spirit's powerful presence is experienced at conversion or after is ultimately irrelevant, and to insist that all must go "one route" is to say more than the New Testament allows.[8] In short, Fee maintains that although Pentecostals need to reformulate their theology, their experience is valid.

Before we move to an assessment of Fee's position, two points need to be made. (1) Although Fee suggests that his critique of subsequence does not impact the essentials of Pentecostalism, this claim is questionable. It should be noted that Fee's position is theologically indistinguishable from that of many other Evangelical scholars, James Dunn in particular. His essential message is that Pentecostals have, in terms of theology, nothing new to offer the broader Evangelical world. While Pentecostal fervor serves as a reminder that Christian experience has a dynamic, powerful dimension, the theology that gives definition and expectation to this dimension is rejected. Furthermore, Fee's critique does not simply call into question the Pentecostal understanding of the timing of Spirit-baptism (i.e., whether it is experienced simultaneously with or after conversion), but it challenges the Pentecostal understanding of this experience at its deepest level.

The central issue is whether or not Spirit-baptism in the Pentecostal sense (Acts 2) can be equated with conversion. Evangelicals affirm that the two are one—and Fee agrees, though he acknowledges that the dynamic, charismatic character of the experience (for a variety of reasons) in our modern context is often lacking. Fee's affirmation, qualified as it is, still undercuts crucial aspects of Pentecostal theology. Pentecostals, as we have noted, have generally affirmed that the purpose of Spirit-baptism is to empower believers so that they might be effective witnesses. This missiological understanding of Spirit-baptism, rooted in the Pentecost account of Acts 1–2, gives important definition to the experience. In contrast to Fee's vague descriptions of Spirit-baptism as "dynamic," "powerful," or even "charismatic," Pentecostals have articulated a clear purpose: power for mission.

When the Pentecostal gift is confused with conversion, this missiological focus is lost. Pentecostalism becomes Christianity with fervor (whatever that means) rather than Christianity empowered for mission. Furthermore, this blurring of focus inevitably diminishes one's sense of expectation. For it is always possible to argue, as most Evangelicals do, that while all experience the soteriological dimension of the Pentecostal gift at conversion, only a select few receive gifts of missiological power. Fee's effort to retain a sense of expectation, though rejecting the distinction between Spirit-baptism and conversion, fails at this point.

The bottom line is this: If Fee is right, Pentecostals can no longer speak of an enabling of the Spirit that is distinct from conversion and available to every believer, at least not with the same sense of expectation, nor can Pentecostals maintain that the principal purpose of this gift is to grant power for the task of mission. To sum up, the doctrine of subsequence articulates a conviction crucial for Pentecostal theology and practice: Spirit-baptism, in the Pentecostal sense, is distinct from (at least logically, if not chronologically) conversion. This conviction, I would add, is integral to Pentecostalism's continued sense of expectation and effectiveness in mission.

(2) Although Fee focuses our attention on an important issue (i.e., the nature of Luke's theological intent), his critique is based on a fundamental presupposition. He repeatedly states that "in the New Testament the presence of the Spirit was the chief element of Christian conversion."[9] Indeed, Fee declares "what we must understand is that the Spirit was the chief element, the primary ingredient," of new covenant existence.[10] This is Paul's perspective *and Luke's as well*! Fee confidently writes that "on this analysis of things, it seems to me, all New Testament scholars would be in general agreement."[11]

Thus, in reality, Fee's article raises two important questions: (1) Did Luke intend for us to understand Spirit-baptism to be a gift distinct from conversion, granting power for effective witness and available to every believer? (2) Is it true that the the New Testament writers uniformly present the gift of the Spirit as the chief element of conversion-finitiation? The remaining portion of this chapter will seek to address these questions. We will begin with the latter question, since this touches on a presupposition fundamental to Fee's argument.

2. The New Context: Defining the Crucial Issue

As noted above, Fee's critique of the Pentecostal position centers on hermeneutical flaws, particularly the use of historical precedent as a basis for establishing normative theology. Fee skillfully demonstrates the weaknesses inherent in traditional Pentecostal arguments based on facile analogies or selected episodes from Acts. Here we hear an echo of James Dunn's timely critique of arguments for subsequence based on a conflation of John 20:22 with Luke's narrative in Acts.[12]

When originally published, Fee's articles, painful though they may have been, served a valuable purpose: They challenged Pentecostals to come to terms with the new and pressing questions raised by their Evangelical brothers. These questions were all the more urgent in view of the rapid assimilation of the Pentecostal movement into mainstream Evangelicalism, a process that by the mid-70s was largely complete. Perhaps because of his position as an "insider," Fee was thus able to give voice to a much needed message: No longer could Pentecostals rely on the interpretative methods of the nineteenth-century Holiness Movement and expect to speak to the contemporary Evangelical world—a world that, with increasing vigor, was shaping the ethos of Pentecostalism.

Yet the theological landscape that Fee surveyed in the mid-70s and 80s has changed considerably. Simplistic arguments from historical precedent, though once the bulwark of Pentecostal theology, have been replaced with approaches that speak the language of modern Evangelicalism. Although perhaps this is not entirely true when it comes to the question of tongues as initial evidence, it is certainly the case for the doctrine of subsequence. Roger Stronstad's *The Charismatic Theology of St. Luke* illustrates this fact. Published in 1984, it marks a key shift in Pentecostal thinking. Stronstad's central thesis is that Luke is a theologian *in his own right* and that his perspective on the Spirit is different from, although complementary to, that of Paul. Unlike Paul, who frequently speaks of the soteriological dimension of the Spirit's work,[13] Luke *consistently* portrays the Spirit as the source of power for service.

My book, *The Development of Early Christian Pneumatology with Special Reference to Luke–Acts*, also highlights the distinctive character of Luke's pneumatology. The book's thesis corroborates that of Stronstad's, for I argued that Paul was the first Christian to attribute soteriological functions to the Spirit and that this original element of Paul's pneumatology did not influence wider (non-Pauline) sectors of the early church until after the writing of Luke–Acts.

The crucial point on which Stronstad and I agree is that Luke never attributes soteriological functions to the Spirit and that his narrative presupposes a pneumatology that excludes this dimension (e.g., Luke 11:13; Acts 8:4–17; 19:1–7). Or, to put it positively, Luke describes the gift of the Spirit *exclusively* in charismatic terms as the source of power for effective witness.[14] Luke's narrative, then, reflects more than simply a different agenda or emphasis; his pneumatology is *different* from, although *complementary* to, that of Paul.

In the previous chapters we have attempted to substantiate this description of Luke's pneumatology. In the remaining portion of this chapter I would like to show how this assessment of Luke's pneumatology provides a biblical foundation for the doctrine of subsequence.

From a biblical perspective, the key question is this: What is the nature of the Pentecostal gift (Acts 2)? As we will demonstrate, it is abundantly clear that Luke *intended* his readers to understand that this gift (whatever its nature) was available to—and indeed, should be experienced by—everyone. Fee and virtually all Evangelicals assert that this gift is the chief element of conversion-initiation. Although most Evangelicals acknowledge that divine enabling is prominent in the narrative, this aspect of Luke's account is generally regarded as a reflection of his special emphasis. It is assumed that Luke and Paul shared essentially the same pneumatological perspective, and thus broader, soteriological dimensions of the Spirit's work are also understood to be present. The universal character of the Pentecostal gift is then easily explained: All should experience the gift because it is the means by which the blessings of the new covenant are mediated.

However, the description of Luke's pneumatology outlined above challenges this Evangelical assessment of the Pentecostal gift. For if Luke views the gift of the Spirit exclusively in charismatic terms, then it is not possible to associate the Pentecostal gift with conversion or salvation. Indeed, by placing the Pentecost account within the framework of Luke's distinctive theology of the Spirit, Pentecostals can argue with considerable force that the Spirit came on the disciples at Pentecost, not as the source of new covenant existence, but rather as the source of power for effective witness. And since the Pentecostal gift is charismatic rather than soteriological in character, it must be distinguished from the gift of the Spirit that Paul associates with conversion-initiation. Here, then, is a strong argument for a doctrine of subsequence—

that is, that Spirit-baptism (in the Pentecostal or Lukan sense) is logically distinct from conversion. This logical distinction reflects Luke's distinctive theology of the Spirit.

Note that this argument is not based on biblical analogy or historical precedent. It does not seek to demonstrate that the disciples had received the Spirit, at least from Luke's perspective, prior to Pentecost. Nor is it dependent on isolated passages from the book of Acts. Rather, drawing from the full scope of Luke's two-volume work, it focuses on the nature of Luke's pneumatology and, from this framework, seeks to understand the character of the Pentecostal gift. The judgment that the gift is distinct from conversion is rooted in the gift's function: It provides power for witness, not justification before God or personal cleansing. The universal character of the gift established in Luke's narrative rather than historical precedent is the basis for its normative character.

All of this indicates that Fee's critique of Pentecostal hermeneutics, focused as it is on naive appeals to historical precedent, fails to address today's crucial question: Does Luke, in a manner similar to Paul, present the Spirit as the source of new covenant existence? Fee, as we have noted, assumes this to be the case, and confidently declares that on this point "all New Testament scholars" would agree. Yet this confident statement, apart from the two Pentecostal studies noted above, ignores a significant group of New Testament scholars. Over a century ago Herman Gunkel reached very different conclusions; and he has been followed in more recent years by E. Schweizer, David Hill, and Gonzalo Haya-Prats, all of whom have written works that highlight the distinctive character of Luke's pneumatology.[15] The real issue centers not on hermeneutics and historical precedent, but rather on exegesis and the nature of Luke's pneumatology.

3. Establishing Luke's Intent

The question of Luke's intent, which looms so large in Fee's argument, is clearly subordinate to the more fundamental question outlined above. For if our description of Luke's distinctive pneumatology is accurate, then Luke's intent to teach a Spirit-baptism distinct from conversion for empowering is easily demonstrated. One need only establish that Luke's narrative was designed to encourage every Christian to receive the Pentecostal gift.

Since Luke highlights Pentecost as a fulfillment of Joel's prophecy concerning an outpouring of the Spirit on "all people" (Acts 2:17–21), this appears to be self-evident. The community of faith is, at least potentially, a community of prophets; and it was Luke's expectation that this potential would be realized in the church of his day as it had been in the past (e.g., 2:4; 19:6). Although numerous other texts can be cited in support of this conclusion, we will limit our discussion to one significant text not previously treated: Luke 11:13.

Luke 11:1–13 forms a section devoted to Jesus' teaching on prayer. It begins with one disciple's request for instruction on how to pray (11:1), which Jesus answers in the form of a model prayer (11:2–4) and parabolic teaching concerning the willingness and certainty of God's response (11:5–13). The section concludes by comparing the heavenly Father with an earthly counterpart: "If you then, though you are evil, know how to give good gifts to your children, how much more will your Father in heaven give the Holy Spirit to those who ask him!" (11:13). This concluding comparison, with its reference to the Holy Spirit, warrants examination.

The similarities in wording between Luke 11:9–13 and Matthew 7:7–11 indicate that the passage stems from a source commonly called Q (a hypothetical document of the Gospel passages that are common only to Matthew and Luke). However, there is a crucial difference: Matthew 7:11b has "good gifts" rather than the "Holy Spirit" (Luke 11:13b). There can be little doubt that Matthew's "good gifts" represents the original wording of the hypothetical Q.[16] Matthew follows his sources closely with reference to the Spirit; he never omits a reference to the Spirit that is contained in his sources and he never inserts *pneuma* ("Spirit") into Mark's or Q material.

Luke, by contrast, does insert *pneuma* into Q material on at least three occasions (Luke 4:1; 10:21; in addition to 11:13) and into Mark's material once (4:14).[17] This data suggests that Luke, rather than Matthew, has altered Q. Our conclusion is confirmed by the awkwardness of Luke's construction: The insertion of "Holy Spirit" breaks the parallelism of the *a minore ad maius* ("from lesser to greater") argument that links the "good gifts" given by earthly fathers (Luke 11:13a = Matt. 7:11a) with the "good gifts" given by the heavenly Father (Matt. 7:11b).

Having established that the "Holy Spirit" of Luke 11:13b is a redactional addition coming from Luke, what is the significance of this alteration for Luke's pneumatology? We observe three things.

(1) Luke's alteration of the Q form of the saying anticipates the postresurrection experience of the church.[18] This is evident from the fact that the promise that the Father will give the Holy Spirit to those who ask begins to be realized only at Pentecost. By contemporizing the text in this way, Luke stresses the relevance of the saying for the post-Pentecostal community to which he writes.

(2) The context indicates that the promise is made to disciples (Luke 11:1). Thus, Luke's contemporized version of the saying is directed to the members of the Christian community. Since it is addressed to those who are already

believers, the promise cannot refer to an initiatory or soteriological gift.[19] This judgment is confirmed by the repetitive character of the exhortation to pray:[20] Prayer for the Spirit (and, in light of the promise, we may presume this includes the reception of the Spirit) is to be an ongoing practice. The gift of the Holy Spirit to which Luke refers neither initiates one into the new age nor is it to be received only once;[21] rather, this pneumatic gift is given to disciples and is to be experienced on an ongoing basis.

(3) Luke's usage elsewhere indicates that he viewed the gift of the Holy Spirit in Luke 11:13b as an enduement of prophetic power. On two occasions in Luke–Acts the Spirit is given to those praying;[22] in both the Spirit is portrayed as the source of prophetic activity. (a) Luke alters Mark's account of Jesus' baptism so that Jesus receives the Spirit after his baptism while praying (Luke 3:21); this gift of the Spirit, portrayed principally as the source of Jesus' proclamation (4:18–19), equipped Jesus for his messianic task. (b) Later, in Acts 4:31 the disciples, after having prayed, "were all filled with the Holy Spirit and spoke the word of God boldly." Again the Spirit given in response to prayer is the impetus behind the proclamation of the word of God.

To sum up, through redactional activity in Luke 11:13b, Luke encourages post-Pentecostal disciples to ask for the gift of the Spirit, which, for Luke, meant open access to the divine Spirit—the source of power that would enable them to be effective witnesses for Christ (Luke 12:12; Acts 1:8) by providing what was required in time of need, whether it be special knowledge or the ability to powerfully proclaim the gospel in the face of persecution. This text, then, reflects Luke's intent to teach a Spirit-baptism for empowering, distinct from conversion. It also supports our Pentecostal claim that Luke's pneumatology is distinct from, although complementary to, that of Paul, for in Luke 11:13 the author presents the Spirit not as the source of cleansing and a new ability to keep the law, but rather as the source of power for effective witness.

4. Conclusion

Pentecostals are seeking to come to terms with their Evangelical heritage. Gordon Fee's book *Gospel and Spirit* represents the quest of one respected scholar. When the essays contained in this book were originally written, they provided a valuable service. They helped Pentecostals recognize their need to address the new and pressing questions raised by their Evangelical brothers. Fee's quest encouraged others to make the journey. Yet the theological landscape has changed considerably since the initial publication of Fee's articles. And although these articles have been updated, they do not show an awareness of the new terrain. Thus they address concerns that have little relevance. Today, the crucial issue centers not on hermeneutics and historical precedent, but rather on exegesis and the nature of Luke's pneumatology. If Fee and Evangelical scholars wish to engage in meaningful dialogue with contemporary Pentecostal scholarship, they will need to address this issue.

Study Questions

1. Why have arguments for a doctrine of subsequence based on historical precedent been unconvincing?
2. Fee suggests that the doctrine of subsequence deals with unimportant matters and thus its rejection does not represent a significant loss for Pentecostals. Is this really the case? Does the doctrine simply seek to deal with matters of timing?
3. What does the doctrine of subsequence tell us about the nature of baptism in the Spirit? How does it impact our sense of expectation?
4. Fee's case rests on a major assumption, one that the authors challenge throughout this book. What is that assumption?
5. Menzies argues that the question of Luke's "intent" is really not the central issue. What then is the key issue in the current Evangelical-Pentecostal debate?

Notes

[1] *Minutes of the 44th Session of the General Council of the Assemblies of God* (Portland, Ore.; August 6–11, 1991), 129.

[2] Gordon Fee, *Gospel and Spirit: Issues in New Testament Hermeneutics* (Peabody, Mass.: Hendrickson, 1991). Chapters 6 and 7 are updated versions of the following articles: "Hermeneutics and Historical Precedent—A Major Problem in Pentecostal Hermeneutics," in *Perspectives on the New Pentecostalism*, ed. R. P. Spittler (Grand Rapids: Baker, 1976), 118–32; "Baptism in the Holy Spirit: The Issue of Separability and Subsequence," *Pneuma* 7:2 (1985): 87–99.

[3] Fee, *Gospel and Spirit*, 92.

[4] Ibid., 108.

[5] Ibid., 94.

[6] Ibid., 97.

[7] Ibid., 98.

[8] Ibid., 111.

[9] Ibid., 98. For statements reflecting this presupposition see 94, 98, 109–17.

[10] Ibid., 114.

[11] Ibid., 115.

[12] Dunn, *Baptism in the Holy Spirit*, 39.

[13] Paul presents the Spirit as the source of cleansing, justification, and sanctification (e.g., 1 Cor 6:11).

[14] Fee states that he strongly agrees "with Stronstad on the 'charismatic nature' of Lukan theology" (*Gospel and Spirit*, 101). Yet Fee does not appear to understand Stronstad at this point, for he says elsewhere that Luke, in a manner similar to Paul,

viewed the gift of the Spirit as "the chief element of conversion and the Christian life" (ibid., 98). These two statements are, in reality, contradictory. When Fee speaks of the "charismatic nature" of Luke's pneumatology, he seems to mean merely that Luke associates charismatic functions, in addition to soteriological functions, to the Spirit.

[15] H. Gunkel, *The Influence of the Holy Spirit*; E. Schweizer, "πνεῦμα," *TDNT*, 6:389–455; D. Hill, *Greek Words and Hebrew Meanings*; G. Haya-Prats, *L'Esprit force de l'église*.

[16] C. K. Barrett, *The Holy Spirit and the Gospel Tradition* (London: SPCK, 1947), 126–27; Schulz, *Q: Die Spruchquelle der Evangelisten* (Zurich: Theologischer Verlag, 1972), 162; Schweizer, "πνευμα," 6:409; T. W. Manson, *The Sayings of Jesus*, 2d ed. (London: SCM, 1949), 81; Fitzmyer, *The Gospel According to Luke* (AB 28; New York: Doubleday, 1982 1985), 2:915–16; Ellis, *The Gospel of Luke* (NCB; London: Oliphants, Marshall, Morgan & Scott, 1974), 164.

[17] See Rodd, "Spirit or Finger," *ExpTim* 72 (1960–61): 157–58.

[18] Fitzmyer, *Luke*, 2:916; Ellis, *Luke*, 164; Stronstad, *Charismatic Theology*, 46.

[19] Montague, *The Holy Spirit: Growth of a Biblical Tradition* (New York: Paulist, 1976), 259–60.

[20] Note, e.g., the repetitive force of Luke 11:2 (lit., "whenever you pray, keep on saying") and the continuous action implicit in the present active verbs in 11:10: "Everyone who keeps on seeking, finds."

[21] Büchsel (*Der Geist Gottes*, 189–90) and Montague (*Spirit*, 259–60) both note the repetitive character of the exhortation.

[22] See Luke 3:31 and Acts 4:31. Note also that in Acts 8:15–17 the Spirit comes upon the Samaritans in response to the prayers of Peter and John. Prayer is implicitly associated with the reception of the Spirit at Pentecost (1:14; 2:4). Here, as in the other passages noted above, the gift of the Spirit is presented as a prophetic endowment.

Chapter Eight

Evidential Tongues

As a missionary educator, I frequently travel to various parts of Asia in order to teach. Wherever I go, irrespective of the course or topic of discussion, I can always count on one question being asked by my Pentecostal students: What about tongues as initial evidence? The fact that the question is asked so frequently and in a variety of settings indicates that Pentecostals have not effectively dealt with this issue. We have failed to provide convincing biblical and theological support for our position that glossolalia is the "initial physical evidence" of Spirit-baptism (Acts 2:4).[1]

This is the case largely because we have failed to speak to this issue in a manner that makes sense in today's hermeneutical context. Too often in the past we have relied on social pressure rather than clear theological arguments. The result is widespread confusion within our churches and unnecessary estrangement from many Christians without. I offer the following chapter with the hope that it might encourage much-needed theological reflection on this important issue. It represents my response to the question I so frequently encounter and my own attempt to integrate my Pentecostal convictions and experience with my Evangelical heritage and schooling.

1. A Tale of Two Questions

In the previous chapter, I suggested that Pentecostals have shed fresh light on an extremely important question: What is the nature of the Pentecostal gift? We now focus our attention on a second, separate question: What is the nature of the relationship between tongues (glossolalia) and the Pentecostal gift? It is imperative to recognize that these are two distinct questions. Indeed, much of the confusion surrounding these questions stems from the failure to distinguish between them. On the one hand, this failure has led many Pentecostals to erroneously equate the Pentecostal gift with tongues. On the other hand, it is the reason why many Evangelicals, with tunnel vision, have focused on the hermeneutics of historical precedent and missed the fundamental question concerning the nature of Luke's pneumatology.

These two questions must be approached and ultimately answered in different ways. The question concerning the nature of the Pentecostal gift is a question of biblical theology. It is a question that Luke himself clearly addresses. Indeed, in previous chapters we have examined evidence from Luke–Acts that supports our contention that Luke consistently presents the Pentecostal gift in charismatic terms as the source of power for effective witness; furthermore, he consciously encourages his readers to experience this gift. Here Luke's intent is clear. But the question of tongues as initial evidence ushers us into the realm of systematic theology.

In biblical theology, we focus on the agenda of the biblical authors. We seek to hear the questions they raise and the answers they offer. G. B. Caird has aptly described the task of biblical theology as one of listening to the dialogue of the biblical authors seated at a roundtable.[2] By contrast, in systematic theology we frequently begin with the agenda and questions of our contemporary setting. We bring the pressing questions of our day to the biblical text, and as we wrestle with the implications that emerge from the text for our questions, we seek to answer them in a manner consistent with the biblical witness. In systematic theology, we do not simply sit passively, listening to the discussion at the roundtable. Rather, we bring our questions to the dialogue and listen for the various responses uttered. Ultimately, we seek to integrate these responses into a coherent answer.

The question concerning the relationship between tongues and Spirit-baptism is a question of systematic theology. Larry Hurtado correctly notes that "the question of what constitutes 'the initial evidence' of a person having received the 'baptism in the Spirit' simply is not raised in the New Testament."[3] Luke, as we shall emphasize, is no exception at this point. That is to say, neither Luke nor any other biblical author deliberately sets out to demonstrate that "tongues" is the initial physical evidence of that empowering experience and dimension of the Spirit's activity that Pentecostals appropriately call, "baptism in the Holy Spirit."

However, as Hurtado notes, this does not necessarily "render the doctrine invalid," nor does it indicate that the questions associated with the doctrine are inappropriate.[4] Nevertheless, Hurtado goes on to suggest that in this instance the doctrine is invalid (we will examine his objections later). For the moment, it is important to note that it is not only legitimate, but often necessary, to bring our questions to the text or (as Caird might put it) the dialogue at the roundtable. Here we must also carefully listen to the voice of

Scripture. Although the biblical authors may not directly address our questions, our goal is to identify the implications for our questions that emerge
from the various theological perspectives they represent.

2. The Limitations of Biblical Theology

The doctrine of evidential tongues is often treated purely in terms of the
categories of biblical theology. This is true of Pentecostal presentations and
non-Pentecostal evaluations. Pentecostals have generally supported the doctrine by arguing that the various accounts in Acts present a normative pattern
for Christian experience. Although it is not always clearly articulated, implicit
in this approach is the notion that Luke consciously crafted his narrative in
order to highlight the normative character of evidential tongues. Yet, as Gordon Fee has pointed out, this sort of argument has not been persuasive.[5] In
the previous chapter we noted that Fee's critique of arguments based on historical precedent was significant because it challenged Pentecostals to deal
with this fact.

Our inability to offer clear theological support for our doctrine of evidential tongues is nowhere more clearly demonstrated than in the recent publication of *Initial Evidence*.[6] The articles by Hurtado and J. Ramsey Michaels
represent further elaborations of the basic message voiced by Fee over a
decade ago.[7] Pentecostals have failed to convince because they have not been
able to demonstrate that Luke intended to present in the key narratives of
Acts a normative model of Christian experience.

The problem is twofold. (1) The evidence is not uniform: If Luke intended
to teach evidential tongues as normative, why does he not consistently present tongues as the immediate result of Spirit-baptism (e.g., Acts 8:17; 9:17–
18)? (2) Even when tongues is connected to Spirit-baptism, it is doubtful
whether this connection is made in order to present evidential tongues as a
normative doctrine. In other words, it is difficult to argue that Luke, through
his narrative, intended to teach this doctrine as articulated by modern Pentecostals. This does not appear to be his concern.

As noted above, we should be careful not to jump immediately to the unwarranted conclusion that this judgment necessarily invalidates the doctrine of evidential tongues. But this is precisely the conclusion that is often drawn. The
reason is clearly articulated by Fee, who suggests that normative theology at
this point must be grounded in Luke's "primary intent" or "intention to teach."[8]
But surely this is overly restrictive. Not all questions of normative teaching are
rooted directly in the intention of the author. Hurtado notes the oft-cited illustration of the doctrine of the Trinity, which is not taught explicitly in the New
Testament but developed on the basis of inferences from biblical teaching. Is

it not valid to inquire about the character of Luke's pneumatology and then to wrestle with the implications that emerge from his pneumatology for our contemporary questions? Only "the most severe form of biblicism" would deny the validity of this sort of exercise.[9]

An exclusive focus on an author's "primary intent" or "intention to teach" too often leads to a form of tunnel vision that ignores the implications of an individual text for the theological perspective of the author. This myopia is illustrated in Fee's treatment of the Samaritan episode in Acts 8:4–17.[10] He argues that this passage is ultimately irrelevant to discussions concerning the doctrine of subsequence, for Luke's "primary intent" lies elsewhere. Now, the primary intent of the narrative, as Fee suggests, may be to stress that the expansion of the gospel beyond the bounds of Judaism had "divine and apostolic approval." And, I would agree, it is unlikely that Luke consciously sought to teach here that the gift of the Spirit is normally separate from saving faith. Yet this does not allow us to ignore the clear implications of the narrative for Luke's pneumatology.

Indeed, the fact that Luke *does* separate the gift of the Spirit from saving faith clearly reveals his distinctive pneumatological perspective. Paul would not—indeed, could not—have interpreted and narrated the event in this way. Furthermore, this separation refutes the commonly accepted interpretation of the Lukan gift as "the climax of conversion-initiation." In other words, the value of a passage for assessing the theological perspective of a given author cannot be reduced to its "primary intent." A passage must be understood in terms of its original setting and intention, but the theological freight it carries may transcend its "primary intent." Each piece of evidence must be taken seriously as we seek to reconstruct the theological perspective of the biblical author.

This leads to an important conclusion regarding theological method. The quest for normative theology is often a twofold task, embracing both the disciplines of biblical and systematic theology. (1) We must reconstruct the theological perspective of the biblical authors, thereby enabling them to take their rightful places at the roundtable. This task of reconstruction cannot be limited to a survey of the "primary intent" of isolated passages; rather, it calls for a careful analysis of the theological significance of the author's entire work. (2) After the task of theological reconstruction is finished, we must bring our questions to the roundtable and listen attentively to the ensuing dialogue. Here we seek to hear the answers (by inference) to our questions that emerge from the various theological perspectives of the biblical authors. In the following sections we will seek to employ this twofold method in an attempt to evaluate the Pentecostal doctrine of evidential tongues.

3. The Contributions of Biblical Theology

Let us then gather the biblical authors together at the roundtable. For our purposes, Luke and Paul will be sufficient. However, before we raise our question, it would be well for us simply to listen. We must listen to their discussion of significant matters related to the manifestation of tongues and prophetic speech. Paul is the first to respond. Although his statement is not definitive for our question, it is significant nonetheless. Paul affirms that *every Christian may—and indeed should—be edified through the private manifestation of tongues*.

This statement is significant, for some have suggested that Paul limits speaking in tongues to a few in the community who have been so gifted. Don Carson's comments in *Showing the Spirit* are representative of this position.[11] On the basis of the rhetorical question in 1 Corinthians 12:30 ("Do all speak in tongues?"), Carson argues that it is inappropriate to insist that all may speak in tongues; not all have the same gift. This principle is central to Carson's dismissal of tongues as evidence of a distinctive postconversion experience.

Yet Carson fails to acknowledge the complexity of the issue, for 1 Corinthians 12:30 must be reconciled with 14:5 ("I would like everyone of you to speak in tongues"). Furthermore, he does not consider whether the reference in 12:30 is limited to the *public* manifestation of tongues. If, as the context suggests, this is the case, then the way is open for every believer to be edified personally through the private manifestation of tongues. It is striking that Carson fails to discuss this exegetical option when he acknowledges that although all are not prophets (12:29), all may prophesy (14:31). Paul's comment in 14:18 ("I thank God that I speak in tongues more than all of you"), coupled with the reference in 14:5 noted above, indicates that Paul considered the private manifestation of tongues to be edifying, desirable, and available to every Christian.[12] Carson has apparently misread Paul and inappropriately restricted tongues-speech to a select group within the Christian community.

We now turn our attention to Luke. His contribution is multifaceted. First, Luke reminds us of *the prophetic character of the Pentecostal gift*. We have noted that Luke describes the gift of the Spirit *exclusively* in charismatic terms as the source of power for effective witness. That is to say, Luke does not, in a manner analogous to Paul, present the Spirit as a soteriological agent (the source of cleansing, justification, and sanctification). If we ask more specifically concerning the impact of the Spirit in Luke–Acts, we see that Luke's perspective is similar to that of the Judaism of his day. First-century Jews identified the gift of the Spirit as the source of prophetic inspiration. This view was dominant for the Judaism that gave birth to the early church, with Wisdom of Solomon and the Hymns of Qumran providing the only exceptions.[13]

As the source of prophetic inspiration, the Spirit grants special revelation and inspired speech. These twin functions are exemplified by the many instances where the rabbis speak of "seeing" or "speaking *in the Spirit*." One early citation (probably pre-Christian), *Aboth de Rabbi Nathan* A.34, is also illustrative: "By ten names was the Holy Spirit called, to wit: parable, metaphor, riddle, speech, saying, glory, command, burden, prophecy, vision."[14] Notice here how the various "names" identified with the Holy Spirit feature charismatic revelation (e.g., "prophecy," "vision") and speech (e.g., "speech," "saying," "command").

Luke also presents the Spirit as the source of prophetic inspiration. This is apparent from the outset of his Gospel, which features outbursts of prophetic speech by Elizabeth (Luke 1:41–42), Zechariah (1:67), and Simeon (2:25–28). It is highlighted in the programmatic accounts of Jesus' sermon at Nazareth (4:18–19) and Peter's sermon on the day of Pentecost (Acts 2:17–18), both of which indicate that the Lukan gift of the Spirit is intimately connected to inspired speech. Furthermore, references to Spirit-inspired speech punctuate Luke's two-volume work (e.g., Luke 10:21; 12:10–12; Acts 4:31; 6:10). Thus, when Luke reminds us of the prophetic character of the gift of the Spirit, he is in fact affirming that the Pentecostal gift is intimately linked to inspired speech.

4. The Contributions of Systematic Theology

We are now in a position to press beyond the initial and foundational contributions of biblical theology, particularly of Paul and Luke. We must now put our questions before them: What is the nature of the relationship between tongues (glossolalia) and the Pentecostal gift? More specifically, is tongues the "initial physical evidence" of the baptism in the Holy Spirit (Acts 1:5; 2:4)?

Paul must remain silent at this point. We have already noted that his theology does not stand in contradiction to evidential tongues. Nevertheless, since he does not speak specifically of the Pentecostal gift,[15] we are unable to reconstruct his contribution to the discussion at this point.

Luke, however, has much to say. Concerning the question of "initial physical evidence," one might be inclined to hear in his answer an allusion to charismatic revelation and inspired speech, including both intelligible and unintelligible (glossolalia) utterances. Certainly Luke presents the Pentecostal gift as the source of prophetic inspiration, and this inspiration includes all three of these activities (charismatic revelation, intelligible speech, and glossolalia).

Yet as we reflect on the question and listen attentively, we can hear that Luke's answer is more precise. After all, "physical evidence" suggests visible or audible signs that verify reception of the Pentecostal gift. Thus, we can, without further ado, eliminate charismatic revelation from Luke's response.

Charismatic revelation, unless uttered in some way, cannot serve as "physical evidence," for it lacks a visible or audible dimension.

Furthermore, how is one to distinguish inspired intelligible speech from that which is uninspired? Although we may all be able to think of instances when intelligible speech was uttered in a manner that indicated the inspiration of the Spirit (spontaneous, edifying, appropriate), the point is that judgments of this kind are rather tenuous or approximate. Tongues-speech, however, because of its unusual and demonstrative character (the very reason it is both often maligned or overesteemed), is particularly well suited to serve as "evidence." In short, if we ask the question concerning "initial physical evidence" of Luke, tongues-speech uniquely "fits the bill" because of its intrinsically demonstrative character.

There is evidence, apart from Luke's larger pneumatology, that suggests this conclusion is harmonious with Luke's perspective. The decisive sign of God's favor on the Gentiles is their reception of the gift of the Spirit, manifested in tongues-speech (Acts 10:46). It is this sign that astonishes Peter's circumcised companions and results in his command to baptize the Gentile converts (10:45–48). This emphasis on the sign value of speaking in tongues is rooted in Luke's prophetic pneumatology. Since according to Luke reception of the Spirit is the exclusive privilege of "the servants" of God and produces miraculous and audible speech, by its very nature glossolalia provides demonstrative proof that the uncircumcised members of Cornelius's household have been incorporated into the community of salvation. The sign value of tongues-speech is also emphasized in the Pentecost account (2:4–5, 17–20). Whether from the lips of a Jew in Jerusalem or a Gentile in Caesarea, the manifestation of tongues-speech marks the speaker as a member of the end-time prophetic community.

We are now in a position to summarize our findings. I have argued that the doctrine of "tongues as initial evidence," although not explicitly found in the New Testament, is an appropriate inference drawn from the prophetic character of the Pentecostal gift and the evidential character of tongues-speech. Although tongues-speech, as a form of inspired or prophetic speech, is integral to the Pentecostal gift, Paul makes a significant contribution to the discussion by highlighting its potentially universal character. Let us now turn to an evaluation of our approach and findings.

5. The Limitations of Systematic Theology

Our approach to the "tongues" question is not based on arguments from historical precedent. I have not, on the basis of an analysis of isolated passages from the books of Acts, sought to demonstrate that Luke intended to teach evidential tongues. Rather, drawing from the full scope of Luke's two-volume work, I have focused on the nature of Luke's pneumatology and, from this theological framework, sought to answer our contemporary question concerning "initial evidence." Significant evidence from Paul has also been considered. The normative character of evidential tongues thus emerges, not from Luke's primary intent, but rather as an implication from his prophetic pneumatology and Paul's complementary perspective.

Larry Hurtado, as we have noted, acknowledges that doctrines cannot be judged invalid simply because they are not explicitly taught in Scripture. In principle, it is valid to base doctrine on inferences drawn from the text. And in practice, although we acknowledge that the doctrine of the Trinity is not explicitly taught in Scripture, we affirm its validity. However, Hurtado suggests that the doctrine of evidential tongues cannot be compared to that of the Trinity and that while the latter is valid, the former is not. The Christian movement, from its earliest stages "was engaged in attempting to understand God in the light of Christ."[16] Thus later Trinitarian statements represent the culmination of a process that can be traced back to the apostolic age. Hurtado contrasts the apostolic origins of Trinitarian thought with the relatively modern origin of evidential tongues:

> Unlike such matters as the Christian doctrine of God, the question of whether there is a separate level of Spirit empowerment subsequent to regeneration, with a required "evidence" of it, seems not to be reflected at all in the New Testament.[17]

Yet Hurtado's judgment needs to be reexamined. As we have noted, a careful analysis of Luke–Acts indicates that from its earliest days the early church was cognizant of "a separate level of Spirit empowerment subsequent to regeneration." This level of empowerment Luke described in terms of the Pentecostal gift and promise. Furthermore, a process of development in the early church's understanding of the work of the Spirit is clearly reflected in the writings of Mark, Matthew, Luke, Paul, and John. The evidence, I have argued, suggests that Paul was the first Christian to attribute soteriological significance to the gift of the Spirit and that his insight did not impact non-Pauline sectors of the early church until after the writing of Luke–Acts (probably around A.D. 70). This means that from its earliest days the early church knew only of "a level of Spirit empowerment subsequent to [or at least logically distinct from] regeneration." Paul's fuller understanding had to be integrated with this more primitive perspective. Thus, the Pentecostal doctrine of Spirit-baptism also has apostolic roots.

I would acknowledge that "initial physical evidence" is a relatively recent theological formulation. Indeed, even the wording of the phrase is conditioned by historical circumstances. The focus on "evidence" reminds us of a day in which the scientific method had seized the imagination of the American people. Nevertheless, this modern formulation is related to a process of doctrinal development that is reflected in the New Testament and that has been largely ignored by modern exegetes: What is the nature of the Pentecostal gift? This question has been with the church since that first Pentecost day.

The question with which we have been wrestling in this chapter—"What is the nature of the relationship between tongues (glossolalia) and the Pentecostal gift?"—undoubtedly generated considerable discussion among Peter's colleagues. Thus it is virtually certain that it accompanied the expansion of the church among the Gentiles.[18] And it appears to be an inevitable question for those who would try to reconcile Paul's gift-language with Luke's Pentecostal gift. In other words, the pedigree of Pentecostal doctrine is not as shabby as Hurtado would suggest.

This is not to suggest that modern Pentecostal formulations are inspired. All theological formulations are the product of human beings and thus, for better or worse, are human attempts to come to terms with the significance of God's Word. All such formulations stand under the judgment of that Word. The phrase "initial physical evidence," as all theological formulations, has its limitations. The focus on "evidence" can easily lead to a confusion of the gift with the sign. The Pentecostal gift is not tongues. It is rather an empowering experience that enables its recipient to participate effectively in the mission of God. The manifestation of tongues is an evidence of the Pentecostal dimension of the Spirit's work, but it is not the gift itself. An inordinate focus on "evidence" may result in Christians who, looking back into the distant past, can remember the moment they "got it," but for whom the Pentecostal dimension of power for witness is presently unknown.[19]

Yet, this human formulation also captures well the sense of expectation called for by Luke and Paul: Speaking in tongues is an integral part of the Pentecostal gift, edifying and universally available. Therefore, when one receives the gift, one would *expect* to manifest tongues. Furthermore, the manifestation of tongues is a powerful reminder that the church is, by virtue of the Pentecostal gift, a prophetic community empowered for a missionary task.

This, of course, does not exhaust the theological significance of glossolalia. Frank Macchia, in a stimulating article, appropriately calls for Pentecostals to reflect further on the theological significance of tongues-speech.[20] In my judgment, he highlights three areas of special significance.

- *Missiology*: Is it not significant that "tongues" accompany (and are a decisive "sign" of) God's initiative in breaking through racial and economic barriers?[21]
- *Eschatology*: The manifestation of tongues reminds us that we, like those

on that first Pentecost, live in the "last days"—that period of God's gracious deliverance that immediately precedes the Day of the Lord (Acts 2:17)—and that God has called us to be a part of his glorious plan of salvation.

- *Ecclesiology*: Tongues have been described as a Pentecostal "sacrament" (a visible sign of a spiritual reality), but one that is not bound to clergy or institution, and therefore one that has a powerful democratizing effect on the life of church. Is it purely coincidental that tongues-speech has frequently accompanied renewed vision for ministry among the laity?

6. Conclusion

We have argued that the Pentecostal doctrine of evidential tongues is an appropriate inference drawn from the prophetic character of Luke's pneumatology (and more specifically, the Pentecostal gift) and from Paul's affirmation of the edifying and potentially universal character of the private manifestation of tongues. Our argument may be summarized as follows:

1. Paul affirms that the private manifestation of tongues is edifying, desirable, and universally available. In short, all should speak in tongues.
2. Luke affirms that the Pentecostal gift is intimately connected to inspired speech, of which tongues-speech is a prominent form, possessing a uniquely evidential character.
3. Therefore, when one receives the Pentecostal gift, one should *expect* to manifest tongues, and this manifestation of tongues is a uniquely demonstrative sign (evidence) that one has received the gift.

Although the doctrine of evidential tongues is formulated in modern language and addresses contemporary concerns, it is linked to a process of doctrinal development that extends back into the apostolic age. Indeed, the question it addresses undoubtedly accompanied the expansion of the church among the Gentiles, and it appears to be unavoidable for those who try to reconcile Paul's gift-language with Luke's Pentecostal gift. The doctrine calls us to retain a biblical sense of expectancy, for it reminds us that the manifestation of tongues is an integral part of the Pentecostal gift, edifying and universally available. Above all, the manifestation of tongues is a powerful reminder that the church is, by virtue of the Pentecostal gift, a prophetic community called and empowered to bear witness to the world.

Study Questions

1. What is the difference between biblical and systematic theology? Why is the question concerning the nature of the Pentecostal gift a question of biblical theology? Why is the question concerning evidential tongues a question of systematic theology?
2. Menzies suggests that none of the biblical authors consciously set out to demonstrate that glossolalia is the initial physical evidence of Spirit-baptism. Does this mean the doctrine must be invalid?
3. According to Menzies, the theological significance of a passage cannot be reduced to its "primary intent." What does he mean? How does this impact the way in which we "do" theology?
4. Menzies suggests that a systematic approach, which seeks to integrate the contributions of Luke and Paul, provides support for the doctrine of evidential tongues. What is Paul's contribution? What does Luke add to the discussion?
5. What are some of the important strengths of the doctrine of evidential tongues? What are some of the potential weaknesses?

Notes

[1] *Minutes of the 44th Session of the General Council of the Assemblies of God* (Portland, Ore., August 6–11, 1991), 130.

[2] Caird's approach is summarized by L. D. Hurst, "New Testament Theological Analysis," *Introducing New Testament Study*, Scot McKnight, ed. (Grand Rapids: Baker, 1989), 145.

[3] Larry W. Hurtado, "Normal, but Not a Norm: Initial Evidence and the New Testament," *Initial Evidence*, G. McGee, ed. (Peabody, Mass.: Hendrickson, 1991), 191.

[4] Ibid.

[5] Gordon Fee, "Hermeneutics and Historical Precedent—A Major Problem in Pentecostal Hermeneutics," *Perspectives on the New Pentecostalism*, R. P. Spittler, ed. (Grand Rapids: Baker, 1976), 118–32; see also Fee, "Baptism in the Holy Spirit: The Issue of Separability and Subsequence," *Pneuma* 7:2 (1985): 87–99.

[6] This is the case in spite of Donald A. Johns' excellent article, "Some New Directions in the Hermeneutics of Classical Pentecostalism's Doctrine of Initial Evidence," in *Initial Evidence* 145–67. Johns' article focuses on methodology and thus, by design, represents a provisional statement.

[7] Hurtado, "Normal," 189–201; J. Ramsey Michaels, "Evidences of the Spirit, or the Spirit as Evidence? Some Non-Pentecostal Reflections," *Initial Evidence*, 202–18.

[8] Fee, "Hermeneutics and Historical Precedent," 83–99.

[9] Hurtado, "Normal," 191.

[10] Gordon Fee and Douglas Stuart, *How to Read the Bible for All its Worth*, 94–96; see also Fee, *Gospel and Spirit*, 97.

[11] Don Carson, *Showing the Spirit: A Theological Exposition of 1 Corinthians 12–14* (Grand Rapids: Baker, 1987).

[12] Note also 1 Cor. 14:4: "He who speaks in a tongue edifies himself. . . ."

[13] Robert Menzies, *The Development of Early Christian Pneumatology*, 52–112.

[14] English translation from J. Goldin, *The Fathers According to Rabbi Nathan* (New Haven, Conn.: Yale Univ. Press, 1955). On the dating of *ARN* A.34, see Menzies, *Development*, 97–99.

[15] Although Paul does not specifically relate the empowering dimension of the Spirit to the Pentecostal gift, this Lukan contribution accords well with Paul's theological perspective.

[16] Hurtado, "Normal," 192.

[17] Ibid.

[18] P. F. Esler, "Glossolalia and the Admission of Gentiles into the Early Christian Community," *BTB* 22 (1992): 136–42.

[19] The phrase "accompanying sign" is a possible useful alternative.

[20] Frank D. Macchia, "The Question of Tongues as Initial Evidence: A Review of *Initial Evidence*, edited by Gary B. McGee," *JPT* 2 (1993): 117–27.

[21] See M. Dempster, "The Church's Moral Witness: A Study of Glossolalia in Luke's Theology of Acts," *Paraclete* 23.1 (1989): 1–7.

Chapter Nine

Tongues: Available to All

In 1 Corinthians 12–14 Paul refers to glossolalia (tongues) as one of the gifts God grants to the church. A thorough reading of these chapters reveals that in spite of the Corinthians' misunderstanding and abuse of this gift, Paul holds the private manifestation of tongues in high regard.[1] Although Paul is concerned to direct these believers toward a more mature expression of spiritual gifts "in the assembly"[2] (12:28; 14:19)—and thus he focuses on the need for edification and the primacy of prophecy over uninterpreted tongues in the corporate setting—Paul never denigrates the gift of tongues.

Indeed, Paul affirms that the private manifestation of tongues is edifying to the speaker (1 Cor. 14:5), and in an autobiographical note, he thanks God for the frequent manifestation of tongues in his own private prayer life (14:18). Fearful that his instructions to the Corinthians concerning the proper use of tongues "in the assembly" might be misunderstood, he explicitly commands them not to forbid speaking in tongues (14:39). And with reference to the private manifestation of tongues, Paul declares: "I would like every one of you to speak in tongues" (14:5).

Paul's words at this point, particularly the wish expressed in 1 Corinthians 14:5, have led many to conclude that Paul viewed the private manifestation of tongues as edifying and available to every believer. As a result, most Pentecostals and many Charismatics believe and teach that every believer can be strengthened through the manifestation of tongues during times of private prayer. This conclusion and reading of Paul has recently been challenged in a thoughtful and engaging article by Max Turner. In my opinion, Turner's article, irenic in tone and addressed to those in the Pentecostal community, serves to stimulate exactly the kind of dialogue that we in the Christian community need. That article and the ensuing responses will undoubtedly help us all better understand each other, our points of commonality, and our differences on certain issues.

This sort of dialogue also challenges all of us to reexamine our positions in light of the Scriptures. Although this process will not always result in agreement, I believe that it will serve to build a sense of unity and mutual respect within the body of Christ. Ultimately, it will help us reflect more faithfully the mind of Christ. It is with this hope that I offer the following response to Turner's article. Three major issues will be treated: (1) the nature of the problem Paul addresses in 1 Corinthians 12–14 and its implications for our question concerning the potential universality of tongues; (2) the force of the rhetorical question in 12:30b, "Do all speak in tongues?" and (3) the significance of Paul's wishful declaration in 14:5, "I would like everyone of you to speak in tongues." I will conclude by responding to Turner's probing questions concerning the present shape of Pentecostal theology, especially his critique of the doctrine of initial evidence.

1. The Problem at Corinth

Turner notes that 1 Corinthians 12–14 is polemical. Paul is attempting here to correct problems in the Corinthians' understanding and use of tongues. At least some of them appear to have viewed tongues as an expression of a superior level of spirituality. Thus, they valued tongues above other gifts, and in the context of corporate meetings, their spiritual elitism often found expression in unintelligible outbursts that disrupted meetings and did not build up the church.[3] This basic reconstruction of the problem at Corinth has found widespread acceptance. However, as Turner notes, one matter is less clear. Were all of the Corinthians caught up in this elitist form of spirituality (and thus standing in opposition to Paul), or was the church itself divided over the issue? The former position has been advocated by Fee, the latter by Forbes.[4]

Turner himself opts for the latter position, following closely the lead of Forbes. Thus he suggests that at Corinth the gift of tongues was exercised by some to establish or reinforce their position as members of the spiritual elite. The exercise of tongues was, then, a part of the "power games" that divided the church in that city. Turner suggests that this in turn indicates that the exercise of tongues at Corinth "was a relatively restricted phenomenon."[5] He reasons, "If all or most could speak in tongues—if only as private prayer and doxology—then manifestation of the gift could provide no grounds for elitist claims."[6]

Yet Turner's reasoning here seems to miss a vital point: The central question is not whether all of the Corinthians *actually* spoke in tongues; rather, did Paul teach or imply that this was potentially the case? It is worthwhile to note that if Turner's reconstruction of the problem is accurate—that is, that an elitist group was disrupting meetings with outbursts of tongues because they felt this marked them off as part of a super-spiritual group—then Paul's references to the potentially universal character of tongues as an edifying dimension of one's private prayer life is readily explicable. An analysis of Paul's argument is instructive in this regard.

Paul seeks to correct the Corinthians' misunderstanding: He highlights the variety and origin of God's gracious gifts (1 Cor. 12, esp. vv. 4–6), that everyone has a role to play (12:11–27), and that edification is the key goal (12:7). Specifically, with reference to tongues, he insists that "in the assembly," unless tongues are interpreted, they do not edify the church and thus prophecy is to be preferred (14:2–5). In the context of his argument that prophecy is greater than tongues in the assembly, Paul also states that the private manifestation of tongues is edifying to the speaker and, furthermore, that it is not limited to an elite group, but rather available to all (14:5, 18).

In other words, just as Paul notes that he is no stranger to tongues and thus qualified to speak of the gift's significance (perhaps here he bests the Corinthians at their own game of elitist claims; 1 Cor. 14:18), so also Paul undermines the Corinthians' sense of superiority with his comments concerning the universality of the gift. If Turner's reconstruction of the problem is correct, this then may indeed be the thrust of 14:5: All can be edified by the private manifestation of tongues (this is not reserved to a select group), but in the gathered assembly it is more spiritual to prophesy (since this is intelligible and edifying).

In short, Turner's reconstruction of the problem does not indicate that Paul viewed the gift of tongues as limited to a select group within the church. In fact, it is quite the opposite. Turner's reconstruction actually offers a positive reason for Paul to affirm the universality of tongues. In the face of elitist claims, we can understand Paul's words in 14:5 ("I would like every one of you to speak in tongues") as a subtle corrective.

While Turner's reconstruction might suggest that only members of the problem group at Corinth actually spoke in tongues, this is by no means necessarily the case. On the one hand, as Fee suggests, it is possible that we should see the entire church standing in opposition to Paul. If this is the case, then tongues may have been widely exercised by the entire church. On the other hand, even if the problem was localized in a group within the church, it is still likely that the private manifestation of tongues was not limited to this select group. The key problem at Corinth with reference to tongues was the abuse of the gift "in the assembly" (that is, when the church gathered together; cf. 1 Cor. 12:28; 14:4–6, 9–19).

It is certainly possible to envision the elitist group reveling in their *public display* of tongues, regardless of whether or not there were others who exercised the gift in private, such as Paul (1 Cor. 14:18).[7] This public display of "speaking mysteries" (14:2) would be sign enough of their special knowledge and position, superior to any private usage. Of course, with this flawed thinking Paul cannot agree. In this case, Paul's words in 14:5 would serve to remind the elitist group of the larger reality reflected in their midst (of which they may or may not have been aware): All can be edified through the private manifestation of the gift.

2. Paul's Rhetorical Question (1 Cor. 12:30b)

Turner next moves to the rhetorical question in 1 Corinthians 12:30b, "Do all speak in tongues?" As the Greek grammar indicates, the anticipated answer is "no." For those not wishing to deal with the complexities of Paul's argument, this statement is often taken as the final word on this issue. However, Paul's treatment of tongues in chapter 14 clearly warns us against making such a premature judgment. Upon closer analysis we see that Paul here is clearly dealing with the exercise of gifts "in the assembly" (12:28). In other words, when Paul asks, "Do all speak in tongues?" he is not asking, "Can all speak in tongues (in private or corporate contexts)?" Rather, he is making a point much in line with what precedes in chapter 12: When we gather together, not everyone contributes to the body in the same way; not everyone speaks in tongues or interprets in the corporate setting, do they?[8] Paul is not discussing the private manifestation of tongues here. Questions pertaining to that sphere of usage are simply not in view.

In the previous chapter I pointed out the faulty logic presented by those who, on the one hand, have been quick to cite 1 Corinthians 12:30 as a clear statement limiting the manifestation of tongues (public or private) to a select group within the church, and yet, on the other hand, have affirmed that everyone can prophesy. If, in spite of the rhetorical question in 12:29 ("Are all prophets?"), it is acknowledged that all can potentially prophesy (usually on the basis of 14:1, 31), why is it so different with tongues? If, as Turner notes, "the distinction between the narrower circle of those recognized as 'prophets' and a broader one of those 'able (occasionally) to prophesy' is ... widely accepted," why is it so difficult to see the distinction between tongues exercised "in the assembly" (the corporate setting) and the exercise of tongues in private, particularly when Paul clearly speaks of these two distinct functions (e.g., public: 14:27–28; private: 14:5, 18)?[9] It is difficult not to feel that factors other than the text are controlling exegesis at this point.

Turner, however, is helpful at this point in that he does offer reasons for his judgment. He argues that there is little in the text that would "prepare the reader to think Paul's question, 'Not all speak in tongues, do they?' refers exclusively or primarily to the use of tongues in public worship."[10] Turner acknowledges that the larger context clearly focuses on problems related to congregational worship (1 Cor. 8–14), with chapters 12–14 focusing specifically on the abuse of tongues "in the assembly."

The immediate context also focuses our attention on the corporate life of the church. Paul, who has just highlighted the importance and uniqueness of each believer's role in the corporate life of the church (note the body metaphor, 1 Cor. 12:12–26), declares in 12:27, "Now you are the body of Christ. . . ." The list of ministries, gifts, and deeds of service and the associated rhetorical questions follow immediately (12:28–30) and are prefaced with the phrase "in the assembly" (12:28). Elsewhere this phrase clearly refers to the corporate gathering of believers, the local assembly (11:18; 14:19, 23, 28, 33, 35). For most this is enough to indicate that Paul has the local congregation at Corinth in view.[11] Fee states the matter clearly: "Since [v. 28] is coordinate with v. 27, with its emphatic 'you are,' meaning the church in Corinth, there can be little question that by this phrase ['in the assembly'] Paul also primarily intends the local assembly in Corinth."[12]

Turner, however, remains unconvinced. In spite of these contextual markers, he argues that Paul here has in mind the church universal rather than the local assembly in Corinth. This judgment follows from Paul's reference to "apostles" (1 Cor. 12: 28–29): "There were not regularly (if ever) a plurality of apostles in the Corinthian meetings."[13] Nevertheless, no doubt feeling the weight of the evidence, Turner largely concedes this point and moves to his major objection:

> Even if Paul has the Corinthian church primarily in mind (cf. 12:27), his description of what God has set "in the church" cannot easily be restricted in reference to what goes on when "the church in Corinth" meets in formal assembly for public worship, as opposed to what happens through believers (individually or as groups) in the variety of contexts that Corinthian life provided.[14]

Turner argues that the rhetorical questions—"Not all are apostles are they?" "Not all are prophets are they?" "Not all work miracles do they?" "Not all have gifts of healings do they?"—indicate that Paul is talking about activities that cannot be restricted to what takes place in the local assembly. Paul is an apostle whether he is shipwrecked at sea, fleeing from persecution, or "in the church." Similarly, prophets often prophesy outside the assembly (cf. Acts 21:4, 11), and the working of miracles and gifts of healings are normally described as happening outside the assembly (e.g., 8:36–41; 28:7–8). In the light of all this, Turner asks, how can the reader be expected to discern that when Paul asks, "Not all speak in tongues do they?" he is asking only about the expression of tongues in the assembly?[15]

Actually, several reasons indicate that this is exactly what we would expect. (1) As we have noted, the context clearly focuses our attention on the corporate life of the church. Paul has stressed the need for diversity in the body of Christ. He now illustrates this with concrete examples from the life of the church in Corinth. The list and rhetorical questions of 1 Corinthians 12:28–30 offer examples of the variety of ministries and gifts that are exercised in the corporate life of the church. In this context, the references to "apostles," "prophets," "teachers," and so on allude to the diverse *functions* these individuals exercise "in the assembly."

This is confirmed by the shift in the list from people (apostles, prophets, teachers) to gifts and deeds (lit., "miracles," "gifts of healing," "helpful deeds," "acts of guidance," "different kinds of tongues").[16] All of the functions listed here could and quite naturally would have taken place in the local assembly in Corinth, and especially in light of verse 28 ("in the assembly"), Paul's readers most naturally would have viewed the list in this way. The thrust of the rhetorical questions is then abundantly clear: When we gather together, do all function in the same way to build up the body of Christ? Of course not.

(2) While Turner correctly notes that some of the ministries noted in these verses (12:28–30) may possibly take place outside of the formal assembly, it must be noted that all of the functions listed here refer to activities that take place in a corporate setting. None of these ministries or actions can take place in a private setting (i.e., by an individual in isolation from others). The only possible exception would be Paul's reference to tongues. However, since elsewhere Paul clearly speaks of a corporate expression of this gift (in contrast to a private expression), his reader would have naturally understood the text in this way. That this is indeed what he intended is confirmed not only by the context, but also by the collocation of rhetorical questions pertaining to tongues and the interpretation of tongues (the latter demands a corporate setting; cf. 1 Cor. 14:5) in 12:30.

(3) Turner's lack of faith in the ability of Paul's readers to pick up on these contextual markers is striking when he himself acknowledges that Paul clearly distinguishes between the private and corporate expressions of the gift of tongues. If Turner can see this distinction in the text, why assume Paul's readers could not? In light of our discussion above, it would be odd if the Corinthians had missed this point. In any event, we need not.

(4) One final point with reference to 1 Corinthians 12:28–30 should be noted. Turner seeks to justify those, like D. A. Carson, who see this passage as restricting tongues to a select few, yet understand prophecy as available to all. He notes that prophecy is "an established ministry," and thus some function in the gift more frequently and profoundly than others. While all might

prophesy (14:31), not all are prophets. The problem with tongues, he suggests, is that there was no established ministry of tongues, or at least the terminology to speak of such a ministry of tongues-speaking was lacking. Yet is not the distinction between those who exercise the gift of tongues in a corporate setting with interpretation for the edification of all and those who exercise the gift in a private setting for their own edification obvious? Although Paul does not coin a special term for individuals who exercise the gift of tongues in the corporate setting, the distinction between these *functions* is clear.

Indeed, a distinction between the corporate exercise of tongues (12:28–30) and the private exercise (1 Cor. 14:4–5) is more easily discerned than the distinction between those who prophesy in a particularly profound way and those who do so only occasionally and less powerfully. Does Paul in 12:28–29 refer to the office of the prophet or the function of prophecy more generally? Fee states "the answer is probably Yes and No."[17] This ambiguous answer makes my point: The distinction here between the office of prophet and the function of prophecy (Paul actually seems to be stressing the latter) is not as clear as the distinction between the corporate and private expressions of tongues.

What is too often missed in this discussion is that Paul's concern, whether in relation to prophecy or to tongues, is *not* to delineate who may or may not function in these gifts. Fee correctly notes that Paul's "rhetoric does not mean, 'May all do this?' to which the answer would probably be, 'Of course.' Rather, it means, 'Are all, Do all?' to which the answer is, 'Of course not.'"[18] In other words, just as Paul in these verses does not intend to exclude anyone from potentially uttering a word of prophecy (all may, but not all do); so also, Paul does not intend to limit anyone from potentially uttering a message in tongues (with interpretation) for the benefit of the church (all may, but not all do). What should be even clearer is that Paul's words here have absolutely nothing to do with limiting the scope of those who manifest tongues in private to a select few.

3. Paul's Wish (1 Cor. 14:5)

We now come to the *crux* of the matter. How shall we interpret Paul's words, "I would like every one of you to speak in tongues, but I would rather have you prophesy" (1 Cor. 14:5a)? This passage has been frequently abused, as Turner correctly notes.[19] Turner, along with Fee, rejects the notion that Paul here, as elsewhere, is "damning tongues with faint praise."[20] Turner specifically rejects the notion that in 14:5a Paul grants "what he will effectively withdraw through the strategy of the *whole* discourse."[21] He acknowledges that Paul values tongues

highly. As we have seen, the apostle explicitly states that the private manifestation of tongues is edifying to the speaker (14:4), and he himself has frequently
exercised the gift and was thankful to God for this fact (14:18). Thus Turner
finds little evidence of irony in Paul's wish and regards it as genuine.

Nevertheless, and this is the key for Turner, all of this does not mean that
Paul felt the wish would actually be realized. It is a genuine wish, but Paul does
not expect it to be fulfilled. According to Turner, this judgment is supported
by Paul's use of the grammatical construction, "I would like ... but rather ...,"
which is also found in 1 Corinthians 7:7. Here Paul expresses the wish that all
could be celibate as he himself is: "I wish that all men were as I am. But each
man has his own gift from God." Turner correctly notes that we would not
want to press this "to mean Paul really does set forth that *everyone can* and (perhaps) *should* be unmarried and celibate." However, I would add that we know
that this wish cannot and should not be universally fulfilled, not because of the
grammatical construction Paul uses, but rather because the context explicitly
tells us this is the case. As Turner notes, 7:2–6 tells us of the need that some
have for sexual relations in the context of marriage, and the wish is qualified
in 7:7 so as to bring out this point. The context of 14:5 is strikingly different,
for there is nothing in chapter 14 that suggests that Paul's wish here cannot
or should not be fulfilled.

The context of 1 Corinthians 14 actually suggests the opposite. Verse 5
forms part of a larger unit (14:2–5). Paul's argument here can be analyzed in
terms of the structure of the passage. The passage contains three couplets,
which consist of parallel statements concerning tongues and prophecy. Paul
has just encouraged the Corinthians to "eagerly desire spiritual gifts, especially the gift of prophecy" (14:1). He then tells them why this should be the
case ("for," 14:2). Each couplet moves from a description of tongues as beneficial for the individual and thus fitting for the private setting to a description of prophecy as beneficial for the body and thus fitting for the corporate
setting. The couplets build to the final point: In the assembly, prophecy is preferred above tongues, unless interpreted, because it is edifying to all.

For

     (a) The one who speaks in tongues speaks to God (private setting)
        Indeed, no one understands him
        He speaks mysteries by the Spirit

     (b) The one who prophesies speaks to people (corporate setting)
        edification, encouragement, comfort

(a) The one who speaks in tongues edifies himself (private setting)

(b) The one who prophesies edifies the church (corporate setting)

⁓

(a) I would like every one of you to speak in tongues (private setting)

(b) but I would rather have you prophesy (corporate setting)

⁓

(Thus in the assembly:)
He who prophesies is greater than he who speaks in tongues, unless he
interprets, so that the church may be edified.

This analysis of the structure of 1 Corinthians 14:2–5 highlights several important aspects of Paul's attitude toward tongues. (1) It is evident that for Paul, tongues is edifying and appropriate in its proper context, the private domain. At least some at Corinth did not properly understand this point. (2) Paul's wish that all would speak in tongues (14:5a), must, as the structure and logic of his argument indicate, refer to the private manifestation of the gift. The contrast with 14:5b indicates that in this part Paul is talking about uninterpreted tongues. It would be incomprehensible for Paul to desire that in the assembly all should speak in tongues without interpretation. (3) Since tongues, like prophecy, has a positive (albeit largely noncongregational and thus lesser) contribution to make, it would appear that both may be exercised by anyone in the community.

As we have noted, nothing in the context suggests Paul's wish that all would speak in tongues cannot or should not be realized. The parallelism between 14:5a and 14:5b (and throughout 14:2–4) suggests that both prophesy and tongues are open to all within the community of believers. That is to say, since Paul seems to believe that all may prophesy and indeed encourages the Corinthians to do so (14:5b; cf. 14:1, 31), it seems most probable that in light of 14:5 (cf. 14:18) that Paul had a similar attitude toward the private manifestation of tongues. Indeed, if the gift of tongues has merit in its private expression, why would God withhold it?[22]

Of course Paul's primary intent in this passage is not to give his readers a detailed treatment of the private manifestation of tongues. He is, as we have noted, seeking to correct misunderstandings and abuses concerning the exercise of tongues in the assembly. Nevertheless, we may properly ask what implications emerge from Paul's instruction at this point for our question. Although his wish in 1 Corinthians 14:5 forms part of a larger argument that seeks to encourage the Corinthians to value prophecy in the assembly, it does offer valuable insight into the mind of the apostle on this issue. In view of his positive attitude toward the private manifestation of tongues (14:2–4, 18) and the lack of any clear limitation for the wish beyond placing tongues in the private setting, Paul most certainly understood this wish not only to be genuine, but to express a potentially realizable state of affairs.[23]

4. Conclusion

Biblical exegesis is the bedrock of sound systematic reflection. Our different and varied systematic formulations reflect our different appraisals of specific texts. In this chapter, I have attempted to explain why I believe Paul encourages us to see the private manifestation of tongues as edifying and available to every believer. Max Turner will probably disagree with my assessment of the biblical data and thus will want to formulate matters differently. Nevertheless, there are substantial areas of agreement. By way of conclusion, I would like to highlight several points I feel are particularly significant.

(1) I do believe that Pentecostals are correctly challenging many to reassess their previous negative reconstruction of Paul's attitude toward the gift of tongues. First Corinthians 12–14 has often been treated as Paul's attempt to put down the practice of glossolalia, even though his rhetorical flourishes contain comments that might at first glance seem to affirm it. This reading of Paul needs to be challenged, and, it is noteworthy, on this point Turner and I are in full agreement.

(2) While I feel confident for the reasons stated above that Paul did believe all could be edified by the private manifestation of tongues, I would also agree that the exercise of this gift does not take us to the center of Christian spirituality. There are a whole range of questions theologians must ponder, and while this question is not insignificant, it is not as significant as many. In short, the question of tongues does not take us to the core of the Christian faith and, indeed, does not in my opinion represent the most important theological contribution Pentecostals have to make to the larger body of Christ. I believe that the Pentecostal appraisal of Spirit-baptism has more far-reaching implications for the life of the church and is more clearly supported in the Scriptures.[24]

(3) When Turner questions the appropriateness of seeing in tongues the "evidence" of Spirit-baptism,[25] he challenges us to recognize the limitations of our human formulations. All theological formulations represent human attempts to come to terms with the significance of the Word of God. These human formulations often have strengths and weaknesses. While I believe that the classical Pentecostal doctrine of tongues as the "initial physical evidence" of baptism in the Holy Spirit captures well the sense of expectation

inherent in Paul's words, I acknowledge that this statement is not without its limitations. The focus on evidence can lead to a preoccupation with a single crisis experience. Evidential tongues can also be easily confused with a badge of holiness, an experience that signifies that one has entered into a higher degree of spiritual maturity. At a popular level, Pentecostals have too often succumbed to this Corinthian temptation. Turner's article may serve as a call for Pentecostals to be clearer on these points.

I have found Turner's proddings on the issue of tongues, and particularly Paul's attitude toward the gift, to be extremely helpful. We Pentecostals have at times simply assumed that our position is correct and thus not always thought through carefully or communicated clearly our various theological positions. We should value friends like Dr. Turner, who through their good-natured proddings challenge us to deal with issues that we may otherwise overlook. This dialogue has challenged me to engage the text in a fresh and rigorous manner and helped me better understand those with whom I disagree. This in turn gives me hope that we may indeed "follow the way of love" (1 Cor. 14:1) and encourage one another to move toward the goal of more faithfully reflecting the mind of Christ.

Study Questions

1. Some feel that Paul's rhetorical question in 1 Corinthians 12:30, "Do all speak in tongues?" clearly indicates that the gift of tongues is limited to a select few. Why does Menzies disagree with this position?
2. Why is the context, which focuses on the corporate setting, so crucial for our understanding of Paul's intent in 1 Corinthians 12:30?
3. Turner argues that while Paul's wish in 1 Corinthians 14:5, "I would like every one of you to speak in tongues," was genuine, it was a wish Paul knew could not be realized. What support does Turner offer for this position? How does Menzies counter?
4. What does the structure of 1 Corinthians 14:2–5 tell us about Paul's perspective?
5. What is Paul's primary intent in 1 Corinthians 14? What are the implications that emerge from Paul's words of instruction for our question concerning the availability of tongues?

Notes

[1] See also Gordon D. Fee, *The First Epistle to the Corinthians*, 659.

[2] The Greek phrase here is *en tē ekklēsia*, which the NIV translates "in the church." In this article I will be translating this "in the assembly," since Paul seems to have the assembled church in mind here.

[3] Max Turner, "Tongues: An Experience for All in the Pauline Churches?" *AJPS* 1 (1998): 235–36.

[4] Fee, *First Corinthians*, 4–15; Christopher Forbes, *Prophecy and Inspired Speech in Early Christianity and its Hellenistic Environment* (Tübingen: Mohr, 1995), 14–16, 171–75, 182–87, 260–64.

[5] Turner, "Experience for All," 237.

[6] Ibid., 237.

[7] The contrast between 1 Cor. 14:18 ("I thank God I speak in tongues more than all of you") and 14:19 ("But, in the church . . .") indicates that Paul's autobiographical comments in 14:18 refer to the private exercise of tongues.

[8] Fee, *First Corinthians*, 623.

[9] The question concerning whether or not there are two distinct gifts of tongues (one for private edification and one for use in the corporate setting) is not germane. What is essential and a point on which Turner and I agree is that "Paul distinguishes two spheres of use of tongues—public and private" (Turner, "Experience for All," 238).

[10] Ibid., 240.

[11] Fee, *First Corinthians*, 618; James D. G. Dunn, *Jesus and the Spirit*, 262–63; R. Banks, *Paul's Idea of Community* (Grand Rapids: Eerdmans, 1980), 35–37.

[12] Fee, *First Corinthians*, 618, n. 13.

[13] Turner, "Experience for All," 240.

[14] Ibid.

[15] Ibid., 241.

[16] Fee, *First Corinthians*, 621–22.

[17] Ibid., 621.

[18] Ibid., 623.

[19] See Turner, "Experience for All," 245, and the references he cites in n. 30.

[20] The quote is from Fee, *First Corinthians*, 653. For Turner's comments, see Turner, "Experience for All," 245.

[21] Turner, "Experience for All," 245 (italics his).

[22] Turner notes that Judaism, and especially the Old Testament, anticipated a universal outpouring of prophecy; yet with respect to tongues, the Jewish traditions are virtually silent. So Paul had "good scriptural grounds" for a universal expectation with respect to prophecy, but not for tongues (Turner, "An Experience for All," 246). However, this misses the important fact that tongues was clearly viewed, at least by Luke, as one expression of prophecy (Acts 2:17–18).

[23] Fee, *First Corinthians*, 623.

[24] See R. P. Menzies, "Evidential Tongues: An Essay on Theological Method," *AJPS* 1 (1998): 122–23.

[25] Turner, "Experience for All," 249–50: "One does not receive the impression that the God of the Bible looks particularly favorably on the human search for 'proofs'. . . ."

Chapter Ten

Signs and Wonders

One striking characteristic of modern Evangelicalism is a growing appreciation for the miraculous. This trend has generated a subgroup within Evangelicalism frequently identified as the "Signs and Wonders Movement" or the "Third Wave." The latter title indicates the close relationship between this movement and Pentecostalism. The "Third Wave" refers to an energizing work of the Spirit among Evangelical Christians, subsequent to the "first wave" of renewal that birthed the classical Pentecostal denominations and the "second wave" that impacted mainline denominations and ignited the Charismatic movement. Third Wavers and Pentecostals clearly hold much in common in that both groups stress the continuing validity and importance of the gifts of the Spirit described by Paul (e.g., 1 Cor. 12), including the more demonstrative gifts, such as healing and prophecy, which many Evangelicals had consigned solely to the apostolic age.

Nevertheless, Third Wavers clearly distinguish themselves from their Pentecostal precursors. The key point of difference is the way in which these two groups view Spirit-baptism. Pentecostals have long affirmed a baptism of the Holy Spirit "distinct from and subsequent to the experience of new birth."[1] By way of contrast, Third Wavers "generally understand the baptism of the Spirit not as a second blessing but as a part of conversion."[2] Thus, while Pentecostals and Third Wavers both highlight the contemporary relevance of the miraculous gifts of God, the Pentecostal emphasis on the distinction between conversion and Spirit-baptism (i.e., the Pentecostal gift of Acts 2) separates this group from their Third Wave counterparts.

This difference in theological perspective reflects differing interpretations of Luke's theology of the Spirit in general and the Pentecostal gift of Acts 2 in particular. The Pentecostal doctrine of "subsequence" flows naturally from the conviction that the Spirit came on the disciples at Pentecost (Acts 2), not as the source of new covenant existence, but rather as the source of power for effective witness. More recent Pentecostal studies have grounded this judgment in the distinctive character of Luke's pneumatology: Luke *consistently* portrays the Spirit as the source of power for service. Third Wavers, by contrast, consistent with their (non-Pentecostal) Evangelical origins, view reception of the Pentecostal gift as the sine qua non of Christian existence, the essential element in conversion.

These differing views have led Pentecostals and Third Wavers to develop their respective emphases on "power evangelism" along different lines. Pentecostals have given special prominence to Luke–Acts, and especially Pentecost, as containing an important promise and paradigm of empowering. Indeed, for Pentecostals, any discussion of "power evangelism" or "signs and wonders" must take as its point of departure Luke's record of that first Pentecost (Acts 1–2).

This is not to suggest that Third Wavers have ignored Luke–Acts. Luke's references to miracles are frequently cited—if often in an anecdotal way— as evidence of the close association between miracles and church growth. Yet the Third Wave appropriation of Luke–Acts is not linked to any distinctive feature of Lukan theology; rather, it simply reflects the large quantity of miracle material contained in this two-volume work. References from Luke–Acts are interspersed with those from other portions of the New Testament, and the homogeneity of the New Testament witness, rather than Luke's distinctive contribution, has been the focus.[3]

In the following chapter I would like to explore some of the implications that Luke's theology of the Spirit may hold for a biblical perspective on "signs and wonders." Then, in view of the unique role that Luke–Acts plays in the formation of Pentecostal theology, I would also like to suggest how Luke's perspective has contributed to a uniquely Pentecostal approach to "power evangelism." I hope by offering this Pentecostal perspective to contribute in some small way to the stimulating discussion concerning "signs and wonders" currently taking place within the larger Christian community.

1. "Signs and Wonders" in Lukan Perspective

1.1. Luke's Advocacy of Power Evangelism

Few would dispute the claim that Luke is an advocate of "power evangelism." In terms of sheer space, Luke's gospel devotes considerable space (over 160 verses) to discussion of miracles. Luke is particularly fond of references to healing, employing the word *iaomai* (to heal) more than any other Gospel writer (Luke, 11x; Acts, 4x; Matthew, 4x; Mark, 1x; John, 3x). When the book of Acts is placed alongside Luke's Gospel, the amount of material featuring miracles is all the more impressive. The phrase "signs and wonders" occurs with special frequency in the book of Acts (Acts, 9x; Matthew, 1x; Mark, 1x; John, 1x; rest of New Testament, 4x). Indeed, because Luke's narrative is so filled with descriptions of miraculous events, often spectacular, his presentation has been described as "crude" and "lopsided."[4]

Quite apart from the sheer bulk of Luke's miracle material, two particularly important texts state the matter explicitly. (1) The promise of Jesus recorded in Acts 1:8 ("you will receive power [*dynamis*] when the Holy Spirit comes on you") clearly includes the ability to perform miracles of healing and exorcisms. Luke repeatedly portrays *dynamis* as the source of miracles of healing, exorcism, and marvelous deeds.[5] Most decisively, whenever Luke employs the collocation of *pneuma* (Spirit) and *dynamis*, he has a combination of prophetic phenomena (inspired speech and/or special revelation) and miraculous activity in view.[6] Since the promise of Pentecostal empowering is extended to all of God's servants (Acts 2:17–18), this text is of special significance for the contemporary Church.

(2) Luke's alteration of the Joel text in Acts 2:19 is particularly striking.[7] In this passage Luke adds three words that are not in the LXX text of Joel: *anō* (above), *sēmeia* (signs), and *katō* (below). Joel's text is thus transformed so as to read: "I will show wonders in the heaven *above*, and *signs* on the earth *below*." The significance of these insertions, which form a collocation of "wonders" and "signs," becomes apparent when one looks at the larger context of Luke–Acts. The Acts verse immediately following the Joel citation reads: "Jesus . . . was a man accredited by God to you by miracles, *wonders and signs*" (2:22). Then, throughout Acts we repeatedly read of the followers of Jesus working "wonders and signs."[8]

Thus, through his alteration of Joel 2 in Acts 2:19, Luke links the miraculous events associated with Jesus (Acts 2:22) and his disciples (e.g., 2:43) together with the cosmic portents listed by Joel (see 2:19b–20) as "signs and wonders" that mark the end of the age. In other words, the miracles of Jesus and his disciples are precursors of those cosmic signs that signal the Day of the Lord. For Luke, "these last days"—that period inaugurated with Jesus' birth and leading up to the Day of the Lord—represents an epoch marked by "signs and wonders." Undoubtedly, Luke is conscious of the significant role that miracles have played in the growth of the early church and anticipates that these "signs and wonders" will continue to characterize the ministry of the church in these "last days." In this respect, Luke certainly is an advocate of "signs and wonders."

Yet we dare not stop here. Luke's perspective is far more developed and complex than this limited sampling suggests. Indeed, although Luke's narrative is replete with miracle stories, his narrative is also filled with material that indicates that he is keenly aware of the danger of placing inordinate emphasis on the miraculous. Luke's narrative, I will argue, is neither "crude" nor "lopsided." His attitude toward "signs and wonders" may be described as positive, but he is not uncritical. Furthermore, the evidence from Luke–Acts suggests that for Luke, the primary manifestation of the Spirit was not miracle-working power, but rather bold and inspired verbal witness, particularly in the face of persecution. To this other facet of Luke's perspective I now turn.

1.2. Spirit and Miracle in Luke–Acts

Any attempt to elucidate Luke's perspective on "signs and wonders" must consider the unique way in which the inspired author relates the Spirit to miracles. An analysis of the way in which he relates the Spirit to prophetic phenomena (inspired speech and/or special revelation) on the one hand, and to miracles (of healing, exorcism, and feats of strength) on the other is particularly instructive.

(1) While Luke frequently presents the Spirit as the exclusive source (without reference to *dynamis*) of prophetic activity, he *never* does so with reference to miracles of healing, exorcism, or marvelous deeds. This is the case although it means that Luke has had to alter his sources on several occasions.[9]

(2) While Luke repeatedly portrays *dynamis* as the exclusive source (without reference to the Spirit) of miracles of healing, exorcism, and marvelous deeds,[10] he *never* does so with reference to inspired speech or esoteric wisdom.

(3) Whenever a combination of prophetic and miraculous activity is in view, Luke is unwilling simply to cite *pneuma* as the source (even if this accords with tradition), but feels compelled to qualify the term with the addition of *dynamis*.[11] In short, the evidence indicates that Luke has consciously distanced the Spirit from direct or exclusive association with miracles by altering his sources (e.g., Mark and Q) and by using *dynamis* as an important qualifying term.[12] Why was Luke reluctant to attribute miracles directly (or exclusively) to the Spirit? What has prompted him to be so cautious in the way he relates the Spirit to miracles? The strong connection Luke makes between proclamation (verbal witness) and the inspiration of the Spirit suggests a motive: Luke considered inspired proclamation rather than miracle-working power to be the primary manifestation of the Spirit's work.[13]

Luke 11:20 and 12:10, in comparison with Matthew 12:22–32, serve as excellent examples of Luke's tendency to associate the Spirit with proclamation rather than with miracles.

Luke 11:20:	Matt. 12:28:
"But if I drive out demons by the *finger of God*, then the kingdom of God has come to you"	"But if I drive out demons by the *Spirit of God*, then the kingdom of God has come upon you"
Luke 12:9–12:	**Matt. 12:22–32:**[14]
v. 9: "But he who disowns me before men will be disowned . . ."	v. 24: "[the Pharisees] said, 'It is only by Beelzebub . . . that this fellow drives out demons.'"
v. 10: " . . . but anyone who blasphemes against the Holy Spirit will not be forgiven."	v. 32: "but anyone who speaks against the Holy Spirit will not be forgiven."
v. 11: "When you are brought before synagogues . . . do not worry . . . what you will say, for the Holy Spirit will teach you."	

Luke's treatment of these texts represents two modifications of a *single* text, the Beelzebub Controversy in Q[15] (Matt. 12:22–30, 32=Luke 11:14–23; 12:10). (1) Luke uses "finger of God" (Luke 11:20) rather than "Spirit of God" (Matt. 12:28). In doing so he has eliminated a reference that attributed Jesus' exorcisms to the agency of the Spirit. (2) Luke has also taken the blasphemy saying (Luke 12:10=Matt 12:32) from its presumed original setting and inserted it into another block of Q material (Luke 12:2–9, 11–12) containing exhortations to bear witness to the Son of Man. Thus, Luke has altered the function it ascribes to the Spirit: No longer the power to exorcise demons as Matthew writes, in its Lukan context the Spirit is the means by which the disciples courageously bear witness to Jesus in the face of persecution.

This evidence, then, lends substantial support to my contention that Luke presents proclamation (verbal witness) rather than miracle-working power as the primary product of the Spirit's inspiration.

1.3. Word and Miracle in Luke–Acts

A survey of Luke's usage elsewhere, particularly his narration of miracle stories, adds further weight to the above-mentioned assessment. While it is true that for Luke "word and sign are complementary" and "both realities belong together in the missionary endeavour,"[16] it is also true that Luke is especially concerned with the "word" or proclamation. We have already noted that his pneumatology emphasizes the primacy of verbal witness. This emphasis is also found in the way in which Luke has appropriated and modified the accounts of miraculous activity found in his sources.[17] On several occasions Luke inserts references to "teaching" into the miracle stories that he adopts from Mark.

In Luke 5:12–16 Luke describes Jesus' healing of a leper. This account follows closely that of Mark and is clearly dependent on it (Mark 1:40–45).[18] Yet Luke deviates from Mark's account at a number of points, one of which is particularly noteworthy. Mark and Luke both record the impact of this marvelous healing: In spite of Jesus' command of silence, news of the miracle spreads dramatically—so much so that "Jesus could no longer [openly] enter a town" (Mark 1:45). Yet Luke writes that although "crowds of people *came to hear him and to be healed* of their sicknesses" (Luke 5:15), Jesus withdrew to the desert. It is striking how Luke specifically notes that as a result of the healing, people came not only to be healed (as we would expect), but also "to hear" Jesus.[19]

This theme is carried forward in Luke 6:6. Again following Mark (Mark 3:1–6=Luke 6:6–11),[20] Luke narrates Jesus' healing of a man with a withered hand. But whereas Mark begins the miracle story by simply stating that Jesus "entered the synagogue" (Mark 3:1), Luke places the miracle in the context of Jesus' teaching: "when he entered the synagogue *and taught*" (Luke 6:6).

Luke's penchant for introducing miracle stories with references to the teaching of Jesus is also reflected in two accounts Luke records that are not found in the other Gospels. Luke introduces the story of the miraculous catch of fish (Luke 5:1–11) with this descriptive phrase: "One day as Jesus was standing by the Lake of Gennesaret, with the people crowding around him and *listening to the word of God*" (5:1). Again, "on a Sabbath Jesus *was teaching* in one of the synagogues" (13:10), where he saw and healed a crippled woman (13:10–17).

Luke's account of the commissioning of the Twelve (Luke 9:1–6) again reflects his special concern to emphasize proclamation in the context of the miraculous. Luke follows Mark 6:6b–13 closely, with one major exception. Mark tells us that after Jesus called the Twelve together, "he sent them out two by two and gave them authority over evil spirits" (Mark 6:7). Luke, by contrast, drawing from Q material that he also uses in the commissioning of the Seventy (Luke 10:9=Matt. 10:7), expands his account so that it reads: "He gave them power and authority to drive out all demons and to cure diseases, and he sent them out *to preach the kingdom of God and to heal the sick*" (Luke 9:1–2). Thus, Luke highlights the fact that the commission to the Twelve was not limited solely to exorcism, but also included preaching and healing.

In other words, Luke is fond of referring both to the teaching and healing activities of Jesus. Repeatedly, he includes material referring to both of these activities into what he has obtained from his sources (Luke 5:15; 6:17–19; 9:1–2).[21] While this tendency certainly indicates that proclamation and miracles are complementary, the fact that these references generally occur in the context of a miracle story suggests that Luke is especially concerned to highlight the significance of proclamation. Luke's penchant for introducing miracle stories with references to Jesus' teaching confirms this judgment (Luke 5:1; 6:6; 13:10).[22] Jesus is more than a miracle-worker, he is the long-anticipated prophet-teacher. His disciples, as a band of end-time prophets (Acts 2:17–21), follow in his footsteps with their inspired witness. In Luke's eyes, word and sign are complementary, but they are not of equal significance.

1.4. Luke's Cautions Concerning Power Evangelism

Luke's concern to present Jesus and his disciples as more than simply miracle-workers is also reflected in a number of texts that seem to warn against a preoccupation with miracles. Here we see clearly that Luke is not uncritical in his acceptance or portrayal of miracles.

Luke alone records the return of the Seventy (Luke 10:17–20). In an account that features the victory and authority of the disciples over "the power of the enemy," Jesus' final words are surprising: "However, do not rejoice in that the spirits submit to you, but rejoice that your names are written in heaven" (10:20). Fitzmyer captures well the essence: "Jesus directs the attention of the disciples away from thoughts about sensational success to a consideration of their heavenly status."[23] Thus, through his utilization of this material, Luke appears to present a warning to his church (and to ours): A preoccupation with power over demons is misguided, for it is "no guarantee of life."[24]

In the midst of the Beelzebub controversy (Matt. 12:22–30/Mark 3:22–27/Luke 11:14–23), Luke has a verse that is not found in either Matthew or Mark: "Others tested [Jesus] by asking for a sign from heaven" (Luke 11:16). The context, particularly in view of the reference to this evil, sign-seeking generation in 11:29, casts this appeal in a decidedly negative light. The request for a dramatic "sign" is denied; instead, Jesus offers the "sign of Jonah" (11:29). As Jonah and his preaching were a sign to Nineveh, so also the preaching of Jesus serves as a "sign" to this generation.[25] The irony is evident, for the crowds who ask for a spectacular display of power have already heard Jesus' message. Once again, Luke is mindful of the limitations of "signs and wonders" and a mentality that seeks after them.

Finally, Luke's record of Simon's attempt to buy the ability to dispense the Spirit (Acts 8:9–24) also serves as a warning against selfish, worldly attitudes toward spiritual power. Luke is not unaware of potential abuses and speaks forthrightly to those who seek to use God's gifts for personal gain.

In short, Luke's perspective on "signs and wonders" is rich and full. He clearly acknowledges the important role that miracles played in the ministries of Jesus and the early church. His narrative is replete with references to the miraculous. At almost every opportunity, he reminds us that word and sign go hand in hand. Furthermore, in Luke's perspective "signs and wonders" should characterize the ministry of the church in these "last days" (Acts 1:8; 2:19). In all of these respects, Luke is an advocate of "signs and wonders."

Nevertheless, Luke is also keenly aware of the danger of placing inordinate emphasis on the miraculous. His narrative is neither "crude" nor "lopsided," but rather sprinkled with statements and stories that speak of the limitations of "signs and wonders" and a mentality that seeks after them. Luke's attitude toward "signs and wonders" may be described as positive, but not uncritical. This is most clearly reflected in his emphasis on proclamation: For Luke, the primary manifestation of the Spirit is not miracle-working power, but rather bold and inspired witness.[26]

With these conclusions in mind, I will now attempt to describe how Luke's perspective provides the basis for a uniquely Pentecostal approach to "power evangelism."

2. "Signs and Wonders": A Pentecostal Perspective

I have already noted how Pentecostals attach special significance to Luke–Acts, especially Pentecost (Acts 2), as a paradigm of God's empowering. This theological foundation provides a unique frame of reference for reflecting on questions generated by the "signs and wonders" movement and has led Pentecostals to develop their own theology of "power evangelism." A Pentecostal perspective differs from that of the Third Wave in three important ways.

2.1. The Diverse Nature of God's Empowering

Pentecostals tend to understand the nature of God's empowering in broader terms than Third Wavers. Third Wavers have sought to recapture the importance of the gifts of the Spirit described by the apostle Paul (e.g., 1 Cor. 12), especially the more demonstrative gifts such as healing and prophecy. Since they do not view the Pentecostal gift as an empowering experience (but rather as conversion), Paul's theological perspective and language rather than Luke's has largely shaped their outlook. Thus, drawing largely from Paul's letters, Third Wavers have sought to reclaim miraculous gifts for the contemporary church. Additionally, they have stressed the significance of such demonstrative gifts for church growth. The fact that the movement is known as the "signs and wonders" movement is no accident. The title reflects this important Third Wave focus on dramatic, demonstrative gifts (e.g., healing and prophecy) as a key to church growth.

However, as we have noted, Luke's perspective on divine enabling is much broader than a narrow focus on dramatic signs. Although Luke acknowledges and even highlights the positive and powerful impact of miracles, his emphasis on verbal witness is even greater. This focus on Spirit-inspired proclamation moves Luke to highlight dimensions of God's enabling that Third Wavers generally fail to mention. The ability to bear bold witness for Christ in the face of persecution or hardship is central to Luke's concept of "power evangelism" (e.g., Luke 12:8–12; Acts 4:31).[27]

This is a theme that Third Wavers have not emphasized. Although miracles facilitated the growth of the early church, this "staying power"—this ability to remain firm in the face of opposition and hardship—is the indisputable focus of the Spirit's work in Luke's narrative. Pentecostals, influenced as they have been by Luke–Acts, have tended to feature this dimension of "power evangelism." Although "signs and wonders" have been a prominent part of the Pentecostal message, the *focal point* of Pentecostal missions has always been the "staying power" made available through the baptism of the Holy Spirit.

This Lukan focus on inspired witness in the face of opposition was undoubtedly shaped by the context of suffering and persecution in which the early church flourished. It is interesting to note the parallels with the modern Pentecostal movement, a movement that also experienced rapid growth in the midst of opposition and hardship. Perhaps here we find an insight into the strength and importance of this focus on "staying power." Does it not serve as a constant reminder of the reality of opposition and suffering on the one hand, and of our vulnerability and weakness on the other? Does it not also remind us that in this life suffering will often not be removed and that this is, in any case, not the goal of God's enabling? I suggest that this is, indeed, a needed reminder as we seek after and receive God's empowering. It helps us, in the midst of our experience of God's miraculous gifts, to avoid a superficial, self-seeking, and ultimately secular perspective. James Bradley speaks forthrightly:

> Charismatic signs of healing are all too often appealed to as an attempt to remove the last vestiges of suffering in areas where modern medicine has not yet devised a means of granting relief. Healing is often linked with an overall preoccupation with material well-being, a preoccupation that most Christians in other times and other countries would have found scandalous.[28]

Certainly, any evaluation of "signs and wonders" in the early church must not forget this context of suffering and persecution. The focus on "staying power" as central to divine enabling has the advantage of offering needed perspective and balance at this point. In short, this Lukan and Pentecostal focus not only offers a broader and fuller perspective on "power evangelism," it may also assist us in our efforts to avoid the danger of triumphalism inherent in "signs and wonders."[29]

2.2. The Expectation of God's Empowering

Third Wave theology is, in one sense, a rejection of earlier Evangelical attempts to limit various Pauline gifts of the Spirit to the apostolic age. Thus Third Wavers retain the basic Evangelical theological framework but simply insist that all of the gifts are available and needed today. This approach has the advantage of making the "signs and wonders" emphasis more palatable to non-Pentecostal Christians. Peter Wagner in particular (not overly concerned with theological distinctions) has done a remarkable job of marketing various Pentecostal themes in a way that appeals to Evangelicals. The result has been an impressive openness on the part of many Evangelicals to God's gracious gifts of the Spirit.

Pentecostals can and should rejoice at this wonderful work of God's Spirit in Third Wave congregations. Nevertheless, the question must be asked (especially by Pentecostals): In the midst of the marketing, what has been lost? My own answer to this question is that Third Wavers, with their rejection of a Pentecostal (and I would add, Lukan) perspective on Pentecost, have lost the theological rationale for a strong sense of expectation. Although Third Wavers today are praying for and seeking God's enabling with fervent expectation, I wonder if they have a theological base sufficient to sustain the movement. Will the Third Wave be able to pass on its spiritual legacy to the next generation? I fear the answer may be no.

My fears are rooted in the fact that Third Wave expectation is based solely on Paul's teaching concerning spiritual gifts. I do not see Paul's teaching on gifts as providing an adequate basis for a truly and fully biblical sense of expectation concerning divine enabling. Luke's perspective is needed at this very point.

A review of Evangelical attitudes toward spiritual gifts is instructive here. The attitude of many Evangelical Christians may be described as follows: All of the gifts of the Spirit are valid for the church today; but since God sovereignly bestows his gifts on selected individuals, we must wait and watch what God chooses to do. We have no assurance that God will give us any particular gift. While we may receive gifts of missiological power, there is always the chance we will not.[30]

Certainly this approach captures an important aspect of Paul's teaching, but it is not the final word concerning God's promise of power. Yet this limited Pauline perspective shapes the theology and expectation of Third Wave and non-Third Wave Evangelicals alike. That is to say, theologically there is nothing concrete that distinguishes Third Wavers from many of their Evangelical brothers and sisters who have remained passive in their approach to divine enabling. The aggressive posture of many Third Wavers appears to be a matter of attitude that has no theological basis. In short, Third Wavers have failed to articulate a theology that adequately represents its posture toward and experience of God's power.

Luke's Pentecost account provides what is needed, a promise of missiological power for every believer. As the citation of Joel makes clear, everyone is included in the promise: sons, daughters, young, old, men, women—all of God's servants (Acts 2:17–21)![31] While it would be false to claim that here Luke promises miracle-working power to every believer, he does promise the Spirit's enabling for every Christian to boldly and effectively bear witness for Christ.[32] This Pentecostal promise, then, is crucial if we are to retain the full biblical sense of expectation.

However, as I have already noted, Third Wavers tend to equate Spirit-baptism (i.e., the Pentecostal gift) with conversion rather than with missiological empowering. This understanding of the Pentecost gift inevitably diminishes one's sense of expectation. It is always possible to argue that while all experience the soteriological dimension of the Pentecostal gift at conversion, only a select few receive gifts of missiological power. The proper Lukan sense of expectancy is thus lost.

In short, a Pentecostal reading of Luke–Acts and particularly Pentecost has the potential to aid Third Wavers as they seek to develop a theological rationale for their aggressive posture toward divine enabling. Indeed, a fully biblical sense of expectation concerning God's promise of missiological power is dependent on it.

2.3. Historical Perspective on God's Empowering

Finally, in view of Luke's cautions concerning the potential abuse of God's miraculous power (Luke 10:20; 11:16, 29; Acts 8:9–24), I would like to note a third distinguishing feature of the Pentecostal approach to "power evangelism": its historical perspective. Although the modern Pentecostal movement is still quite young, it does have almost one hundred years of first-hand experience to draw upon as it approaches this subject. Its own experience of past abuses and extremes offers much needed insight into many of today's issues.

This historical perspective appears to be lacking in Third Wave discussions of "signs and wonders." Some Third Wave leaders, newcomers as they are to charismatic gifts, exhibit the spiritual equivalent of a *nouveau riche* mentality and uncritically accept anything that appears miraculous. A bit of reflection on experiences from the recent Pentecostal past may encourage a more sober and discerning approach. For example, the current emphasis on prophecy for the purpose of personal guidance should be tempered by an examination of the abuse of personal prophecy in "the latter rain" movement of 1948–1949.[33] And the salvation-healing movement of the 1950s offers further valuable insight into potential pitfalls for the "signs and wonders" movement.[34] Just as Luke encourages his readers to learn from the mistakes of the past, so also Third Wavers can profit from the past errors of Pentecostals.

3. Conclusion

I have suggested that Luke's theology has much to contribute to a biblical perspective on "signs and wonders." He clearly acknowledges the importance of miracles in the apostolic church and affirms their continuing significance for the church today. Significantly, his Pentecostal narrative contains a promise of divine enabling that extends to every believer (Acts 1:8; 2:19). Yet, Luke is also keenly aware of inherent dangers. His narrative is neither "crude" nor "lopsided," but rather sprinkled with words of caution. Luke's attitude toward "signs and wonders" may be described as positive, but not uncritical. Most significant, Luke adds breadth to a biblical perspective on "power evangelism" by highlighting fearless and effective witness as the primary manifestation of the inspiration of the Spirit.

Because of the special significance Pentecostals attach to Luke–Acts, and especially Pentecost (Acts 2), as a paradigm of God's empowering, Pentecostals have been able to appropriate in a unique way the richness of Luke's perspective. The resulting theological perspective has much to contribute to Third Wavers seeking to ground their experience in the Scriptures: It offers a broad and full understanding of "power evangelism," a solid rationale for a high sense of expectancy with respect to divine enabling, and encouragement to avoid inherent dangers.

Study Questions

1. How do Third Wavers differ from Pentecostals?
2. What is the key difference between a Third Wave and a Pentecostal approach to "power evangelism"?
3. Why does Menzies suggest that Luke is an advocate of "power evangelism"?
4. How does Luke present a balanced perspective on "signs and wonders"?
5. Menzies suggests that although word and sign are complementary, they are not of equal significance. Which is more important and why?
6. What lessons concerning "power evangelism" does Luke strive to

teach? Why are Pentecostals in an especially good place to hear and appropriate Luke's words of wisdom?

Notes

[1] *Minutes of the 44th Session of the General Council of the Assemblies of God* (Portland, Ore., August 6–11, 1991), 129.

[2] Gary S. Greig and Kevin N. Springer, eds., *The Kingdom and the Power* (Ventura, Calif.: Regal, 1993), 21. See also the Third Wave literature cited there.

[3] See, e.g., the articles and appendixes in Greig and Springer, *The Kingdom and the Power.*

[4] Dunn, *Jesus and the Spirit*, 190–91.

[5] Luke 4:36; 5:17; 6:19; 8:46; 9:1; Acts 4:7; 6:8.

[6] Luke 1:17; 1:35; 4:14; 24:49; Acts 1:8; 10:38.

[7] Acts 2:17–21=Joel 2:28–32 (LXX, Joel 3:1–5).

[8] Or sometimes "signs and wonders." The collocation of *sēmeia* and *terata* is found in Acts 2:19, 22, 43; 4:30; 5:12; 6:8; 7:36; 14:3; 15:12.

[9] See Luke 4:18; 11:20; 12:10.

[10] Redactional: Luke 4:36; 6:19; 9:1; traditional: Luke 5:17; 8:46; Acts 4:7; 6:8.

[11] See Luke 1:17, 35; 4:14; 24:49; Acts 1:8; 10:38.

[12] For a more detailed treatment of Luke's usage at this point see Menzies, *Development*, 124–28, M. Turner's thoughtful critique, "The Spirit and the Power of Jesus' Miracles in the Lucan Conception," *NovT* 33 (1991): 124–52, and my response to Turner (R. P. Menzies, "Spirit and Power in Luke–Acts: A Response to Max Turner," 11–20).

[13] The Spirit is frequently described as the agent of inspired speech in Acts (see Acts 1:8, 16; 2:4, 14, 17–18, 33; 4:8, 25, 31; 5:32; 6:10; 7:51; 9:31; 10:44–45; 13:9; 18:25; 19:6; 28:5).

[14] Cf. Mark 3:22–29.

[15] Q represents those verses that are common to Matthew and Luke but are not found in Mark. Most scholars think that both Matthew and Luke used some such document in writing their respective Gospels.

[16] L. O'Reilly, *Word and Sign in the Acts of the Apostles: A Study in Lucan Theology* (Rome: Editrice Pontificia Università Gregoriana, 1987), 217.

[17] I accept the two-document hypothesis as axiomatic. Therefore, I have assumed that Luke knew Mark and a written source Q (cf. Luke 1:1–3). I limit my analysis of Luke's use of source material to his Gospel since our knowledge of sources for the book of Acts is so limited.

[18] See I. H. Marshall, *The Gospel of Luke: A Commentary on the Greek Text* (NIGTC; Grand Rapids: Eerdmans, 1978), 206.

[19] See also J. Nolland, who sees Luke here "correcting a one-sided attention to healing" (Nolland, *Luke 1–9:20* [WBC 35; Dallas: Word, 1989]), 228.

[20] Ibid., 259–60.

[21] Note also other passages where Luke retains references to both proclamation and miracles as found in his sources (Luke 4:40–44; 7:18–22; 8:1–3; 9:6; cf. Acts 6:7). In Luke 4:40–44 Luke retains references to exorcisms and healings found in Mark 1:32–34, but omits Mark's reference to exorcisms in his final summary statement (Mark 1:39=Luke 4:44) so that "all the stress lies on . . . preaching" (Marshall, *The Gospel of Luke*, 198).

[22] See also Luke 4:31 and 5:17 for similar references that follow Mark.

[23] J. A. Fitzmyer, *The Gospel According to Luke*, 1:860.

[24] Ibid.

[25] Ibid., 933.

[26] See Nelson Estrada's fine thesis, "A Redactional Critical Study on the Relationship of the Spirit, Proclamation, and Miracle-Working Power in Luke–Acts" (unpublished Th.M. thesis; Manila: Asia Graduate School of Theology, 1994). Estrada also argues that proclamation is the primary product of the inspiration of the Spirit in Luke–Acts.

[27] Other dimensions of God's enabling stressed by Luke include the ability to bear witness with special power and effectiveness, charismatic insight, and a special awareness of and sensitivity to God's redemptive plan.

[28] J. Bradley, "Miracles and Martyrdom in the Early Church: Some Theological and Ethical Implications," *All Together in One Place*, ed. H. Hunter and P. Hocken (Sheffield: JSOT Press, 1993), 240.

[29] Admittedly, this potential has not always been realized in Pentecostal circles.

[30] See, e.g., the comment of M. Erickson, *Christian Theology*, 881: " . . . whether the Bible teaches that the Spirit dispenses special gifts today is not an issue of great practical consequence. For even if he does, we are not to set our lives to seeking them."

[31] On the universality of the Pentecostal gift, see Menzies, *Development*, esp. 227–29.

[32] As we have noted, Luke's use of Spirit and power in Acts 1:8 suggests that this enabling will often include miracle-working power. However, the activities envisioned in this promise are broader in scope and include inspired speech and special revelation as well as miracle-working power.

[33] For a discussion of this movement see W. Menzies, *Anointed to Serve*, 321–25.

[34] See ibid., 330–35.

Chapter Eleven

Healing in the Atonement

I had always affirmed that healing flowed from the cross and, as a matter of course, regularly prayed for the sick. Yet I remember the day when I was forced to reexamine the basis of my belief and practice. A colleague asked me to present a lecture to his class on "healing in the atonement." He had watched a relative struggle with a cancer that ravaged her body. He had witnessed many prayers for healing. He knew that the one standing in need of healing and, for the most part, those who prayed on her behalf were people of strong faith. He had heard the words of encouragement and counsel. And through it all he watched this loved one die a slow and agonizing death. My colleague, a man whom I respect, asked me to present the lecture because he knew that he could not. As he witnessed his relative's suffering, he became convinced that the doctrine of healing in the atonement was flawed.

His own struggle with the doctrine, even more than the teaching assignment I accepted, presented me with a challenge. As I look back on this situation, I now see that my friend's objections to the doctrine reflect the viewpoint, and at times also the experience, of many: How can God's gift of healing be rooted in the atonement, when our experience of it is so uncertain, so limited, so infrequent?[1]

When it comes to our experience of divine forgiveness and the spiritual dimensions of salvation, my friend declared, matters are relatively clear. We respond to Christ in faith and we are saved. There are no exceptions, no delays. Christ has provided for our spiritual salvation (i.e., the forgiveness of our sins) on the cross, so we may apprehend salvation through faith. However, with physical healing it is very different. We may pray for healing in faith, but we do not always apprehend the gift. Unlike the spiritual dimensions of salvation, our experience of physical healing is sporadic and uncertain. My friend felt that the inevitable conclusion was clear: Physical healing cannot be linked to the atonement.

A sampling from any church pew will reveal that the doctrine of healing in the atonement—that is, that physical healing flows from the atoning work of Christ on the cross—continues to be a source of contention in many churches. Although Pentecostals have traditionally affirmed this doctrine, even in Pentecostal circles the doctrine has sparked controversy. There are many who speak passionately on its behalf, while others reject it outright as a dangerous misunderstanding. Why has this doctrine polarized so many?

There appear to be two reasons for this division. (1) Extreme views by some proponents of the doctrine have discredited it in the minds of many. In some circles, the doctrine means that we should all be healed here and now.[2] Healing has been provided for us, they argue; thus, it is our right and responsibility to receive it by faith. If we are not healed, then there must be something wrong with our faith, with our inability to apprehend the healing. Of course, the realities of life as well as a careful reading of Scripture speak against this simplistic approach. Nevertheless, its lingering legacy reminds us that the doctrine of healing in the atonement and its implications have not always been carefully thought through or developed in a coherent manner.[3]

(2) There is a second reason for division over this doctrine. Frequently the discussion has been shaped by differing understandings of Christ's atonement. Those opposed to the doctrine tend to focus more narrowly on the semantic range of "atonement" and related words in the Bible.[4] Thus, they generally define atonement as a "covering of sin" and interpret the significance of the cross in forensic terms. On the cross, Jesus took upon himself the sins of a guilty world. He bore the punishment that we all justly deserve. Atonement, then, has to do with eradicating the problem of sin. If one views the atonement in this way, its relationship to physical healing is easily dismissed or minimized.

The key point to note is this: How one understands the atonement will inevitably shape the way in which he or she answers the question at hand. A narrow focus on the semantic range of isolated words translated or related to "atonement" may allow one to focus exclusively on the forgiveness of sins and thereby exclude physical healing from the discussion. Yet, as Gustaf Aulen notes, this limited conception of the atonement hardly does justice to the biblical witness or to the historical understanding of the church. To this crucial point we now turn.

1. The Starting Point

We have noted that those opposed to healing in the atonement tend to understand Christ's atoning work in forensic terms as the means by which God deals with the problem of sin. The picture is that of a law court. God the Father sits before us as the wise and righteous judge. We sit in the chair of the accused and are justly declared guilty. But just when it appears our fate is sealed, God himself provides the means by which we can be declared innocent, and at the same time, the requirements of his justice are met. How does it happen? Jesus, the Righteous One, takes our place. He bears the penalty that was rightfully ours. It is a powerful picture of God's grace and one clearly traced in Scripture. This picture, rooted as it is in the imagery of the law court, has been aptly described as the forensic view of the atonement.

Beyond doubt this forensic view offers significant insights into Christ's work on the cross. But a crucial question must be raised: Does the forensic view do justice to the *full* biblical witness concerning the significance of Christ's death? Is this view alone adequate to explain the full meaning of Christ's death? In his insightful book, *Christus Victor,* Gustaf Aulen argues that this is not the case.[5] He outlines three approaches to understanding Christ's work on the cross. (1) We encounter the Latin or forensic view, just outlined. Christ as the sinless man appeases the moral demands of a righteous God. As we have noted, this viewpoint captures an important and powerful aspect of biblical teaching.

(2) There is the liberal view. Here Christ's selfless death on the cross is presented as an example of the highest form of love. Such an act calls for a response, compelling others to live in a similar way. This view, though certainly limited, adds another dimension to our understanding of the atonement, in that Christ's sacrificial death on the cross does constitute a challenging model of love. Nevertheless, Christ's death represents much more than this. It actually impacts our relationship with God. Our position before God is, through faith, fundamentally altered by virtue of Christ's sacrificial death.

(3) Aulen describes the classic view of the atonement, which he aptly terms *Christus Victor* (Christ the Victor). This view emphasizes that by virtue of his death and resurrection, Christ has overcome the powers. The cross is not simply presented as the means for dealing with the problem of sin; it is now viewed in larger terms as the point at which the powers (the powers of the devil, death, and sin) are decisively defeated. Here the cross is seen to have cosmic significance, releasing all of creation from its captors. This perspective connects the incarnation with Jesus' death by presenting Jesus' entire life and ministry, as well as his death and resurrection, as meaningful. Christ's ministry, culminating in his death and resurrection, is thus presented as a devastating defeat of the powers—a victory that liberates all of creation so that it might fulfill its God-ordained destiny. Aulen argues that this "classic" view was dominant in the early church. His book is a call to recapture this important dimension of the biblical witness concerning the atonement.

Aulen's work is significant in that it reminds us that no single view of the atonement is sufficient. The classic, Latin, and liberal views all have something important to say to us concerning the significance of Christ's death. It also serves to warn us against narrowly focusing on the semantics of one particular word group. It calls us to integrate into our discussion of the atonement other elements of the biblical witness. To sum up, the starting point for our discussion of healing in the atonement cannot simply be the lexical meaning of "atonement." If we are to do justice to the full breadth of the biblical witness, we must broaden our view and ask: What is the full significance of Christ's death on the cross? Only then can we adequately address the question at hand.

2. Healing and the Cross: Theological Reflections

We will offer three interrelated propositions that help clarify the significance of Christ's work on the cross. Together, these propositions call us to recognize that physical healing, like all of the benefits of salvation, flows from the cross.

2.1. The Cross and the Lordship of Christ

Opponents of the doctrine often make a distinction between healings sovereignly wrought by God and healing as a work of grace rooted in the cross. They acknowledge that God occasionally performs miracles of healing, but they are quick to add that this miraculous activity is rooted in the sovereign will of God. The essential point here is that healing cannot be located in the atonement; otherwise, all who are sick could, indeed should, expect to be healed. If healing is located in God's sovereign choice rather than his gracious provision, the uncertainty of healing is more easily explained.

The logic of this argument is clear enough. But it simply does not fit the New Testament data. Equally significant, the contrast between the certainty of spiritual salvation and the uncertainty of physical healing breaks down, for it rests on a false analogy. Let us examine our first proposition, one that calls into question the dichotomy between healing as a sovereign act of God and healing as a gracious gift that flows from the cross.

Proposition 1: Jesus is Lord and Savior by virtue of his work on the cross (Rev. 5:9).

The distinction between the gifts of God that flow from his sovereign choice and those that issue from Christ's atoning work is a false one. This is particularly apparent when we begin to recognize that God's reign, his sovereignty, is inextricably tied up with the cross. This is clearly stated in Revelation 5:9. The praises from the throne room in heaven resound with these words:

> *You are worthy to take the scroll*
> *and to open its seals,*
> *because you were slain,*
> *and with your blood you purchased men for God*
> *from every tribe and language and people and nation.*

Notice the link between the cross of Christ and his sovereign rule. Christ is able to take up the scroll, which represents the destiny of the nations, *because* he was slain. It is the cross, then, that leads to the praises recorded in Revelation 11:15: "The kingdom of the world has become the kingdom of our Lord and of his Christ, and he will reign for ever and ever." This message resonates well with the words of Paul in 1 Corinthians 1:24, where he describes the cross of Christ as "the power of God and the wisdom of God." Perhaps the message is nowhere so powerfully stated as in Colossians 2:13–15:

> When you were dead in your sins and in the uncircumcision of your sinful nature, God made you alive with Christ. He forgave us all our sins, having canceled the written code, with its regulations, that was against us and that stood opposed to us; he took it away, nailing it to the cross. And having disarmed the powers and authorities, he made a public spectacle of them, triumphing over them by the cross.

John in Revelation, Paul throughout his letters, and virtually the entire New Testament call us to see the cross as the center point of history, the means by which Christ defeated the power of the evil one and assumed his rightful place as sovereign Lord. All the saints who lived prior to the cross and all the events of salvation history that preceded it look forward to the cross in anticipation. Thus John speaks of the "Lamb that was slain from the creation of the world" (Rev. 13:8). And as the texts cited above indicate, all those believers and events that have followed look back to this crucial event.

The cross is indeed the central reason why Christ reigns as Lord. It should be clear, then, why distinctions between actions rooted in God's sovereignty and those rooted in the cross are meaningless. Jesus is the sovereign Lord, he acts as the King, because he is the Lamb who was slain! All of the blessings of God's reign flow from this crucial event, the center of salvation history.

2.2. The Progressive Nature of Salvation

We have noted that opponents of the doctrine of healing in the atonement see a distinction between our experience of the spiritual dimensions of salvation and our experience of physical healing. When we repent and believe, through God's transforming grace we are immediately forgiven and granted a new relationship with God. But our experience of physical healing is of a different order, more ambiguous and sporadic. Yet this argument ultimately rests on a flawed analogy. In reality, our experience of the spiritual dimensions of salvation is not so immediate and complete as we might assume. This point is elaborated in our next proposition.

Proposition 2: The salvation provided by Jesus as Lord and Savior is progressive in nature (2 Cor. 3:18).

All aspects of the blessings of the kingdom (i.e., salvation), whether spiritual or physical, are mediated to us in a progressive way. Paul makes this point powerfully in 2 Corinthians 3:18: "And we, who with unveiled faces all reflect the Lord's glory, are being transformed into his likeness with ever-increasing glory, which comes from the Lord, who is the Spirit." According to Paul, when one becomes a Christian, one embarks on a journey of transformation through the Spirit—a journey that is progressive in nature and culminates in the ultimate transformation, the resurrection of the body (1 Cor. 15:42–54). This is why Paul speaks of the gift of the Spirit as a "deposit, guaranteeing what is to come" (2 Cor. 5:5).

This, of course, indicates that it is not entirely adequate to speak of being "saved" as if salvation were apprehended in a single moment in the past. The reality is more complex: We enter into the life of the Spirit (or the kingdom) at a given point in time, but this merely constitutes the beginning of a journey whereby we are progressively transformed into his image. I like to ask my students: Do you now know Christ like you will know him in heaven? The correct answer, of course, is, "No, we do not." Just as our relationship with Christ matures and deepens, so also all of the blessings of the kingdom are progressively deepened and realized in our life.

This is true of the spiritual dimensions of salvation (e.g., our sense of sonship) as well as the physical. Remember, our ultimate goal includes a resurrected body transformed by the Spirit (1 Cor. 15:42–54). We are in the process of moving from death to life. In short, all of the dimensions of salvation are progressively appropriated and realized in our lives. Just as our present experience of the Spirit is a "deposit, guaranteeing what is to come," so also our present experience of healing is a foretaste of the glorious resurrection body that awaits us.

This, of course, does not mean that our bodies will be gradually strengthened and energized until we obtain immortality. Our bodies will grow frail and weak and ultimately die. However, in a larger sense, it is true to say that we—that is, our entire being (body and spirit)—are being transformed; we are moving toward our ultimate destiny in Christ, which includes physical wholeness. Currently, we see but a shadow, the firstfruits of the glory that awaits us. But then we will see in fullness (1 John 3:2). Although the physical transformation may be less conspicuous than the spiritual, it is nevertheless an important part of the process, an important aspect of our glorious destiny in Christ. Those who deny this physical dimension of salvation have more in common with the Gnostics than the early church.

2.3. The Cosmic Nature of Salvation

A key weakness in the perspective of those who deny healing in the atonement is a truncated view of salvation. The attempt to limit the atonement to the "spiritual" dimensions of life appears to rest in a soteriology that misses key aspects of the biblical witness. Although we commonly speak of "saving souls" and picture the future hope as disconnected from this world, in reality God's plan for his creation is far greater, far more comprehensive. This leads us to our third proposition.

Proposition 3: The salvation provided by Jesus as Lord and Savior is cosmic in nature and includes physical wholeness (Rom. 8:23; 1 Cor. 15:42–54).

God's plan for us and his world—indeed, all of creation—is breathtaking in its scope. History's end will not be complete until God accomplishes his purposes for creation, the restoration of all things. On a personal level, Paul calls us to see ourselves in the future, not as disembodied spirits floating off into an ethereal world, but rather as transformed people whose lives, including our bodies, are shaped by the Spirit—people who are whole. Thus Paul declares, "the body that is sown is perishable, it is raised imperishable; it is sown in dishonor, it is raised in glory; it is sown in weakness, it is raised in power; it is sown a natural body, it is raised a spiritual body" (1 Cor. 15:42–43). Paul gives us little reason to disregard the body as inconsequential. In fact, much of his ethical teaching that combats proto-gnostic hedonism is grounded in the importance of the body (e.g., 1 Cor. 6:12–20).

Paul also gives us little reason to disregard our world. Although popular apocalyptic sermons frequently leave us with the impression that our world should hold little concern for us (will it not all be destroyed in a massive ball of fire?), the biblical reality is far different. Paul reminds us that God is at work restoring all of creation, and his purposes will not be frustrated. The scope of his salvific work is not limited to the redemption of people (although this is indeed the centerpiece), but it includes the transformation of the world. This marvelous hope is described in Romans 8:20–22:

> The creation was subjected to frustration, not by its own choice, but by the will of the one who subjected it, in hope that the creation itself will be liberated from its bondage to decay and brought into the glorious freedom of the children of God.
>
> We know that the whole creation has been groaning as in the pains of childbirth right up to the present time.

This theme is also taken up in the book of Revelation, which pictures the future hope both in terms of continuity with this world (Rev. 20, the Millennium) and discontinuity (Rev. 21, the new heaven and new earth). John calls his church (and ours by extension) to rejoice in the hope that we await: a hope that includes the transformation of this present world, but that is so great that ultimately it transcends any of our feeble attempts to comprehend it. No, it simply will not do, to dismiss the world in which we live, *God's world*, as if it held little significance for the Creator.

The implications of the foregoing are apparent. God's purposes, his concerns, include the physical body, our environment, and the world in which we live. Thus, these dimensions of creation should also be of concern to us. Physical healing is a powerful reminder of this fact—a reminder of the holistic nature of God's redemptive purposes. And, as we have seen, the center point of God's redemptive work is the cross of Jesus Christ.

3. Healing and the Cross: Exegetical Reflections

Much of the biblical support for the above-mentioned assertions has already been discussed. In this section we will deal with one central passage not previously cited: Matthew 8:14–17.

Discussions of healing in the atonement generally begin with Isaiah 53:4–5, the Old Testament text cited in Matthew 8:14–17. These studies usually examine Isaiah's text in order to determine whether these verses have physical healing in view. Some scholars have concluded that the passage is simply a metaphor that refers to the manner in which the Messiah will bear our sins and that any link to physical healing was not a part of Isaiah's original intent. Such discussions are largely irrelevant for our purposes and need not be examined. The crucial question is this: How does Matthew understand Isaiah 53:4? His understanding need not be limited to that of Isaiah. He, like the other New Testament writers, writes in the light of the cross and the resurrection. Thus, he reads many Old Testament passages with an eye for fresh insights inspired by the Christ event.

As we examine Matthew 8:14–17, and particularly Matthew's reference to Isaiah 53:4, three important points emerge. (1) The context indisputably centers on physical healing (Matt. 8:16, "he healed all the sick") and presents this as a fulfillment of Isaiah 53:4. Thus, the fulfillment formula, so prominent in Matthew's gospel, is applied to Jesus' healing ministry.

(2) Matthew's use of "infirmities" (*asthenia*) and "diseases" (*nosos*) in Matthew 8:17 clearly points to physical healing. The term *nosos* occurs in 4:23, 24; 8:17; 9:35; 10:1 and always refers to physical maladies. The term *asthenia* is found only in this text in Matthew's Gospel, but elsewhere in the New Testament it too refers to sickness.

(3) A comparison of Matthew's citation of Isaiah 53:4 with the LXX is instructive. Matthew does not follow the Greek translation of the Hebrew

text commonly used in the Hellenistic synagogues; rather he offers his own rendering of the Hebrew text. Indeed, if Matthew had simply followed the LXX, as he often does, he could not have made the link to physical healing. The LXX renders the Hebrew loosely and interprets the text as a reference to sins. By way of contrast, Matthew "translates independently in order to make the quotation apply to physical maladies cured by Jesus."[6]

Matthew 8:17 (lit. trans.)	Isaiah 53:4 (lit. trans. of LXX)
In this way the word spoken through the prophet Isaiah was fulfilled, "He took up our infirmities and carried our diseases."	He bears our *sins*, and is pained for us.

In other words, regardless of how Isaiah understood Isaiah 53:4, Matthew understood it messianically and applied it to the healing ministry of Jesus. In so doing, Matthew, writing after the cross and the resurrection, bears witness to the faith of the early church. Matthew 8:14–17 establishes that the early church understood Isaiah 53:4–5 as a messianic prophecy fulfilled in Jesus' atoning work on the cross (cf. 1 Peter 2:24) and, furthermore, that his prophecy included the gift of physical healing.

If we place Matthew 8:17 in the larger context of Matthew's Gospel, we can see its full significance. It is more than simply a description of Jesus' earthly ministry in terms of healing; rather, it is Matthew's summary of the significance of Jesus' messianic mission, which culminates on the cross. Matthew presents Jesus as the Messiah in word (chapters 5–7) and deed (chapters 8–9), and he connects this to the ongoing mission of the disciples (10:1–11:1). Jesus is the Messiah-King, who ushers in the kingdom of God. The blessings of God's reign flow from the cross and are multifaceted. The salvation the Messiah-King brings includes physical wholeness; and healing now, as during the ministry of Jesus, is a testimony to this fact.[7]

4. Conclusion

We have argued that healing, as every good gift from God, is mediated to us by virtue of Christ's work on the cross. Although this does not encourage us to disregard the complexities of our life between the ages—this present evil age and the age to come, which has already broken into our world in Jesus—and to demand in simplistic fashion that all receive physical healing now, it does call us to recognize that God is vitally concerned with all of his creation, including our bodies. This in turn challenges us, as do the words of James in James 5:13–16, to take an aggressive posture when it comes to physical suffering. The church is called to pray for the sick to be healed and to come against physical suffering.[8] Indeed, unless God directs otherwise, we are called to do just this.

A biblical approach, then, to the ministry of healing in the church should begin by identifying with the revealed will of God to move against physical suffering. This means actively identifying people with specific needs and praying earnestly for them. Occasions in the life of the church that provide for anointing with oil and gathering church elders together to pray for the afflicted represent a clearly biblical method for engaging physical suffering in a concrete way. Prayer for the sick by the church elders, including anointing with oil, is a beginning. Intercession for healing should follow. This continued engagement with the mystery of suffering should be discontinued only when the spiritual leaders in the community of faith surrounding the sick person have a collective sense that God is not going to bring deliverance in this instance. At this point, and only at this point, is it appropriate to pray a prayer of relinquishment.

Pentecostals, who see themselves as ministering between the times, recognize that there is a mystery between the brokenness of a fallen world and the in-breaking of God's future full redemption. In this interim, believers are called upon to move against sin and suffering. Yet, as we have noted, it is a mixed age, and we still see only through a glass darkly. People still die; in fact, this is the destiny of all living unless the Lord returns quickly. Our age is indeed marked by brokenness. But, healings, even if they are not routine, are an announcement that Christ did triumph at the cross and that ultimately he will restore all things. Rather than complain when all are not healed, we should rejoice when *any* are healed! Many Evangelicals (and many Pentecostals, too) are too quick to pray in a resigned fashion.

The doctrine of healing in the atonement not only calls us to take an aggressive posture toward physical suffering, it also challenges us to see the largeness of God's cosmic plan and concern. God is concerned about the physical dimensions of life, about physical suffering, and about the world he created. Healing, although but a foretaste of the ultimate transformation we await, is a powerful reminder of this larger purpose. It serves, then, as a catalyst for our involvement in Christ's ministry to a broken world.

Study Questions

1. Why has the doctrine of healing in the atonement been so controversial?
2. Why is the *Christus Victor* dimension of the atonement so important to our discussion?

3. Some seek to distinguish between healing as a result of God's sovereign will and healing as a result of the cross. Why does Menzies feel this is a false dichotomy?

4. Some have rejected the doctrine because, unlike our prayers for forgiveness, our prayers for healing, even when offered with a sincere heart, are not always answered. How does Menzies deal with this objection?

5. Does the doctrine of healing in the atonement necessarily imply that all may or should expect to be healed here and now?

6. How does the doctrine of healing in the atonement as presented here impact our posture toward prayer for the sick?

7. What is the significance of this doctrine for our understanding of God's plan? The nature of salvation? The mission of the church?

Notes

[1] This concern clearly led John Wilkinson, in his article "Physical Healing and the Atonement," *EvQ* 63 (1991): 149–67, to reject the doctrine. See also the similar concerns expressed by David Petts in his essay, "Healing and the Atonement," *EPTA Bulletin* 12 (1993): 23–37 (esp. 34).

[2] For a helpful overview of the history of the doctrine, see Wilkinson, "Physical Healing," 149–54.

[3] The Assemblies of God Statement of Fundamental Truths #12 reads: "Divine healing is an integral part of the gospel. Deliverance from sickness is provided for in the atonement, and is the privilege of all believers (Isa. 53:4–5; Mt. 8:16–17; James 5:14–16)." The phrase, "the privilege of all believers" is somewhat ambiguous.

[4] See, e.g., the discussions of Wilkinson, "Physical Healing," 156–59; John R. W. Stott, *The Cross of Christ* (Downers Grove, Ill.: InterVarsity, 1986), 244–45. Key terms in the New Testament include *hilastērion* ("sacrifice of atonement" or "propitiation," Rom. 3:25) and *lytron* ("ransom," Mark 10:45).

[5] Gustaf Aulen, *Christus Victor: An Historical Study of the Three Main Types of the Idea of the Atonement*, trans. by A. G. Hebert (London: SPCK, 1931).

[6] Robert Gundry, *Matthew: A Commentary on His Literary and Theological Art* (Grand Rapids: Eerdmans, 1981), 150.

[7] Why does God heal? In the ministry of Christ, sometimes Jesus healed for no other apparent reason than out of compassion for human suffering (Matt. 14:14; 20:34). There is another objective that appears, not only in the ministry of Jesus but in the bold outreach of the apostolic church. The healing of the sick and the deliverance of oppressed people are frequently cited as drawing attention to the person of Christ and thus become an important key to effective evangelism. It does seem that there are more healings at the frontiers of faith than in comfortable, routine Christian settings. Evidently the supernatural intervention of God is linked to the cause of world mission.

[8] There are actually three ways biblically that God is pictured as healing people in our age. (1) There is the providential intervention of God out of his unfathomable grace. In many instances, no human instrumentality can be discerned; God just breaks

in. (2) Healing is listed in the catalog of charismatic gifts (1 Cor. 12:9). God does seem to give a special ministry in praying effectively for the sick to some within the circle of faith. (3) In answer to the prayer of faith of elders, in the routine gathering together of believers, God is often pleased to intervene. This is an act of obedience, mixed with faith (James 5:13–16).

Chapter Twelve

The Providence of God

Pentecostals have been frequently chided for failing to develop an adequate theology of suffering. Our theology has appropriately and correctly emphasized the dynamic presence and power of God active in the lives of Christians. We have rarely, however, developed the breadth of perspective needed to handle suffering. In the minds of many, Pentecostals have a theology of glory, but not a theology of the cross.[1]

Although these criticisms can be overstated, most would agree that Pentecostals do need to think more deeply, more carefully about suffering. This chapter represents an attempt to do just this. Furthermore, I am convinced that this goal is best achieved by way of reflection on the providence of God.

When we speak of the providence of God, we simply affirm that God protects, guides, and cares for believers. Many of us can look back to moments in our lives when we sensed God's intervention, when we felt his hand holding us up so that we were not shattered by the chaotic events around us, when we felt his protective power—sometimes in truly miraculous ways. On other occasions we have sensed that God has ordered the events of the day, bringing unanticipated opportunities for service our way. Although the details of our lives are quite different, most Christians unequivocally affirm that God does indeed care for us in unique and wonderful ways.

Yet how do we affirm the truth of God's providence, the reality of his intimate involvement in our lives, in the context of the pain and suffering we see around us and experience in our own lives? How do we, on the one hand, rejoice in divine protection from that fatal crash and, on the other hand, make sense of the suffering of those who were not so blessed?

This question was posed to me several years ago by a missionary friend. My friend is a medical doctor, the former editor of a journal devoted to medical insurance issues, and a man of deep faith. During one conversation, he raised a probing question. "I believe that God guides, protects, and provides for his children. He cares for us. I firmly believe this," my friend declared. "But as a medical person and an expert in medical insurance matters, I also know that if God intervened in the life of just one out of ten Christians— extending their life through miraculous protection—this would be statistically significant. Insurance companies would reflect this fact in their statistical analyses, policies, and rates. But this is not what we find. The research indicates that, apart from matters of choice (e.g., whether one chooses to smoke, drink, etc.), there is no significant difference in the life span and disease rates of believers and unbelievers. How do we reconcile this fact with our belief in the providence of God?"

As I wrestled with this question, I immediately began to think of Mark's Gospel, particularly his account of the transfiguration. Does God protect, guide, and provide? If so, why is it not more apparent? I believe that Mark 9:2–10 helps us answer this question. In this passage Mark describes the transfiguration of Jesus. But he does so with a pedagogical or teaching motive, to teach us lessons of discipleship. Specifically, as we see how God reveals his glory in and through Jesus, as we see how he works in the life of Jesus, we come to learn important lessons concerning how he desires to work in and through our lives. Here is the text (using the NRSV):

> Six days later, Jesus took with him Peter and James and John, and led them up a high mountain apart, by themselves. And he was transfigured before them, and his clothes became dazzling white, such as no one on earth could bleach them. And there appeared to them Elijah with Moses, who were talking with Jesus. Then Peter said to Jesus, "Rabbi, it is good for us to be here; let us make three dwellings, one for you, one for Moses, and one for Elijah." He did not know what to say, for they were terrified. Then a cloud overshadowed them, and from the cloud there came a voice, "This is my Son, the Beloved; listen to him!" Suddenly when they looked around, they saw no one with them any more, but only Jesus.
>
> As they were coming down the mountain, he ordered them to tell no one about what they had seen, until after the Son of Man had risen from the dead. So they kept the matter to themselves, questioning what this rising from the dead could mean.

These verses present two perspectives on God's care: One is Peter's view, the view from the mountaintop; the other is the perspective of Jesus, the view from the valley.

1. The View from the Mountaintop

Peter's perspective is given voice in verse 5: "Rabbi, it is good for us to be here." Peter is awed by the awesome display of glory (who can blame him?).

In fact, he is so awed that he suggests that they all stay on the mountain. This is the point of his remark concerning building tents. Peter's words might be paraphrased like this: "Forget the journey down the mountain to Jerusalem with all of its potential for trouble. Let's stay here. The nations will see the glory of the Lord. They will come to us. Let's establish our headquarters here."

It is apparent that Peter's perspective is limited at best and self-centered at worst. Note how Mark characterizes Peter's words as a gaffe produced by fear (v. 6). Peter here still appears to have in mind not "the things of God but the things of men" (cf. 8:33). His reaction is a classic example of what I call the "Three Stooges" motif in Mark's Gospel.

Throughout Mark's Gospel the disciples, and especially Peter, are constantly bungling, constantly misunderstanding what Jesus is up to. It seems that Jesus, at almost every step, must correct or rebuke them. A clear pattern emerges.

- Mark 7:18: "Are you so dull?" The disciples fail to understand Jesus' words about "uncleanness."
- Mark 8:21: "Do you still not understand?" The disciples fail to understand Jesus' words about "the yeast of the Pharisees."
- Mark 8:33: "Get behind me, Satan!" Jesus rebukes Peter for suggesting he need not suffer.
- Mark 9:10: The disciples fail to understand Jesus' comments concerning "rising from the dead."
- Mark 9:32: The disciples do not understand that Jesus must suffer.
- Mark 10:35: James and John seek their own glory and do not understand what it means to follow Jesus.
- Mark 14:41: "Are you still sleeping?" The disciples fall asleep while Jesus prays at Gethsemane.
- Mark 14:50: "Everyone deserted him and fled." Jesus is utterly abandoned when arrested.
- Mark 14:68: Peter disowns Jesus.

This motif becomes especially meaningful when we remember that, as Papias states, Mark passes on to us the memoirs of Peter.[2] All of the bungling, all of the mistakes—it is as if Peter is calling us to learn from his past.

Well, once again in Mark 9:5, Peter misses the point. Once again Peter's perspective is shortsighted. It is, however, so human that all of us can identify with it. All of us long for God's glory to be revealed visibly and powerfully in our lives. We long for his healing power to flow through us to bring healing and grace to others. We long for his glory to be revealed in a dazzling display of power.

Yet here we see that the mountaintop experience is intentionally short-lived; it gives way (as it must) to the experience of the valley. Certainly we can be thankful for those moments when the dazzling display occurs, when God's glory is made visible. However, the dazzling display of glory, wonderful though it may be, is not the primary way God has chosen to reveal himself, either in Jesus or in us.

2. The View from the Valley

As we look to the valley and the perspective of Christ, we see three truths about God's providential care.

2.1. The Goal of God's Care

Peter had wanted Jesus to stay on the mountain, but in Mark 9:9 we read that Jesus descended from the mountain into the valley. The travel notice comes almost as an aside, "As they were coming down the mountain...." In this brief remark we see the difference between the perspective of Peter and that of Jesus. Peter is still focused on "the things of men." Jesus, however, is committed to his Father's redemptive plan. He understands the *true goal* of God's care. Jesus sees that the goal of God's providential care is not necessarily his well-being here and now; rather, the goal of God's care is that the Father's redemptive plan might be fulfilled.

This insight helps us understand why God's protective care is not immediately obvious to the world, why statistically Christians may not fare better than non-Christians. Although as Christians we sometimes do experience God's protection, at other times we experience suffering and hardship because we are seeking to follow Christ; our experiences of both protection and suffering are a result of his ordering of events. Both are arranged to further his redemptive plan.

This is an important lesson, for when we understand the goal of God's providential care, then we can begin to see the fullness of God's working in our lives. We can sense his working in the difficult circumstances as well as the good. We can look with expectancy and thanksgiving for his guidance in the midst of tragedy as well as good fortune.

We often think that difficult circumstances come our way in order to prepare us for God's future work. But is it not also true that frequently it is in the midst of difficulty that God's power is most beautifully displayed (cf. 2 Cor. 12:7–10)? Let us be mindful that the goal of God's care is not our well-being, but his glory.

2.2. The Character of God's Care

As Jesus and the disciples walk down the mountain, Jesus orders them "not to tell anyone what they had seen until the Son of Man had risen from the dead" (Mark 9:9). Jesus orders silence. Why? Why not let the nations know of his glory? I believe that Peter's misunderstanding provides the clue. If Peter and the disciples—those who had lived with Jesus, who had seen the miracles, and who had heard his teaching—if they had a hard time understanding the nature of the kingdom (and we know they did, as Acts 1:6 clearly indicates), how much more the crowds? The call to silence reminds us of a startling fact: Jesus intentionally veiled his glory.

If Jesus veiled his glory, should we assume that it will be any different with us? Should we not expect that God's providential care in our lives will also be intentionally veiled? This appears to be the manner in which God often chooses to work. Although God is unfolding his plan through our lives, this incredible divine action is not necessarily visible to the world. His care is usually veiled.

Here again we see why statistics cannot capture God's care. Imagine for a moment what would happen if Christians really did lead charmed lives. What if Christians really did live longer than non-Christians? What if our insurance rates really were lower than the rates of the unbelieving masses? What would the church look like? It is unlikely that the Church would be strengthened by this public display of glory. Rather, it would be filled with "sign-seekers," people obsessed with their own well-being and clueless concerning "the things of God."

Perhaps here we see why God intentionally hides or veils his glory. He does it so that his glory is discernible only through the eyes of faith. Mark calls us to look at the events of our lives not merely in a superficial way, not merely focusing on the outer circumstances, but to look deeper with eyes of faith and to see God's steadying hand at work. His care is there, though not visible to all and, indeed, often missed by us.

2.3. The Reality of God's Care

As the disciples move down the mountain, they discuss "what rising from the dead" might mean (Mark 9:10). Of course we, the readers, who know how the story ends, cannot help but chuckle at this line. Boy, are the disciples in for a big surprise! Here I see a reminder that God does order our lives and that he delights to bring surprises our way. Just as God brought about the ultimate surprise in the resurrection—life from death, what greater reversal of events can be imagined?—so also he delights to bring unexpected opportunities into our lives as well.

God orders the events of our lives so that we may bring him glory, so that his plan may be fulfilled in our lives. He delights to bring about unusual, unexpected events through which we can extend the kingdom. Of course, it takes faith to see his hand at work. His work is not obvious to all, perhaps least of all to us. But because God does order our lives, we can live with a sense of expectation that he will regularly bring "delightful surprises" into our lives. And when our vision is broad and clear and not narrowly focused on dazzling displays of power, we can see the richness, the fullness of his providential care. Then we will see his hand in all kinds of circumstances, good and bad. Then we will recognize the many "delightful surprises" he brings our way.

3. Conclusion

Pentecostals have tended to feature the dazzling displays of God's glory, the mountaintop experiences. Perhaps this is why Pentecostals have not always been good at seeing the full range of God's providential care. This may also be the reason why we, like Peter and the disciples, have often failed to understand the goal of God's care. Mark, who offers insights from the memoirs of Peter, calls us to learn from the mistakes of the disciples and to grasp hold of the true goal of God's care. He calls us to see that God orders the events of our lives not simply for our well-being, but so that his redemptive purposes may be fulfilled.

Mark also encourages us to see the true character of God's care, that although dazzling displays may come our way, this is not the normal way God reveals his glory. It was not the way he normally worked in and through Jesus, and it is not his usual method for us. Although we can rejoice when the dazzling displays come, our expectation and vision must be broader. We need to cultivate the ability to anticipate and rejoice in the many "delightful surprises" that come our way, those unexpected and seemingly ordinary events in our lives that bear the mark of his loving hand. We also need to cultivate the ability to see that sometimes God speaks loudest to us through suffering, for through times of weakness comes the necessity of leaning most heavily on the gracious hand of God.

Study Questions

1. Why have Pentecostals generally not been good at dealing with suffering?
2. Menzies speaks of the "Three Stooges" motif in Mark. What does he mean? How does this shed light on Peter's response in Mark 9:5–6?

3. What is the central weakness of Peter's perspective? Why is Jesus' view so radically different?
4. Why is grasping the purpose of God's care so crucial? How does it impact our faith, our sense of expectation? How does it help us deal more adequately with suffering?
5. Menzies suggests that we should give thanks for the dazzling displays of God's glory, but God normally does not reveal himself in this way. How does God normally reveal his glory in and through our lives?

Notes

[1] One of the important themes that runs through the theology of Martin Luther is the set of opposites known as the "theology of glory" and the "theology of grace." By the first term, Luther sought to identify the self-assertive triumphalism that tends to infect much of religion. The latter term points away from humanity to the source of all our blessings, to the grace that centers in the cross of Christ.

[2] Papias, the bishop of Hierapolis, cites the testimony of an elder concerning the association between Mark and Peter: "Mark, having become the interpreter of Peter, wrote down accurately whatever he remembered of the things said and done by the Lord" (Eusebius *Hist. Eccl.* 3.39.15).

Chapter Thirteen

Spiritual Gifts:
Essential Principles

Many churches take their names from places in the Bible. Bethanys, Bereans, and Antiochs dot the landscape. But I have yet to find a church named after Corinth. The First Corinthian Baptist Church, it just doesn't happen. And for good reason: The church at Corinth was riddled with problems. Who wants to identify with such an infamous church? Divisions, sexual immorality, lawsuits, heretical teaching—the church there had it all. This makes Paul's words in 1 Corinthians 1:4–7 all the more remarkable:

> I always thank God for you because of his grace given you in Christ Jesus. For in him you have been enriched in every way—in all your speaking and in all your knowledge—because our testimony about Christ was confirmed in you. Therefore you do not lack any spiritual gift as you eagerly wait for our Lord Jesus Christ to be revealed.

"You do not lack any spiritual gift." These words are particularly striking. Did Paul get the address wrong? Is he really writing to the church at Corinth? Most of us would have simply dismissed the Corinthians as devoid of spiritual qualities.

But that is not Paul's perspective. He will not deny that the church possessed spiritual gifts. He refuses to denigrate the gifts even though clearly the church had much to learn in its exercise of them. All of this highlights the importance that the apostle attached to spiritual gifts. If gifts were so significant in his sight, certainly they should be in ours. Yet 1 Corinthians reminds us that gifts do not come without the possibility of abuse or misunderstanding. How can we see God's gifts used in such a way that truly brings glory to him, in such a way that truly builds up the body of Christ? I would like to answer this question by focusing on three principles found in 1 Corinthians 12:1–11.

1. The Grace Principle

Gifts are not a badge of spiritual maturity (1 Cor. 12:4).

In 1 Corinthians 12:1, Paul begins to address questions pertaining to spiritual gifts raised by members of the church at Corinth in their letter to him (cf. 1 Cor. 7:1). It is instructive to note that Paul begins by using what was likely the Corinthian term for spiritual gifts, *pneumatika*. This term builds on the root word *pneuma*, the Greek word for "Spirit." The term *pneumatika* literally refers to "the things of the Spirit" and highlights the association between the Spirit and spiritual gifts. The Corinthians apparently viewed the gifts—particularly the more demonstrative ones, such as speaking in tongues—as a mark of spirituality, a sign of the Spirit's inspiration. But Paul quickly shifts from this Corinthian language to the term of his preference, *charismata* ("gifts," 12:4). This word builds on *charis*, the Greek word for "grace." With this shift in vocabulary, Paul skillfully emphasizes that spiritual gifts are, above all, gifts of grace.

This subtle shift in terminology reflects an important aspect of Paul's perspective. Gifts of the Spirit are not a badge of spiritual maturity. Rather than marking one off as a member of the spiritual elite, spiritual gifts are a reflection of God's grace to the church and made available to every believer. Paul's description of the immature Corinthians as a church that did not lack any spiritual gift (1 Cor. 1:7) highlights this truth. Although spiritual maturity through a life of love may enable one to exercise the gifts in a more effective and edifying manner (cf. ch. 13), spiritual gifts are not reserved for those who are spiritually mature. The whole thrust of Paul's argument in chapters 12–14 suggests that gifts are freely given by God to every believer (12:11).

Paul's perspective is unambiguous: Christians do not have to attain some level of holiness or spirituality in order to receive spiritual gifts. Thus, spiritual gifts do not serve as a badge of spiritual maturity. Some in the church at Corinth appear to have adopted this position, and this is precisely the sort of elitist understanding of the gifts that Paul seeks to correct.

I remember as a young boy attending a series of evangelistic meetings held in my home town. The meetings were dynamic and inevitably included extended times of prayer at the altar. A number of people made public professions of faith, and there were many reports of healing. Several weeks after the meetings ended, we received word that the evangelist who apparently had been so mightily used by God had been living an immoral life. This news disturbed me and raised numerous questions. Were the spiritual gifts I had witnessed genuine? Had God used this man to touch others in spite of his own weakness? I asked my father what he thought, and I still remember his response, "Spiritual gifts are not necessarily given to those who are spiritually mature." This response, I believe, captures well a central thrust of Paul's teaching.[1]

This response has two significant implications for the life of the church today. (1) The fact that spiritual giftedness is not necessarily linked to spiritual maturity serves as a warning against being too awed by displays of spiritual power. Spiritual gifts are not necessarily a mark of spiritual leadership. Thus, churches should be careful not to accept gifts as the chief criterion for leadership. On a personal or individual level, we should be careful not to equate our giftedness with spiritual depth. Pride was at the heart of the problems at Corinth, and it is equally dangerous today.

(2) The fact that God freely bestows his gift to believers—even to those of us who are far from perfect—should encourage us to be open to the gifts God might bring our way. If gifts are granted only to the mature or the spiritual elite, few of us would qualify. It is all too easy to dismiss our role in the life of the church with depreciating thoughts of personal inadequacy. How can God use me? After all, I have my own problems, my own spiritual struggles. But the liberating message of Paul meets us precisely at this point. In spite of our weakness, God delights to use us to bless others. God delights to lavish his gifts of grace on us. So Paul encourages the entire church, not simply the leaders or the spiritual elite, to "eagerly desire spiritual gifts" (1 Cor. 14:1).

2. The Edification Principle

Gifts are given so that we may edify others (1 Cor. 12:7).

The Corinthians had lost sight of the true purpose of spiritual gifts. Thus, Paul's corrective includes clarification of this important point. The message is communicated throughout 1 Corinthians 12–14, but nowhere more clearly than in 12:7: "Now to each one the manifestation of the Spirit is given for the common good." Spiritual gifts are given so the body of Christ may be built up. In a word, edification is the goal. This is why in chapter 14 Paul encourages the Corinthians to value prophecy over speaking in tongues in the corporate setting: "He who speaks in a tongue edifies himself, but he who prophesies edifies the church" (1 Cor. 14:4). In the assembly, prophecy is greater because it is consistent with this magnificent goal. It builds up the church.

An important corollary flows from this central point: Gifts are to be exercised and evaluated with the edification of the body in view. Is the utterance really an inspired word? Was the gift exercised in a proper way? The key to answering these questions is found in this simple question, this fundamental standard: Did the gift edify the church?

I remember one well-meaning gentleman who frequently, in a rather bombastic manner, marched to the front of the church and issued in authoritative tones his "prophetic" message. After this happened on several occasions, people began to feel a bit uncomfortable with these displays. They began to inquire how they should respond to his utterances. The content of the messages was rather innocuous. They certainly did not contain outright heresy, although the words were often couched in language that was not appropriate to the setting. The key problem was that, generally, the messages were simply not edifying. Eventually the leadership encouraged the man to submit his prophecies to one of the elders prior to making them public. This was intended to help him learn how to exercise the gift in an edifying way. The decision was appropriately made on the basis of this key Pauline principle, and the result was positive.

On many occasions I have witnessed the beauty and power of Spirit-inspired words of encouragement. When a group of believers gathers together, frequently a word is given, often from an unexpected source, which ministers precisely to the needs of those present. This sort of prophetic utterance is generally unanticipated and offers encouragement appropriate to the situation and specific to the setting. It is beautiful to see how the Spirit blesses the body through its individual members. Paul was much aware of the church's need of this kind of spontaneous, Spirit-inspired edification. He understood that edification was its chief goal. Perhaps this is also why he highlighted the necessity of love (1 Cor. 13). Love is not "self-seeking"; rather, it seeks the good of others. Paul recognized that when gifts are exercised in the context of love, this goal will certainly be achieved.

3. The Participation Principle

Everyone has something to contribute (1 Cor. 12:11).

Finally, Paul reminds us that everyone has a role to play in the body of Christ. No one is excluded from the dynamic interplay produced by the Spirit that edifies the church. In 1 Corinthians 12:11 Paul declares: "All these are the work of one and the same Spirit, and he gives them to each one, just as he determines." The implications of this verse ("he gives them to *each one*") are fleshed out in the "body metaphor" that follows: Everyone has an important contribution to make.

Why is God not more selective? How is it that he uses everyone, including those of us who have shortcomings and weaknesses? Because God delights to give gifts. He longs to use us to encourage and build up others. The important corollary should be obvious: We should seek to be used by God. Indeed, as Paul implores, "eagerly desire spiritual gifts" (1 Cor. 14:1).

At this point, perhaps a word of caution is needed. It is often easy to get hung up on which of the gifts we have or should have. As we analyze our situation and compare ourselves with others, we needlessly waste energy and time in activities that are not helpful. My advice is this: Rather than analyzing the nature of your gifting, simply respond to needs around you. Bathe this activity in prayer. Ask for the Lord's guidance and power; but, by all means, respond to needs. Step out in areas of service and ministry and see what God will do.

When we do this we will find that God's gifts are not limited to a select list. Certainly the gift list in 1 Corinthians 12:8–10 is not an exhaustive list, but merely a sampling of the gifts, a sampling "taken from an infinite supply."[2] How many gifts are there? There are as many gifts available as there are needs in the life of the church. God delights to use us to meet these needs.

The Corinthians remind us that it is also possible to become preoccupied with the spectacular or supernatural character of spiritual gifts. Of course some spiritual gifts are more spectacular than others, and at Corinth pride of place was given to these gifts, particularly the public manifestation of tongues. Nevertheless, Paul clearly states that all of the gifts originate from the same Spirit and thus all are, in some sense, supernatural in character.

It may be possible to draw a continuum of the gifts, moving from those gifts that involve more natural ability and less supernatural power (e.g., gifts of administration) to those which have little or no human element and are overtly supernatural (e.g., gifts of healing). But regardless of how Paul's gift lists are analyzed, it is evident that for him all of the gifts—whether they be natural talents dedicated to God and thus heightened or strengthened by the Spirit or gifts that require God's dynamic intervention in a particularly visible way—all of the gifts flow from the Spirit, are intended to meet concrete needs, and thus are important to the life of the church. Perhaps the key question to ask is not, What gifts do I have? but rather, What need does God want me to meet?

4. A Postscript on Gifts and Worship

The most important teaching in the New Testament on the proper use of gifts of the Spirit is found in 1 Corinthians 12–14. It is significant that the setting in which gifts are pictured is the church gathered for worship. Certainly there are occasions when gifts of the Spirit operate outside the worship setting, but it is clearly within the worshiping community that the manifestations of the Spirit are expected to occur with some regularity.

The vocabulary Paul uses for expressing the way the Holy Spirit moves among the people of God is instructive. The expression "different kinds of gifts" (1 Cor. 12:4) focuses attention not on the gift as a thing deposited, but on the source of this outpouring of grace. Throughout the passage, the word *dōron*, the Greek term employed for bestowing on an individual a thing or an object in the sense that it is possessed by the recipient, is notably missing. Paul uses terms such as "manifestation" (v. 7) to describe how the Spirit works. And it is the sovereign Spirit who chooses when and how the *charismata* will function and, in fact, through whom the blessing may flow to the gathered body.

What we see, then, is that attention is centered on the corporate sphere in which the Spirit functions rather than on individuals who "own" one or more gifts. In a real sense, the gifts are the possession of the body of believers more than of specific individuals within the group. The Spirit is in charge! And the worshiping body is the arena in which the Spirit speaks and moves among the people of God.

This emphasis is important for preventing an unwarranted spiritual elitism. If one has entered by faith into the manifestation of a gift of the Spirit, on another occasion that individual may find it easier to exercise that gift, having already experienced this ministry previously. Eventually one may learn to cultivate an openness to the nudging of the Holy Spirit and thus to develop grace in the manifestation of that particular gift over time. Rather than saying that this person possesses such and such a gift, is it not more biblical to report that this individual has cultivated a ministry in the gift? In effect, the individual is possessed by the Spirit for ministry rather than the individual possessing a gift of the Spirit.

This concept fits well with the clear intention of Paul to elevate worship above ritual and religious routine. The emphasis on variety opens the door to others entering into ministries of the Spirit, rather than a group of believers depending on one or two known practitioners who have been known to exhibit frequently a given manifestation of the Spirit. The emphasis should be on spontaneity and freshness. Could it be that God may choose to use me in this service today to bless the group?

That Paul considered the worship of the church to embrace more than the subjective manifestations of the Spirit is evident from passages such as 1 Timothy 4:11–16. In this cluster of admonitions, Paul instructs his younger colleague, among other matters, to seek a balance between the objective and the subjective, between the reading and teaching of Scripture and the manifestation of spiritual gifts.

Luke does something similar in Acts 13:1–3. The church in Antioch is pictured as being comprised of three emphases:

verse 1: the church's ministering to believers through prophets (those
whose ministries were spontaneous, immediate, and unstudied, clearly
embracing the category we call "gifts of the Spirit") and teachers (the
didactic role requiring study of the Scriptures and the ability to expli-
cate the objective teaching contained therein);

verse 2: the church's ministering to the Lord in worship;

verse 3: the church's addressing the world.

The picture presented here is of a church exhibiting the functions of inter-
nal nurturing and of worshiping, and out of this edifying environment, a
people called to serve as missionaries beyond their borders. The principle is
clear: The ideal church, as pictured in Antioch, is a learning center, but more
than a school. It is a worship center. It is not to be content with its own blessing but is called to serve those outside. Edification and worship are integrally
linked with reaching the lost of this world. Worship and missions coalesce in
a truly spiritual church.

A mystery in God's dispensing of spiritual gifts is that these treasures are
contained in "jars of clay" (2 Cor. 4:7). Adding to the surprise is that the
prophetic utterances for the blessing of the gathered worshipers is a phenomenon that admits of a human component. It is within the province of the
one who has a manifestation of the Spirit to choose at what point his or her
contribution will be most edifying (1 Cor. 14:32). Paul admonishes his readers to exercise restraint as they operate in the gifts, acknowledging that
prophetic utterances must be limited (14:26–28). This is the wonder that God
the Spirit should minister through jars of clay!

This is all the more reason that believers are called to humility in speaking of the operation of the gifts of the Spirit. It is his grace that he chooses
to use any of us at all! Exercising the gifts does not announce to the congregation that an individual is more pious than others, only that that individual
has had faith to be used of God, that he or she is available for divine service.[3]

Because of the propensity of the Holy Spirit to intervene in worship settings, interventions that by their very character are spontaneous, Pentecostals
tend to plan worship services with a degree of tentativeness. Following the
guidelines of such passages as 1 Timothy 4:11–16, a basic form of worship
service is usually arranged so that the participants have a general sense of what
to expect. The service makes room for prayer, for the preaching of the Word,
for singing, and frequently for sharing testimonies. At the conclusion of most
services an altar call is given, so that the goal of the preaching can be sealed
with a season of prayer, usually around the front of the auditorium. It is during this time that special requests may be ministered to, accompanied by

anointing the sick with oil and believers gathering about the individual, by laying on of hands, and by interceding. Those desiring to be baptized in the Spirit are likewise surrounded by believers to provide a supporting environment of faith.

What is conspicuous in the order of service, however predictable the outlines may be, is that at any time—even on occasion during the preaching of a sermon—there may be a divine interruption. This may be an utterance in the Spirit, sometimes a word of prophecy in the vernacular, sometimes an utterance in tongues, followed by an interpretation. That the manifestations of the Spirit are administered through frail human vessels requires astute spiritual leadership in such meetings.

First Corinthians 14:29 indicates that the manifestations of the Spirit, mediated as they are through human instruments, require others to judge. This means that when a manifestation that is discerned by the spiritual leadership to be of the flesh and not edifying, not of the Spirit, such behavior is to be corrected. This discipline is to teach the fellowship and to make clear that not everything purporting to be of the Spirit is really valid. By exercising prudence in this matter of spiritual oversight, excesses are controlled and error is corrected.

Some are inclined to say that if these manifestations are subject to such abuse, why bother with them at all? Are they really necessary? The answer is evident from Scripture. The picture of the apostolic church is a church that did not despise prophesying, a church that sought to make room for the moving of the Holy Spirit.

By the end of the first century, a problem churches were facing was how to recognize true itinerant prophets from self-serving hucksters of religion. A study of the following centuries discloses that the church routinized the offices and ministries of the Spirit and rid itself of the spontaneous element of public worship. Few would report that the medieval church was improved by this excision. So it has always been. Things of the Spirit (*pneumatika*) are precious and easily abused. Is it not a higher ideal to emulate the apostolic church and to learn how to nurture spiritual manifestations, allowing for the very real possibility of occasional human mistakes along the way?

5. Conclusion

God doesn't have to use us. He could use others. But remarkably and wonderfully, he delights in using us. Thus, he calls us to participate in his work and equips us for this task. Paul's discussion of spiritual gifts encourages us to live with a sense of expectancy, a sense that God will use us to meet the pressing needs around us. The stance of the Christian, every Christian, should be one of expectancy, asking God, How are you going to bless others through my life this day?

Study Questions

1. Are gifts of the Spirit only granted to people who are spiritually mature?
2. How do we know whether an utterance or a particular gift is truly of the Spirit?
3. Are gifts of the Spirit limited to a select few within the church?
4. What does the author mean by the principle of "balance" in the operation of the gifts of the Spirit in the worship setting?
5. Why does the author insist that a gift of the Spirit is not "owned" by an individual?
6. Why is spiritual oversight important in settings where manifestations of the Spirit are encouraged?
7. If the operation of spiritual gifts is so problematic, why not just get rid of them? Would it not be much easier if the church did not have to bother with such matters?

Notes

[1] For further reading on this topic see John White, *When the Spirit Comes with Power: Signs and Wonders Among God's People* (Downers Grove, Ill.: InterVarsity, 1988).

[2] Stanley Horton, *What the Bible Says About the Holy Spirit* (Springfield, Mo.: Gospel, 1976), 209.

[3] See David Lim, *Spiritual Gifts: A Fresh Look* (Springfield, Mo.: Gospel, 1991). This is an excellent handbook for those interested in pursuing the topic of the operation of the gifts of the Spirit, combining biblical exegesis and practical insights.

Chapter Fourteen

Baptism in the Spirit and Spiritual Gifts

Since the earliest days of the modern Pentecostal revival, Pentecostals have advocated a baptism in the Holy Spirit distinct from conversion (Acts 1:5, 8; 2:4) and the present reality of spiritual gifts (1 Cor. 12:8–10). These twin themes of Spirit-baptism and spiritual gifts have decisively marked the movement. Yet surprisingly, the nature of the relationship between Spirit-baptism and the gifts of the Spirit has never received much attention. Early Pentecostal writers generally described baptism in the Holy Spirit as the "door" or gateway to the gifts, but this position was stated or assumed rather than developed in a significant way.[1] More recent Pentecostal writings have shed little light on this subject, and the implicit assumptions of an earlier generation still appear to be determinative. Today, Pentecostals generally affirm that Spirit-baptism is the "gateway" to the gifts, but a clear biblical rationale for this position has never been articulated.[2]

This understanding of Spirit-baptism as the gateway to the gifts was generally linked to an emphasis on the "nine special gifts" of 1 Corinthians 12:8–10.[3] Yet today few speak of only nine gifts. Donald Gee reflects what is today a consensus among students of the Bible: "I now think it is a mistake to always refer to the 'nine gifts' as though the catalogue there [1 Cor. 12:8–10] is exhaustive."[4] The recognition of a rich variety of spiritual gifts has led many Charismatics to reject the "gateway" position of Pentecostalism. H. I. Lederle states the matter directly: "There is no biblical support for any particular crisis experience or event being the gateway to the functioning of the gifts of the Spirit.... Every Christian is, and should be increasingly, charismatic."[5]

More recently the Pentecostal position has been challenged on another front. A large and rapidly growing group of non-Pentecostal Evangelicals are seeking after and experiencing spiritual gifts. This fresh emphasis on the charisms is remarkable in that it is occurring in Evangelical circles, which, in the past, rejected the continuing validity of spiritual gifts. This new out-pouring of charismatic vitality has been designated the "Third Wave."[6] Third Wavers consciously reject the Pentecostal understanding of Spirit-baptism, yet affirm the importance and availability of all of the spiritual gifts listed in 1 Corinthians 12:8–10.[7] Their theology and experience thus represent a sig-nificant challenge to the Pentecostal "gateway" position.

Thus, Pentecostals are being challenged today to reassess previous assumptions and to articulate more clearly the biblical basis for their position. Indeed, the Charismatic emphasis on the diverse nature of the gifts, coupled with the explosion of gifts among non-Pentecostal Evangelicals, raises cru-cial questions: Is it true that one must be baptized in the Holy Spirit before one can experience any of the charisms? What is the nature of the relation-ship between Spirit-baptism and the gifts of the Spirit? We will seek to answer these questions by first critiquing the "gateway" position outlined above and then suggesting an alternative approach that does justice to the distinctive the-ological perspectives of both Luke and Paul.

1. Pentecost: Gateway to the Gifts?

The Pentecostal position that the baptism in the Holy Spirit constitutes a necessary prerequisite for the operation of the gifts (indeed, any gift) faces three insurmountable obstacles. (1) As we have noted, this position was gen-erally associated with an exclusive focus on the "nine gifts" listed in 1 Corin-thians 12:8–10. Today, even in classical Pentecostal circles, most acknowledge that Paul's gift list here is suggestive rather than definitive. A comparison of Paul's gift lists (Rom. 12:6–8; 1 Cor. 12:8–10; 12:28; 12:29–30; Eph. 4:11), which describe a rich variety of gifts, virtually demands such a conclusion. Stanley Horton, a leading Pentecostal scholar, speaks for many when he con-cludes: "It seems better to take all of these lists [the lists in 1 Cor. 12:8–10; 12:28; and 12:29–30] as merely giving samplings of the gifts and callings of the Spirit, samplings taken from an infinite supply."[8]

This judgment, however, represents a significant obstacle for the "gate-way" position. It is one thing to suggest that Spirit-baptism is the "gateway" to specific gifts such as speaking in tongues or prophecy. But it is quite another to suggest that all the gifts, including gifts of "administration" (1 Cor. 12:28), "serving" (Rom. 12:7), or "giving" (12:8), necessarily flow from a prior Spirit-baptism. That is to say, if Paul was speaking only of a select group of gifts, it might be plausible to suggest that a baptism in the Spirit distinct from conversion functions as the "gateway" to their operation. But his emphasis on the variety of charisms encourages us to see his gift language as embracing the entire range of enablings that the Spirit grants to members of the Christian community for the common good. The rich diversity of the gifts thus suggests that they cannot be described as the result of a specific experience distinct from conversion.

(2) This leads us to another obstacle. Paul not only highlights the diverse character of the charisms, but he also declares that every Christian has a role to play. This conclusion is confirmed by Paul's words in 1 Corinthians 12:11: "All these are the work of one and the same Spirit, and he gives them *to each one*, just as he determines" (italics added). In Paul's perspective then, every Christian is charismatic. Nor does Paul speak anywhere of a baptism in the Spirit distinct from conversion that might serve as a "gateway" to the gifts. While he encourages every Christian to "be filled with the Spirit" (Eph. 5:18), this experience is related to Christian maturity rather than the operation of charisms. It centers on the fruit of the Spirit rather than the gifts.[9] Thus it is all but impossible to argue that Paul viewed such an experience as a necessary precondition for entering into the charismatic dimension of the Spirit.

(3) The third obstacle takes us to the heart of the matter, for it explains why the "gateway" position fails to adequately understand Paul. This position is based on a fundamental methodological error. It uncritically blends together theological concepts from Luke (Spirit-baptism) and Paul (spiritual gifts) with little regard for the context in which they are used by their respective authors. Thus, "gateway" proponents have *assumed* that the Spirit-baptism distinct from conversion described by Luke (Acts 1:5, 8; 2:4) represents the "gateway" to the Pauline gifts (Rom. 12:6–8; 1 Cor. 12:8–10; 12:28; 12:29–30; Eph. 4:11), even though Paul never explicitly speaks of Luke's Spirit-baptism (i.e., the Pentecostal gift) and thus never relates it to spiritual gifts. The weakness of this approach is apparent. A framework alien to the perspective of the biblical authors has been imposed on the biblical data, producing a system that is essentially extrabiblical.

There is a better way. A truly biblical theology develops only when we treat "each biblical author or book separately and ... outline his or its particular theological emphases." Only after we have "set a text in the context of its author's thought and intention ... can the biblical-theologian feel free to let that text interact with other texts from other books."[10] Thus, to answer the question concerning the nature of the relationship between Spirit-baptism and spiritual gifts, we must first place these concepts within their proper Lukan and Pauline contexts. To this task we now turn.

2. Two Trajectories: The Perspectives of Paul and Luke

As we have seen, an analysis of the pneumatologies of Paul and Luke reveals a number of significant differences. Each pneumatology appears to have a distinct trajectory, moving in a unique and significant direction. For this reason, it is important to outline the basic characteristics of each trajectory. Then, against this backdrop, we will seek to define the concepts of Spirit-baptism and spiritual gifts.

2.1. The Pauline Trajectory

At the outset, it is evident that Paul presents a fuller, larger picture of the Spirit's work than Luke. For Paul, the Christian life in its entirety is an outworking of the Spirit of God. The Spirit is the source of cleansing (Rom. 15:16; 1 Cor. 6:11), righteousness (Rom. 2:29; 8:1–17; 14:17; Gal. 5:5, 16–26), intimate fellowship with God (Rom. 8:14–17; Gal. 4:6), knowledge of God (1 Cor. 2:6–16; 2 Cor. 3:3–18), and ultimately, eternal life through the resurrection (Rom. 8:11; 1 Cor. 15:44–49; Gal. 6:8).

Thus, it is not surprising that Paul describes each believer's ability to contribute to the life of the community as a manifestation or gift of the Spirit (Rom. 12:6–8; 1 Cor. 12:8–10; 12:28; 12:29–30; Eph. 4:11). More specifically, the rich variety of the gifts granted to each believer for the common good appears to be a natural extension of Paul's larger pneumatological perspective. Since from his viewpoint the Christian life from the outset is shaped by the Spirit of God, there is little reason to suggest that spiritual gifts are transmitted or actualized by some experience subsequent to conversion. The gift of the Spirit, which brings Christian life, also brings the ability to bless the community.

2.2. The Lukan Trajectory

Luke's perspective is considerably different from that of Paul. Unlike Paul, who frequently speaks of the soteriological dimension of the Spirit's work, Luke *consistently* portrays the Spirit as the source of prophetic inspiration. From the outset of his two-volume work, Luke emphasizes the prophetic dimension of the Spirit's activity. The profusion of Spirit-inspired pronouncements in the infancy narratives herald the arrival of the era of fulfillment (Luke 1:41–45, 67–79; 2:25–32). This era is marked by the prophetic activity of John, the ministry of Jesus, and the mission of his church, all of which are carried out in the power of the Spirit.

Filled with the Spirit from his mother's womb (Luke 1:15, 17), John the Baptist anticipates the inauguration of Jesus' ministry. By carefully crafting his narrative, Luke ties his account of Jesus' pneumatic anointing (3:22) together with Jesus' dramatic announcement at Nazareth (4:18–21), thus indicating that the Spirit came on Jesus at the Jordan in order to equip him for his task as messianic herald. Literary parallels between the description of Jesus' anointing at the Jordan and that of the disciples at Pentecost suggest that Luke interpreted the latter event in light of the former: The Spirit came on the disciples at Pentecost to equip them for their prophetic vocation.

This judgment is supported by the Baptist's prophecy concerning the coming baptism of Spirit and fire (Luke 3:16), for Luke interprets the sifting activity of the Spirit of which John prophesied as being accomplished in the Spirit-directed and Spirit-empowered mission of the church (Acts 1:5, 8). It is confirmed by Luke's narration of the Pentecost event (Acts 2:1–13), his interpretation of this event in light of his slightly modified version of Joel 2:28–32 (3:1–5a in the LXX),[11] and his subsequent description of the church as a prophetic community empowered by the Spirit. Whether it be John in his mother's womb, Jesus at the Jordan, or the disciples at Pentecost, the Spirit comes on them all as the source of prophetic inspiration, granting special insight and inspiring speech.

Thus, in Luke's perspective, the disciples receive the Spirit not as the source of cleansing and a new ability to keep the law, nor as the essential bond by which they (each individual) are linked to God, nor even as a foretaste of the salvation to come. Rather, the disciples receive the Spirit as a prophetic anointing that enables them to participate effectively in the missionary enterprise of the church.[12]

Several significant implications emerge from this survey of Lukan pneumatology. (1) Pentecostals are right to speak of a baptism of the Holy Spirit "distinct from and subsequent to the experience of new birth."[13] This Pentecostal understanding of Spirit-baptism as distinct from conversion flows naturally from the conviction that the Spirit came on the disciples at Pentecost and throughout the books of Acts not as the source of new covenant existence, but rather as the source of prophetic inspiration.

(2) Luke describes the work of the Spirit in a strikingly different— although ultimately complementary—manner from that of Paul. For Luke, the Spirit comes exclusively as the source of prophetic inspiration, granting special revelation and inspiring speech.

(3) Although Luke never uses key Pauline terms such as *charismata* and *pneumatika*, he does associate phenomena found in Paul's gift lists with the inspiration of the Spirit. Luke's narrative is filled with references to prophecy and speaking in tongues.

3. Theological Synthesis

We must now define more specifically the concepts of Spirit-baptism and spiritual gifts by placing them against the theological backdrop provided by our survey of the pneumatologies of Paul and Luke. Our goal is to synthesize our findings into a coherent answer that does justice to the perspectives of both Paul and Luke. We will begin by defining the concepts of Spirit-baptism and spiritual gifts and then seek to describe the nature of their relationship.

3.1. Spirit-Baptism

We have seen that the concept of a baptism in the Spirit distinct from conversion flows from Luke's theology of the Spirit. In Luke's perspective, the Spirit comes on the disciples as the source of prophetic inspiration rather than justification, cleansing, or a new sense of filial relationship to God. This indicates that the Lukan gift of the Spirit should not—indeed, cannot—be equated with the Pauline gift of the Spirit, which forms the climax of the conversion experience and mediates the soteriological blessings of Christ (i.e., justification, cleansing, filial relationship) to the believer. Spirit-baptism in the Lukan sense (i.e., the gift of the Spirit or the Pentecostal gift) must be distinguished from the gift of the Spirit that Paul associates with conversion.

This concept of a Spirit-baptism distinct from conversion, while not specifically articulated by Paul, is consistent with (and complementary to) his theological perspective. Paul frequently alludes to the power of the Spirit enabling his own ministry (Rom. 15:19; 1 Cor. 2:4; 1 Thess. 1:5). And he also refers to special anointings that energize the ministry of others (1 Tim. 4:14; 2 Tim. 1:6–7; cf. 1 Thess. 5:19). In view of the ad hoc nature of Paul's letters, it should not surprise us that he nowhere speaks of the Pentecostal gift. He has not set out to write a comprehensive theological treatise delineating the dynamics of spiritual life. Nevertheless, it is evident that Luke's emphasis on the significance of the Pentecostal gift (Acts 1:8; 2:17–18) for the vitality of the church and the missionary enterprise resonates well with Paul's perspective.

If we ask more specifically concerning the impact of Spirit-baptism in Luke–Acts, we immediately note that Luke's perspective is similar to that of the Judaism of his day. As we have noted in other chapters, first-century Jews identified the gift of the Spirit with prophetic inspiration.

Luke also presents the Spirit as the source of prophetic inspiration. This is apparent from the outset of his Gospel, which features outbursts of prophetic speech. It is highlighted in the programmatic accounts of Jesus' sermon at Nazareth (Luke 4:18–19) and Peter's sermon on the day of Pente-cost (Acts 2:17–18). Both accounts indicate that the Lukan gift of the Spirit is intimately connected to special revelation and inspired speech. Further-more, references to charismatic revelation and speech punctuate Luke's two-volume work (e.g., Luke 10:21; 12:10–12; Acts 4:31; 6:10; 7:55; 10:19; 13:2). Thus, Luke affirms that Spirit-baptism is intimately connected to the bestowal of charismatic wisdom and speech.

The connection to Paul's language and perspective is immediately appar-ent. In relation to the Pentecostal gift, Luke actually refers to specific gifts named by Paul: glossolalia and prophecy (e.g., Acts 2:4, 18; 10:46; 19:6). And, of course, Paul alludes to spiritual gifts that center on Spirit-inspired revela-tion and speech. To this significant fact we now turn.

3.2. Spiritual Gifts

Paul's gift language is, in reality, nuanced. In 1 Corinthians, he uses two Greek words to refer to gifts granted by the Spirit: *charismata* ("gifts")[14] and *pneumatika* ("spiritual gifts").[15] The masculine word *pneumatikos* ("spiritual man," 1 Cor. 2:15; "spiritually gifted," 14:37) is also prominent.

The significance of Paul's language at this point is debated. Earl Ellis has argued that the term *charismata* has a broad range of meaning and can be used to refer to any or all of the gifts. The term *pneumatika*, by way of contrast, refers to a more restricted grouping of spiritual gifts, the "prophetic-type gifts."[16] Ellis suggests that the terms *pneumatika* and *pneumatikos* "denote, respectively, gifts of inspired utterance or discernment and men who exercise such gifts."[17] Sev-eral points suggest that Ellis' judgment may indeed be correct.

(1) The way Paul alternates between *pneumatika* (1 Cor. 12:1; 14:1) and *charismata* (12:4; 12:31) in 1 Corinthians 12–14 suggests the former denotes a subcategory of the latter. The *peri de* ("now about") construction of 12:1 indicates that the Corinthians, in their letter to Paul, have raised questions concerning the exercise of the *pneumatika*. It would be natural for the Corinthians, enamored as they were with glossolalia, to focus on this more specific grouping of gifts. Paul, on the other hand, seeks to broaden the Corinthians' perspective by referring to the larger grouping of gifts, the *charismata*. The parallelism between 12:31, "eagerly desire the greater gifts [*charismata*]" and 14:1, "eagerly desire spiritual gifts [*pneumatika*]" supports this reading of the text. Here the *pneumatika* are identified as a subclass of the *charismata* and closely linked to prophecy. The "greater gifts" of 12:31 are prophetic-type gifts that edify the body (and thus, as Paul emphasizes, they must communicate an intelligible message).

(2) A second point in favor of Ellis's thesis emerges in 1 Corinthians 14:37: "If anybody thinks he is a prophet or spiritually gifted [*pneumatikos*]. . . ." This text identifies or closely associates those who possess the *pneumatika* (i.e., the *pneumatikos*) with prophets.

(3) Finally, the discernment characteristic of prophets is, in 1 Corinthians 2:6–16, ascribed to the *pneumatikos*: "The spiritual man [*pneumatikos*] makes judgments about all things, but he himself is not subject to any man's judgment" (2:15). However, Gordon Fee challenges the notion that this passage distinguishes between a special group of pneumatics and believers in general. According to him, the contrast is between unbelievers without the Spirit and believers, all of whom possess the Spirit of God.[18] Nevertheless, even if Fee's reading is accepted at this point, Ellis's thesis remains plausible as a description of Paul's language in chapters 12–14.

Ellis's thesis is not without its critics,[19] but it does highlight significant texts that appear to link the *pneumatika* with gifts of special revelation and inspired speech. If Ellis is correct, then the Pauline category of *pneumatika* is strikingly similar in function to the Lukan gift of the Spirit. Even if Ellis is wrong and the *pneumatika* do not refer to a special cluster of prophetic-type gifts, it is evident that Paul's lists in 1 Corinthians 12 do contain a number of gifts that are prophetic in character. Gifts associated with special revelation and/or inspired speech include: "a message of wisdom" (v. 8), "a message of knowledge" (v. 8), "prophecy" (v. 10), "the ability to distinguish between spirits" (v. 10),[20] "the ability to speak in different kinds of tongues" (v. 10), and "the interpretation of tongues" (v. 10).

We have already noted that Spirit-baptism in the Lukan sense also grants special revelation and inspired speech. Here, then, is the key intersection where the trajectories of Luke and Paul meet, the point of contact between Spirit-baptism in Luke–Acts and spiritual gifts in Paul. Although Paul does not explicitly refer to this Pentecostal gift, he does acknowledge that the Spirit functions in a similar manner. Paul's language and categories are different from those of Luke, but the overlap is apparent. The Lukan gift of the Spirit and the prophetic-type gifts (whether these be described as the *pneumatika* or not) that Paul enumerates have virtually the same impact on their recipients.

4. Conclusion

We are now in a position to answer our question concerning the nature of the relationship between Spirit-baptism and spiritual gifts. While it cannot be maintained that Spirit-baptism is the "gateway" to every spiritual gift, the biblical evidence suggests that Spirit-baptism is the "gateway" to a special cluster of gifts described by Paul, the prophetic-type gifts that are associated with special revelation and inspired speech. Certainly it is true that, in one sense, every Christian "is, and should be increasingly, charismatic."[21] Paul highlights this fact: Every believer has something to contribute; everyone is enabled by the Spirit to contribute to the common good (1 Cor. 12:11).

Yet it is also true that there is a dimension of the Spirit's enabling that one enters by virtue of a baptism in the Spirit distinct from conversion. This dimension might be properly called the prophetic dimension. In Luke's perspective, the community of faith is potentially a community of prophets; and it is by reception of the Pentecostal gift (Spirit-baptism) that this potential is realized. It was Luke's expectation that this potential would indeed be realized in the church of his day as it had been in the past (e.g., Luke 3:16; 11:13; Acts 2:17–18). Paul's letters reveal a similar sense of expectation, although it is frequently found in the guise of a challenge: "Eagerly desire spiritual gifts [*pneumatika*], especially the gift of prophecy" (1 Cor. 12:31).

Study Questions

1. Earlier Pentecostals often spoke of baptism in the Spirit as the "gateway" to the gifts of the Spirit. How has the experience of Third Wavers challenged this position?
2. It is now generally recognized that the gifts of the Spirit cannot be limited to the nine listed in 1 Corinthians 12:8–10. How does this recognition undermine the "gateway" position?
3. The "gateway" position is based on a fundamental methodological error. What is this methodological problem?
4. How does Menzies seek to relate the Pauline gifts of the Spirit to Luke's baptism in the Spirit? How do these concepts overlap?
5. Every Christian is charismatic and should be increasingly so. In what sense is this statement true? In what sense would Pentecostals want to qualify this statement?

Notes

[1] Thus Myer Pearlman declares that the baptism in the Holy Spirit enables Christians to experience "the charismatic operation of the Spirit" (*Knowing the Doctrines of the Bible* [Springfield, Mo.: Gospel, 1937], 313). See also Willard Cantelon, *The Baptism of the Holy Spirit* (Springfield, Mo.: Acme, 1951), 15; Ernest S. Williams, *Systematic Theology* (Springfield, Mo.: Gospel, 1953), 3:63–75; Ralph Riggs, *We Believe* (Springfield, Mo.: Gospel, 1954), 28; Donald Gee, *Spiritual Gifts in the Work of the Ministry Today* (Springfield, Mo.: Gospel, 1963), 18.

[2] See P. C. Nelson, *Bible Doctrines* (Springfield, Mo.: Gospel, 1962), 78; Stanley M. Horton, *What the Bible Says About the Holy Spirit*, 261; G. Raymond Carlson,

Our Faith and Fellowship (Springfield, Mo.: Gospel, 1977), 65–67. Note also the Assemblies of God Statement of Fundamental Truths #7, The Promise of the Father: "All believers are entitled to and should expect and earnestly seek the promise of the Father, the baptism in the Holy Ghost and fire, according to the command of our Lord Jesus Christ. This was the normal experience of all in the early Christian Church. With it come the enduement of power for life and service, the bestowment of the gifts and their uses in the work of the ministry."

[3] For a focus on the "nine gifts" of 1 Cor. 12:8–10 see Pearlman, *Knowing the Doctrines of the Bible*, 321–27; Carl Brumback, *What Meaneth This?* (Springfield, Mo.: Gospel, 1947), 153; Cantelon, *The Baptism of the Holy Spirit*, 15; Riggs, *We Believe*, 28–29.

[4] Donald Gee, *Spiritual Gifts*, 5. See E. Williams, *Systematic Theology*, 3:75–82; Stanley M. Horton, *What the Bible Says About the Holy Spirit*, 209, who also acknowledge that the "nine gifts" of 1 Cor. 12:8–10 are suggestive.

[5] H. I. Lederle, *Treasures Old and New: Interpretations of "Spirit-Baptism" in the Charismatic Renewal Movement*, 218, 228. See also Dennis and Rita Bennett, *The Holy Spirit and You* (Plainfield, N.J.: Logos, 1971), 81, who argue that believers who have not been baptized in the Spirit may manifest seven of the nine gifts listed in 1 Cor. 12:8–10 (tongues and interpretation of tongues are the exception).

[6] For more on the Third Wave, see chapter 10.

[7] See, e.g., Gary S. Greig and Kevin N. Springer, eds., *The Kingdom and the Power*, 21; C. Peter Wagner, *The Third Wave of the Holy Spirit* (Ann Arbor, Mich.: Vine, 1988), 18–19; John Wimber and Kevin Springer, *Power Points* (New York: Harper-Collins, 1991), 135–36, and *Power Evangelism* (San Francisco: Harper & Row, 1991), 148.

[8] Horton, *What the Bible Says About the Holy Spirit*, 209.

[9] Note the context, esp. Eph. 5:15: "Be very careful, then, how you live—not as unwise but as wise."

[10] James Dunn, *Baptism in the Holy Spirit*, 39.

[11] See chapter 10 for an analysis of these changes.

[12] Note that Luke not only refrains from attributing soteriological functions to the Spirit in a manner analogous to Paul, his narrative presupposes a pneumatology that excludes this dimension (e.g., Luke 11:13; Acts 8:4–17; 19:1–7). For detailed argumentation supporting this analysis of Luke's pneumatology see R. P. Menzies, *Empowered for Witness*.

[13] *Minutes of the 44th Session of the General Council of the Assemblies of God* (Portland, Ore., August 6–11, 1991), 129.

[14] Normally the plural form of *charisma* or "gift" is used; see 1 Cor. 1:7; 7:7 (sg.); 12:4, 9, 28, 30, 31.

[15] The plural form of *pneumatikon* appears in 1 Cor. 12:1 (probably neuter) and 14:1. In both instances the NIV translates "spiritual gifts."

[16] E. Ellis, "Prophecy in the New Testament Church—And Today," *Prophetic Vocation in the New Testament and Today*, ed. J. Panagopoulos (Leiden: Brill, 1977), 48.

[17] E. Ellis, "'Spiritual' Gifts in the Pauline Community," *NTS* 20 (1973–1974): 128.

[18] Gordon Fee, *The First Epistle to the Corinthians* (NICNT; Grand Rapids: Eerdmans, 1987), 97–120.

[19] Note, e.g., the objections raised to this perspective by D. A. Carson, *Showing the Spirit: A Theological Exposition of 1 Corinthians 12–14*, 23–24; S. Schatzmann, *A Pauline Theology of the Charismata* (Peabody, Mass.: Hendrickson, 1987), 7.

[20] This is especially true if we see this gift closely linked to the weighing of prophecy described in 1 Cor. 14:29. Note that the Greek word *diakrinō* occurs both in 1 Cor. 12:10 and 14:29.

[21] Lederle, *Treasures Old and New*, 228

Chapter Fifteen

Baptism in the Spirit and the Fruit of the Spirit

We have argued that Paul was the first Christian to connect the Spirit with the broader, soteriological dimensions of the life of faith. Unlike Luke, who viewed the Spirit in a more limited way as the source of prophetic inspiration, Paul saw that the Spirit is at work in the believer's life from the very beginning, progressively transforming the old nature, prone to sin as it is, into a new creation. This transformation includes a radical reworking of one's ethical patterns and behavior. The Spirit, Paul declares, infuses our lives with the very character of Christ. "Those who belong to Christ Jesus have crucified the sinful nature with its passions and desires" (Gal. 5:24). This new life of discipleship is produced by the Spirit (5:25), the fruit of which is described by Paul in concrete terms: "The fruit of the Spirit is love, joy, peace, patience, kindness, goodness, faithfulness, gentleness and self-control" (5:22–23).

Exactly how this ethical dimension of the Spirit's work that Paul highlights relates to the Lukan baptism in the Spirit has rarely been discussed. Although Hermann Gunkel and others have noted that Paul and Luke have differing theological perspectives, no one has attempted to relate the two in a coherent fashion. This has been largely due to the fact that until recently, for the most part, Luke was interpreted through the lenses of Pauline categories and the uniqueness of his message was lost. But more recent scholarly study, especially that produced within Pentecostal circles, calls us once again to recognize the distinctive character of the pneumatologies of Paul and Luke. These new insights, then, raise an intriguing question, one of considerable importance for the life of the believer and the church: What is the relationship between the fruit of the Spirit and the baptism in the Spirit? Put differently, what is the connection between Spirit-baptism and Christian maturity?

To many within the Pentecostal tradition this question may at first sound strange. The link between Spirit-baptism and holiness or Christian maturity has been assumed for generations. The modern Pentecostal revival emerged in a context shaped by the Holiness Movement, and this Holiness legacy continues to exert a strong influence in many circles. Most popular preaching in Pentecostal circles asserts a causal connection between Spirit-baptism and holiness. And many personal testimonies imply a similar link. Does not our own experience suggest that Christian maturity is bolstered through this dynamic experience of the Spirit we call baptism in the Spirit?

More recently the link has been made explicit in the popular and influential *Full Life Study Bible*. The article entitled "Baptism in the Holy Spirit" in this study Bible states that baptism in the Holy Spirit results in, among other things, "enhanced sensitivity to sin," "a greater seeking after righteousness which conforms to Christ," and "a deeper awareness of the judgment of God against all ungodliness."[1]

Popular preaching, the testimonies of believers, and recent literature present baptism in the Spirit as a boost to a higher level of Christian living. Nevertheless, the question must be asked: Is this association between baptism in the Spirit and Christian maturity consistent with the teachings of Scripture? In this chapter, we will seek to answer this question.

1. Corinthian Problems

The notion that Spirit-baptism necessarily leads to greater holiness sounds remarkably similar to the sort of claims that Paul sought to counter in the church at Corinth. At least some of the Christians at Corinth viewed tongues-speech as an expression of a superior level of spirituality. By virtue of their special spiritual experience and knowledge, these people believed they had entered into a "deeper" or "higher" level of spiritual existence. They formed a spiritual elite and their spiritual gifts, especially their ability to speak in tongues, confirmed their special status.

Paul challenges this elitism at every point. He rebukes this attitude of pride when he writes, "Knowledge puffs up, but love builds up. The man who thinks he knows something does not yet know as he ought to know" (1 Cor. 8:1–2). More specifically, he repeatedly challenges the notion of a spiritual elite within the church. This message is communicated with special clarity and force through the use of the body metaphor in 12:12–31, where Paul stresses that all were "given the one Spirit to drink" (v. 13) and that all are of equal importance, for each member of the body has a significant contribution to make.

Because the same Spirit is at work in every believer, transforming them into the image of Christ, Paul understood that there could be no elite class of Christians. Although some may indeed be more mature than others, Christian maturity cannot be linked to a single experience or marked by some special sign as some Corinthians maintained. In Paul's view, to draw divisions or comparisons at this point misses the whole point of Christian community. Thus Paul declares:

> God has combined the members of the body and has given greater honor to the parts that lacked it, so that there should be no division in the body, but that its parts should have equal concern for each other. If one part suffers, every part suffers with it; if one part is honored, every part rejoices with it.
>
> Now you are the body of Christ, and each one of you is a part of it. (1 Cor. 12:24–26)

All of this indicates that when Pentecostals link Spirit-baptism with Christian maturity, we are much closer in our thinking to the prideful Corinthians than to the apostle Paul. If we are to be consistent with his teaching, we must reject the notion that the church is composed of two classes of Christians: the mature who have been baptized in the Spirit and the immature who have not. Spirit-baptism cannot serve as a badge of holiness, a mark of Christian maturity. Rather, it must be seen for exactly what Luke describes it to be, the source of boldness and power in our Christian service and witness. *It should not be confused with Christian maturity.* Just as gifts of the Spirit are often granted to the immature—and the church at Corinth was filled with Christians who verify this claim (cf. 1 Cor. 1:7)—so also it is with the baptism in the Spirit. God's gracious gifts are not limited to an elite few.

The elitist theology of the Corinthians had a devastating impact on the life of the church. Modern forms of elitist theology that confuse Spirit-baptism with holiness often lead to similar problems. Let me suggest three that are particularly common today.

(1) An elitist theology often produces unnecessary spiritual causalities. Pentecostals have correctly, I believe, emphasized the importance of being baptized in the Spirit (i.e., to receive the Pentecostal gift). Although Spirit-baptism (in the Lukan sense) is merely the entry point into a dimension of the Spirit's enabling, which must be appropriated on an ongoing basis, it is nevertheless a significant beginning or experience available to every believer (Acts 1:8; 2:17).

Yet, not all who seek God's gifts immediately receive what they seek or even what they ultimately need. This is true of the gift of Pentecost as well as other gifts. God has his own timing, his own plan, which transcends ours. Not all who pray for the Pentecostal gift receive it without delay. The early Christians waited fifty days; we too may require a season of waiting.

Often those who do not receive have questions. I have prayed with many at altars. I have also participated in numerous prayer meetings, filled with ardent believers reaching out for all that God had for them. I treasure these experiences and joyfully testify that these times of prayer have had and continue to have a powerful and positive impact on my life. Nevertheless, I have also seen men and women walk away from an altar of prayer frustrated and dejected. They had not received from God what they knew he had for them and were filled with questions. "Why was I not baptized in the Spirit? What is wrong with me?"

I have found that these questions are not difficult to deal with when we simply acknowledge that God's gifts are not necessarily given to the spiritually mature. Encouragement to persist in prayer and to live with a sense of expectancy easily follow. But when the link to holiness is made—and it matters little whether Spirit-baptism is viewed as the cause or the result of Christian maturity—pastoral questions and the ensuing casualties abound.

(2) The link between Spirit-baptism and holiness also leads to the confusion of spiritual power with Christian maturity. The church at Corinth should be proof enough that spiritual power is not necessarily linked to spiritual maturity. As we have noted, the Corinthians were spiritually gifted (cf. 1 Cor. 1:7). Our own experience is no less revealing. How many men or women have been used powerfully by God in spite of their weakness and shortcomings?

There is a danger here, however, that must be faced. When spiritual power and spiritual maturity are linked, our vision becomes blurred and we are rendered incapable of distinguishing between the two. This makes the church vulnerable to carnal leaders who possess spiritual power, but little else. On a personal level, the confusion of power with holiness can also have devastating results. How many church leaders have justified their sinful lifestyles by pointing to the effectiveness of their ministry? In order to safeguard our spiritual health, we need to grasp this important point: Spiritual power is no guarantee that all is well.

(3) The link between Spirit-baptism and holiness leads to a repudiation of the Pentecostal message. When we depict baptism in the Spirit as the source of personal holiness, our theology is quickly dismissed as falling into the Corinthian trap of elitism. The criticisms of Wayne Grudem, an Evangelical scholar who is open to the full range of the gifts of the Spirit, illustrates this point. In his *Systematic Theology: An Introduction to Biblical Doctrine*, Grudem dismisses the Pentecostal understanding of baptism in the Spirit as distinct

from conversion because of its elitist overtones. Speaking of the distinction between those who have been baptized in the Spirit and those who have not, Grudem writes, "The problem is that it contributes to a 'we-they' mentality in churches, and leads to jealousy, pride, and divisiveness."[2] This critique is clearly justified if Pentecostals present baptism in the Spirit as a general boost to the Christian life, the source of the fruit of the Spirit.

2. Theological Issues

Although the pastoral concerns related above are real, the fundamental problem with establishing a necessary, causal link between Spirit-baptism and Christian maturity is that it runs counter to the teaching of Scripture. We have already noted how the doctrine conflicts with Paul's theology. Now, I would like to focus on the heart of the problem.

The Holiness position outlined above is based on a fundamental methodological error. It confuses Paul's language, which speaks of fruit of the Spirit (Gal. 5:22–23) and the ethical dimension of the Christian life in terms of being "filled with the Spirit" (Eph. 5:18), with Luke's language of Pentecost (Acts 1:8; 2:17–18). As we have already noted in the preceding chapters, sound theological method demands that we first outline the distinctive theological emphases of a particular biblical author. Only after we have done this may we feel free to relate these theological themes to those that emerge from other biblical authors. In this case, it should be noted that it is not immediately obvious that Paul's "fruit of the Spirit" or his ethical language in general are related to Luke's Pentecostal baptism in the Spirit. Indeed, if our exegetical work in the preceding chapters is sound, the two cannot be linked in a causal relationship.

Certainly Luke describes a powerful experience of the Spirit that is now available to every believer. This experience, which may be appropriately termed a baptism in the Spirit (Acts 1:5), initiates a believer into the prophetic dimension of the Spirit's power. As the source of prophetic inspiration, the Spirit inspires bold witness for Christ, especially in the face of opposition, and guides and encourages the church in its mission (e.g., Acts 1:8; 2:17–18; 4:31; 9:31). The Spirit of Pentecost is, then, above all, the Spirit of mission. As we have noted, Luke does not present the Spirit as a soteriological agent, nor does he describe the Spirit as the direct source of ethical transformation. Spirit-baptism in the Lukan sense, then, cannot be linked with holiness or Christian maturity.

As we have noted, Paul's perspective is larger than Luke's. Paul recognized that the Spirit was more than simply the source of inspired speech and charismatic wisdom; the Spirit was also present from the very beginning of the

Christian life, progressively bringing ethical transformation, shaping the believer into the image of Christ. According to him, the Christian life in its entirety is shaped by the Spirit. As such, the Spirit is a soteriological agent that infuses life-changing power into every believer. In Paul's scheme, this life-changing power is present from the beginning of the Christian life. With regeneration and the reception of the Spirit, the process of ethical transformation begins (Rom. 8:1–17; 2 Cor. 3:8–18).

Luke and Paul, then, speak of two dimensions of the Spirit, which, although they may overlap, are distinct. Luke describes the missiological dimension of the Spirit's work and relates this to the Pentecostal gift. Paul highlights the ethical dimension and associates it with regeneration. It is evident that the two cannot be equated or uncritically linked. Yet, how shall we integrate these two, complementary perspectives? How shall we relate the missiological and the ethical impulses of the Spirit's work? To these questions we now turn.

3. The Way Forward

Several years ago, I found myself riding on a train from Shanghai to Nanjing. I was traveling with the deans and presidents of two seminaries. The five of us were scheduled to visit church leaders in these two historic cities. As the train thundered down the track, we began to discuss various aspects of theology. The discussion shifted to the general topic at hand. More specifically, we began to discuss the problem of relating experience to theology. If the relationship between baptism in the Spirit and Christian maturity cannot be viewed in a necessary, causal way, how do we explain the testimonies of so many believers—believers who describe the baptism in the Spirit as a catalyst to their spiritual growth?

My colleague and, at that time, my academic dean, John Carter, drawing on his training in psychology, suggested the helpful concept and term *co-relational*, which describes the relationship between two things that are frequently found together but do not have a necessary, causal relationship. Birds and squirrels are often found together, but there is no causal relationship. One might be found without the other, however rare that occasion may be.

As Dr. Carter described the term *co-relational*, I began to see that this was a helpful way to speak of the relationship between Spirit-baptism and Christian maturity. Generally, our spiritual life is shaped by two dimensions of the Spirit's work: the prophetic or missiological, and the ethical or soteriological. These two are often experienced in our lives simultaneously. Indeed, this is the biblical ideal. Thus, when we have a powerful spiritual experience, such as when we are baptized in or filled with the Spirit (in the Lukan sense), we frequently experience both dimensions of the Spirit's work in our lives. The prophetic and the ethical flow together in our experience.

However, it is important to remember that although these two dimensions are frequently experienced together (and indeed, this is the ideal), this is not necessarily the case. One dimension may be experienced independently of the other. That is to say, although we may sense the Spirit's encouragement in our lives more broadly in moments of prophetic inspiration (e.g., when one utters a prophetic message or speaks in tongues), this does not mean that the two are always or necessarily related in a causal way. The one does not necessarily serve as a marker or cause of the other. Spirit-baptism and an enhanced sensitivity to sin may often go together. Indeed this is the ideal, but it is important to note that they are not inseparably linked in a causal way.

4. Conclusion

Theological precision on this point is of vital importance. If we base normative theology on general experiences, we run grave risks. We have already discussed the dangers inherent when Spirit-baptism is confused with Christian holiness. An examination of the New Testament, however, calls us to pursue a more excellent way. We can with an open heart seek and expect God to pour out his Spirit on us in such a way as to transform the old nature, with its bent toward sinful ways, and to grant power and boldness to be the witnesses he has called us to be. These two dimensions in our lives may frequently appear as one. As we walk forward in the ways of the Spirit, we will likely encounter moments of refreshment that are ethically transforming and missiologically inspiring. But one dimension may develop without the other.

Let us pray that God will grant us both. May we seek to exhibit the fruit of the Spirit as well as the power of the Spirit.

Study Questions

1. Many Pentecostals link baptism in the Spirit to spiritual maturity. Why does Menzies suggest that this perspective has more affinities with the theology of the Corinthian elitists than that of the apostle Paul?
2. What are some of the problems caused by presenting Spirit-baptism as the source of spiritual maturity?
3. According to Menzies, the linkage between baptism in the Spirit and spiritual maturity rests on a faulty assumption. What is this assumption?

4. What does the term *co-relational* mean? Why does Menzies feel that
   this term can help us more clearly describe and understand the nature
   of the relationship between baptism in the Spirit and spiritual maturity?

Notes

[1] *The Full Life Study Bible—The New Testament*, Donald Stamps, ed. (Grand Rapids: Zondervan, 1990), 244.
[2] Wayne Grudem, *Systematic Theology: An Introduction to Biblical Doctrine* (Grand Rapids: Zondervan, 1994), 777.

Conclusion

Pentecostals have traditionally been long on *action* and short on *reflection*. It is evident that Pentecostals have emphasized *experience* over *theology*. This is a pattern typical of revival movements. Who is to say that this has been wrong? Certainly Pentecostals in the twentieth century have brought to the attention of much of the larger church world the privilege and opportunity of deep experiences with God. The work of the Holy Spirit has been visibly demonstrated around the world at the cutting edges of the Christian mission.

In an earlier day when Pentecostals were uniformly rejected by other Christian believers, not much was required but to proclaim faithfully the basic message of Pentecostalism—that Jesus is the Savior, that he heals people today, that all believers should ardently seek the baptism in the Holy Spirit, and that Jesus is coming soon. Few questions surfaced within the ranks of the faithful; they were too busy reaching the lost for Christ to quibble over theological matters.

Furthermore in those early years, those outside the Pentecostal fold were not interested enough in Pentecostalism to ask questions. Until the middle of the twentieth century, Pentecostals were preoccupied with proclamation. Filled with zeal, confident of the rightness of their cause, Pentecostals connected successfully with common people around the world with a message of deliverance and hope. Serving in virtual isolation from the larger church world, they were not burdened by a need to argue fine points of theology.

But the picture is changing. By mid-century, the surprising growth and vitality of Pentecostalism had begun to attract more than passing interest within a broad range of Christian believers. Evangelicals came to accept Pentecostals as orthodox brothers and sisters (except for some Fundamentalists, who have continued to reject Pentecostalism out of hand as a serious distortion to biblical truth), and mainline Protestants no longer were prone to eject automatically ministers and laypeople who reported receiving the Pentecostal experience.

With the emergence of the Charismatic renewal, which by the decade of the 1960s included not only mainline Protestants but a significant penetration of the Roman Catholic Church, literature related to the person and work of the Holy Spirit has appeared in a veritable explosion on the Christian world. By the 1980s, Evangelicals were to some degree involved with the revival. They, too, were writing thoughtful books, seeking to discover fresh ways to understand the theology of spiritual experience.

The fascination of the Christian world in the latter part of the twentieth century with the empowering and gifting of the Holy Spirit and what this means for the church has changed the environment in which Pentecostals function. The schools Pentecostals operate for the training of ministers for years have employed textbooks written largely by Evangelicals, since so few scholarly works have been provided from their own ranks. Virtually abdicating the theological agenda to Evangelicals, Pentecostals are now confronted with the problems surfacing in such important basic fields as hermeneutics and the exegesis of Scripture resting on these rules for Bible study.

It is evident that basic presuppositions driving Evangelicals do not necessarily serve the interests of Pentecostals in all respects. Largely the product of Evangelical scholars who are sympathetic to Pentecostalism (howbeit critical of basic Pentecostal beliefs), questions have surfaced that challenge a Pentecostal response. Serious Pentecostal students and thoughtful pastors see their faith challenged, not by caustic lampooners as in yesteryear, but by sympathetic Evangelical friends who are appreciative of the great evangelistic and missionary success of Pentecostalism, but who are not persuaded of the biblical soundness of Pentecostal teaching.

It is evident that the earlier pronouncements of Pentecostal advocacy are no longer adequate to meet the challenges sweeping through the church world today. Truth does not change, but the target shifts over time. Thoughtful questions require equally thoughtful responses. This requires a fresh look at values long held dear by a revival movement. This book is a modest effort at engaging the issues raised by recent scholarship with a view to providing a stronger base of support for Pentecostal experience.

At a major juncture in history, at the dawn of a new century and a new millennium, the opportunities and prospects for Pentecostal ministry are exceedingly bright. No longer burdened by the rejection and condescension of days gone by, Pentecostals can take heart in the collegial support enjoyed at many levels. The near term looks bright indeed. Continued rapid growth and increasing influence can be expected.

There are but few shadows on the horizon. One is the possibility of losing the intellectual battle to critics whose questions are not answered. It would be sad if the brightest and most promising among our students and pastors turn away simply because of not having in their hands substantial materials with which to undergird their Pentecostal faith and experience. It is for this reason that this book is presented—to contribute, at least in a small way, to the theological debate impacting the Pentecostal revival.

Select Bibliography

Allen, Roland. "The Revelation of the Holy Spirit in the Acts of the Apostles." *IRM* 7 (1918): 160–67.

Atkinson, W. "Pentecostal Responses to Dunn's *Baptism in the Holy Spirit*: Luke–Acts." *JPT* 6 (1995): 120–24.

Aulen, Gustaf. *Christus Victor: An Historical Study of the Three Main Types of the Idea of the Atonement*. Trans. A. G. Hebert. London: SPCK, 1931.

Banks, Robert. *Paul's Idea of Community*. Grand Rapids: Eerdmans, 1980.

Barrett, C. K. "Acts and the Pauline Corpus." *ExpTim* 88 (1976): 2–5.

_____. *The Holy Spirit and the Gospel Tradition*. London: SPCK, 1947.

Barrett, David, ed. *World Christian Encyclopedia: A Comprehensive Survey of Churches and Religions in the Modern World A.D. 1900–2000*. Oxford: Oxford Univ. Press, 1982.

Beasley-Murray, G. R. *Baptism in the New Testament*. Exeter: Paternoster, 1962.

Bennett, Dennis. *Nine O'Clock in the Morning*. Plainfield, N.J.: Logos, 1970.

Bennett, Dennis, and Rita Bennett. *The Holy Spirit and You*. Plainfield, N.J.: Logos, 1971.

Blomberg, Craig. *Interpreting the Parables*. Downers Grove, Ill.: InterVarsity, 1990.

Bloom, Allan. *The Closing of the American Mind*. New York: Simon & Schuster, 1987.

Bock, Darrell L. *Luke*. 2 vols. Grand Rapids: Baker, 1994.

Bornkamm, Günther, G. Barth, and H. J. Held. *Tradition and Interpretation in Matthew*. Philadelphia: Westminster, 1963.

Bovon, F. *Luc le théologien*. Paris: Delachaux & Niestlé, 1978.

Bradley, J. "Miracles and Martyrdom in the Early Church: Some Theological and Ethical Implications." Pp. 227–41 in *All Together in One Place*, ed. H. Hunter and P. Hocken. Sheffield: JSOT Press, 1993.

Bresson, Bernard. *Studies in Ecstasy*. New York: Vantage Press, 1966.

Brown, S. "'Water-Baptism' and 'Spirit-Baptism' in Luke–Acts." *ATR* 59 (1977): 135–51.

Bruce, F. F. *Commentary on the Book of Acts*. NICNT. Grand Rapids: Eerdmans, 1984.

_____. "The Holy Spirit in the Acts of the Apostles." *Int* 27 (1973): 166–83.

Brumbach, Carl. *What Meaneth This?* Springfield, Mo.: Gospel, 1947.

Bruner, F. D. *A Theology of the Holy Spirit: The Pentecostal Experience and the New Testament Witness*. Grand Rapids: Eerdmans, 1970.

Büchsel, F. *Der Geist Gottes im Neuen Testament*. Gütersloh: C. Bertelsmann, 1926.

Cantelon, Willard. *The Baptism of the Holy Spirit*. Springfield, Mo.: Acme, 1951.

Cargal, Timothy B. "Beyond the Fundamentalist-Modernist Controversy: Pentecostals and Hermeneutics in a Postmodern Age." *Pneuma* 15 (Fall 1993): 163–87.

Carlson, G. Raymond. *Our Faith and Fellowship*. Springfield, Mo.: Gospel, 1977.

Carson, D. A. *Showing the Spirit: A Theological Exposition of 1 Corinthians 12–14*. Grand Rapids: Baker, 1987.

Chevallier, M. A. *Souffle de Dieu*. Paris: Éditions Beauchesne, 1978.

Cole, Stewart G. *The History of Fundamentalism*. Westport, Conn.: Greenwood, 1931.

Conzelmann, Hans. *The Theology of St. Luke*. Philadelphia: Fortress, 1982.

Dayton, Donald. *Theological Roots of Pentecostalism*. Grand Rapids: Francis Asbury Press, 1987.

Dempster, M. "The Church's Moral Witness: A Study of Glossolalia in Luke's Theology of Acts." *Paraclete* 23.1 (1989): 1–7.

Derrett, J. D. M. "Simon Magus (Acts 8:9–24)." *ZNW* 73 (1982): 52–68.

Dunn, James D. G. *Baptism in the Holy Spirit*. London: SCM, 1970.

_____. "Baptism in the Spirit: A Response to Pentecostal Scholarship." *JPT* 3 (1993): 3–27.

_____. *Jesus and the Spirit*. Philadelphia: Westminster, 1975.

_____. "Spirit-Baptism and Pentecostalism." *SJT* 23 (1970): 397–407.

_____. "They Believed Philip's Preaching (Acts 8:12): A Reply," *IBS* 1 (1979): 177–83.

Ellis, E. E. *The Gospel of Luke*. NCB. London: Oliphants, Marshall, Morgan, & Scott, 1974.

_____. "Prophecy in the New Testament Church—and Today." Pp. 46–57 in *Prophetic Vocation in the New Testament and Today*, ed. J. Panagopoulos. Leiden: Brill, 1977.

_____. "'Spiritual' Gifts in the Pauline Community." *NTS* 20 (1973–1974): 128–44.

Erickson, M. *Christian Theology*. Grand Rapids: Baker, 1985.

Ervin, Howard. *Conversion-Initiation and the Baptism in the Holy Spirit*. Peabody, Mass.: Hendrickson, 1984.

Esler, P. F. "Glossolalia and the Admission of Gentiles into the Early Christian Community." *BTB* 22 (1992): 136–42.

Estrada, Nelson. "A Redactional Critical Study on the Relationship of the Spirit, Proclamation, and Miracle-Working Power in Luke–Acts." Unpublished Th.M. thesis; Manila: Asia Graduate School of Theology, 1994.

Ewert, D. *The Holy Spirit in the New Testament*. Kitchener, Ont.: Herald, 1983.

Fee, Gordon D., and Douglas Stuart. *How to Read the Bible For All Its Worth*. Grand Rapids: Zondervan, 1981.

Fee, Gordon D. "Baptism in the Holy Spirit: The Issue of Separability and Subsequence." *Pneuma* 7:2 (1985): 87–99.

_____. *The First Epistle to the Corinthians*. NICNT. Grand Rapids: Eerdmans, 1987.

_____. *Gospel and Spirit: Issues in New Testament Hermeneutics*. Peabody, Mass.: Hendrickson, 1991.

_____."Hermeneutics and Historical Precedent—A Major Problem in Pentecostal Hermeneutics." Pp. 118–32 in *Perspectives on the New Pentecostalism*, R. P. Spittler, ed. Grand Rapids: Baker, 1976.

Fitzmyer, J. *The Gospel According to Luke*. 2 vols. AB 28. New York: Doubleday, 1981, 1985.

Foakes-Jackson, F. J., and K. Lake, eds. *The Beginnings of Christianity*. 5 vols. London: Macmillan, 1920–1933.

Forbes, Christopher. *Prophecy and Inspired Speech in Early Christianity and its Hellenistic Environment*. Tübingen: Mohr, 1995.

The Full Life Study Bible—The New Testament. Donald Stamps, ed. Grand Rapids: Zondervan, 1990.

Gee, Donald. *Spiritual Gifts in the Work of the Ministry Today*. Springfield, Mo.: Gospel, 1963.

Gelpi, Donald. *Pentecostalism: A Theological Viewpoint*. New York: Paulist, 1971.

Giles, K. "Is Luke an Exponent of 'Early Protestantism'? Church Order in the Lukan Writings (Part 1)." *EvQ* 54 (1982): 193–205.

Gordon, A. J. *The Ministry of the Holy Spirit*. Philadelphia: Judson, 1894.

Green, Joel. *The Theology of the Gospel of Luke*. Cambridge: Cambridge Univ. Press, 1995.

Green, M. *I Believe in the Holy Spirit*. Grand Rapids: Eerdmans, 1975.

Greig, Gary S., and Kevin N. Springer, eds. *The Kingdom and the Power*. Ventura, Calif.: Regal, 1993.

Grudem, Wayne. *Systematic Theology: An Introduction to Biblical Doctrine.* Grand Rapids: Zondervan, 1994.

Gundry, Robert. *Matthew: A Commentary on His Literary and Theological Art.* Grand Rapids: Eerdmans, 1981.

Gunkel, H. *The Influence of the Holy Spirit.* Trans. R. A. Harrisville and P. A. Quanbeck II. Philadelphia: Fortress, 1979.

Haenchen, Ernst. *The Acts of the Apostles: A Commentary.* Philadelphia: Westminster, 1971.

Haya-Prats, G. *L'Esprit force de l'église.* Paris: Cerf, 1975.

Hengel, Martin. *Acts and the History of Earliest Christianity.* Trans. J. Bowden. London: SCM, 1979.

_____. *Judaism and Hellenism: Studies in Their Encounter in Palestine During the Early Hellenistic Period.* 2 vols. Trans. J. Bowden. London: SCM, 1974.

Hill, D. *Greek Words and Hebrew Meanings.* Cambridge: Cambridge Univ. Press, 1967.

_____. *New Testament Prophecy.* London: Marshall, Morgan & Scott, 1979.

Horton, Stanley M. *What the Bible Says About the Holy Spirit.* Springfield, Mo.: Gospel, 1976.

Hull, J. H. E. *The Holy Spirit in the Acts of the Apostles.* London: Lutterworth, 1967.

Hunter, H. D. *Spirit-Baptism: A Pentecostal Alternative.* Lanham, Md.: Univ. Press of America, 1983.

Hurst, L. D. "New Testament Theological Analysis." Pp. 133–61 in *Introducing New Testament Study.* Ed. Scot McKnight. Grand Rapids: Baker, 1989.

Hurtado, Larry W. "Normal, but Not a Norm: Initial Evidence and the New Testament." Pp. 189–201 in *Initial Evidence.* Ed. G. McGee. Peabody, Mass.: Hendrickson, 1991.

Johns, Donald A. "Some New Directions in the Hermeneutics of Classical Pentecostalism's Doctrine of Initial Evidence." Pp. 145–67 in *Initial Evidence.* Ed. G. McGee. Peabody, Mass.: Hendrickson, 1991.

Keener, Craig. *The Spirit in the Gospels and Acts: Divine Purity and Power.* Peabody, Mass.: Hendrickson, 1997.

_____. *3 Crucial Questions about the Holy Spirit.* Grand Rapids: Baker, 1996.

Klein, William W., Craig L. Blomberg, and Robert L. Hubbard. *Introduction to Biblical Interpretation.* Dallas: Word, 1993.

Lampe, G. W. H. *God as Spirit: The Bampton Lectures, 1976.* Oxford: Clarendon, 1977.

_____. "The Holy Spirit in the Writings of Saint Luke." *Studies in the Gospels.* Ed. D. D. Nineham. Oxford: Blackwell, 1957.

_____. *The Seal of the Spirit.* London: Longmans, Green & Co., 1951.

Lederle, H. I. *Treasures Old and New: Interpretations of "Spirit-Baptism" in the Charismatic Renewal Movement.* Peabody, Mass.: Hendrickson, 1988.

Lim, David. *Spiritual Gifts: A Fresh Look.* Springfield, Mo.: Gospel, 1991.

Ma, Wonsuk, and Robert P. Menzies, eds. *Pentecostalism in Context: Essays in Honor of William W. Menzies.* JPTSup 11. Sheffield: Sheffield Academic, 1997.

Macchia, Frank D. "The Question of Tongues as Initial Evidence: A Review of *Initial Evidence,* edited by Gary B. McGee." *JPT* 2 (1993): 117–27.

Maddox, R. *The Purpose of Luke–Acts.* Göttingen: Vandenhoeck & Ruprecht, 1982.

Manson, T. W. *The Sayings of Jesus.* 2d ed. London: SCM, 1949.

Marsden, George M. *Understanding Fundamentalism and Evangelicalism.* Grand Rapids: Eerdmans, 1991.

Marshall, I. Howard. *The Acts of the Apostles: An Introduction and Commentary.* TNTC. Leicester: InterVarsity, 1980.

_____. "An Evangelical Approach to 'Theological Criticism.'" *Them* 13 (1988): 79–85.

_____. *The Gospel of Luke: A Commentary on the Greek Text.* NIGTC. Grand Rapids: Eerdmans, 1978.

_____. *Luke: Historian and Theologian.* Grand Rapids: Zondervan, 1970.

Marxsen, W. *Mark the Evangelist.* New York: Abingdon, 1965.

McDonnell, Kilian. *Presence, Power, Praise: Documents on the Charismatic Renewal.* 3 vols. Collegeville, Minn.: Liturgical, 1980.

McGee, G., ed. *Initial Evidence: Historical and Biblical Perspectives on the Pentecostal Doctrine of Spirit Baptism.* Peabody, Mass.: Hendrickson, 1991.

Menzies, Robert P. *The Development of Early Christian Pneumatology with Special Reference to Luke–Acts.* JSNTSup 54. Sheffield: JSOT Press, 1991.

_____. *Empowered for Witness: The Spirit in Luke–Acts.* JPTSup 6. Sheffield: Sheffield Academic, 1994.

_____. "Evidential Tongues: An Essay on Theological Method." *AJPS* 1 (1998): 111–23.

_____. "James Shelton's *Mighty in Word and Deed*: A Review Article." *JPT* 2 (1993): 105–15.

_____. "Spirit and Power in Luke–Acts: A Response to Max Turner." *JSNT* 49 (1993): 11–20.

Menzies, William W. *Anointed to Serve.* Springfield, Mo.: Gospel, 1971.

Metzger, B. *A Textual Commentary on the Greek New Testament*. 2d ed. London: United Bible Societies, 1975.

Michaels, J. Ramsey. "Evidences of the Spirit, or the Spirit as Evidence? Some Non-Pentecostal Reflections." Pp. 202–18 in *Initial Evidence*. Ed. G. McGee. Peabody, Mass.: Hendrickson, 1991.

Montague, G. T. *The Holy Spirit: Growth of a Biblical Tradition*. New York: Paulist, 1976.

Muhlen, Heribert. *A Charismatic Theology*. Trans. Edward Quinn and Thomas Linton. New York: Paulist, 1978.

Nelson, P. C. *Bible Doctrines*. Springfield, Mo.: Gospel, 1962.

Nolland, J. *Luke 1–9:20*. WBC 35a. Dallas: Word, 1989.

O'Neill, J. C. *The Theology of Acts in Its Historical Setting*. 2d ed. London: SPCK, 1970.

O'Reilly, L. *Word and Sign in the Acts of the Apostles: A Study in Lucan Theology*. Rome: Editrice Pontificia Università Gregoriana, 1987.

Osborne, Grant R. *The Hermeneutical Spiral: A Comprehensive Introduction to Biblical Interpretation*. Downers Grove, Ill.: InterVarsity, 1991.

_____. *The Resurrection Narratives: A Redactional Study*. Grand Rapids: Baker, 1984.

O'Toole, R. F. "Christian Baptism in Luke." *RevRel* 39 (1980): 855–66.

Pearlman, Myer. *Knowing the Doctrines of the Bible*. Springfield, Mo.: Gospel, 1937.

Penney, John Michael. *The Missionary Emphasis of Lukan Pneumatology*. JPTSup 12. Sheffield: Sheffield Academic, 1997.

Petts, David. "Healing and the Atonement." *EPTA Bulletin* 12 (1993): 23–37.

Pinnock, Clark H. "The Work of the Holy Spirit in Hermeneutics." *JPT* 2 (1993): 3–23.

Ramm, Bernard. *Protestant Biblical Interpretation*. 3d ed. Grand Rapids: Baker, 1970.

Riggs, Ralph. *We Believe*. Springfield, Mo.: Gospel, 1954.

Robeck, Cecil M. "Splinters and Logs, Catholics and Pentecostals." *Pneuma* 12 (1990): 77–83.

Rodd, C. S. "Spirit or Finger." *ExpTim* 72 (1960–61): 157–58.

Russell, E. A. "'They Believed Philip Preaching' (Acts 8.12)." *IBS* 1 (1979): 169–76.

Russell, W. "The Anointing with the Holy Spirit in Luke-Acts." *TJ* n.s. 7 (1986): 47–63.

Sandeen, Ernest R. *The Roots of Fundamentalism*. Chicago: Univ. of Chicago Press, 1970.

Schatzmann, S. *A Pauline Theology of the Charismata*. Peabody, Mass.: Hendrickson, 1987.

Schulz, S. *Q: Die Spruchquelle der Evangelisten*. Zürich: Theologischer Verlag, 1972.

Schweizer, E. "πνεῦμα." *TDNT*, 6:389–455.

Shelton, J. *Mighty in Word and Deed*. Peabody, Mass.: Hendrickson, 1991.

Spittler, R. P., ed. *Perspectives on the New Pentecostalism*. Grand Rapids: Baker, 1976.

Stein, Robert. *The Synoptic Problem: An Introduction*. Downers Grove, Ill.: InterVarsity, 1987.

Stott, John R. W. *The Baptism and Fullness of the Holy Spirit*. Downers Grove, Ill.: InterVarsity, 1964.

_____. *The Cross of Christ*. Downers Grove, Ill.: InterVarsity, 1986.

Stronstad, Roger. *The Charismatic Theology of St. Luke*. Peabody, Mass.: Hendrickson, 1984.

Synan, Vinson. *The Holiness-Pentecostal Tradition*. 2d ed. Grand Rapids: Eerdmans, 1997.

Thomas, J. C. "Max Turner's *The Holy Spirit and Spiritual Gifts: Then and Now* (Carlisle: Paternoster Press, 1996): An Appreciation and Critique." *JPT* 12 (1998): 3–21.

Tiede, D. L. "The Exaltation of Jesus and the Restoration of Israel in Acts 1." *HTR* 79 (1986): 278–86.

Turner, Max. *The Holy Spirit and Spiritual Gifts: Then and Now*. Carlisle: Paternoster, 1996.

_____. "Luke and the Spirit" Ph.D. diss. University of Cambridge, 1980.

_____. *Power from on High*. Sheffield: Sheffield Academic, 1996.

_____. "Readings and Paradigms: A Response to John Christopher Thomas." *JPT* 12 (1998): 23–38.

_____. "The Spirit and the Power of Jesus' Miracles in the Lucan Conception." *NovT* 33 (1991): 124–52.

_____. "Tongues: An Experience for All in the Pauline Churches?" *AJPS* 1 (1998): 235–36.

Wagner, C. Peter. *The Third Wave of the Holy Spirit*. Ann Arbor, Mich.: Vine, 1988.

Webb, R. L. "The Activity of John the Baptist's Expected Figure at the Threshing Floor (Matthew 3.12 = Luke 3.17)." *JSNT* 43 (1991): 103–11.

Weiser, A. *Die Apostelgeschichte*. OTKNT 5. Gütersloh: Gütersloher Verlagshaus, 1981.

White, John. *When the Spirit Comes with Power: Signs and Wonders Among God's People*. Downers Grove, Ill.: InterVarsity, 1988.

Wilkinson, John. "Physical Healing and the Atonement." *EvQ* 63 (1991): 149–67.

Williams, Ernest S. *Systematic Theology*. 3 vols. Springfield, Mo.: Gospel, 1953.

Wimber, John, and Kevin Springer. *Power Evangelism*. San Francisco: Harper & Row, 1991.

_____. *Power Points*. New York: HarperCollins, 1991.

Subject Index

Scripture Index

We want to hear from you. Please send your comments about this book to us in care of the address below. Thank you.

ZondervanPublishingHouse
Grand Rapids, Michigan 49530
http://www.zondervan.com